50 BEST PLANTS ON THE PLANET

melissa's®

50 BEST PLANTS ON THE PLANET

The Most Nutrient-Dense Fruits and Vegetables, in 150 Delicious Recipes

Cathy Thomas

Foreword by **Cheryl Forberg, RD**
Photographs by **Angie Cao**

CHRONICLE BOOKS
SAN FRANCISCO

Library of Congress Cataloging-in-Publication Data available.

ISBN 978-1-4521-0284-9 (hc)
ISBN 978-1-4521-0283-2 (pbk)

Manufactured in China

Designed by **CELERY DESIGN COLLABORATIVE**
Typesetting by **HELEN LEE**
Prop styling by **CHRISTINE WOLHEIM**
Food styling by **FANNY PAN**
The photographer wishes to thank her excellent stylists, **CHRISTINE** &
FANNY, as well as **CATHRYN LOVECRAFT**, **TREVOR ADAMS**, and **KIZZY
VATCHARAKOMONPHAN**.

Alouette is a registered trademark of Léon Hatot SA; Baby Dutch Yellow
Potatoes is a registered trademark of Melissa's/World Variety Produce, Inc.;
Grand Marnier is a registered trademark of Societe des Produits Marinier
Lapostolle SA; Japonica is a registered trademark of Wehah Farm, Inc. DBA
Lundberg Family Farms; Microplane is a registered trademark of Grace
Manufacturing Inc.; Sriracha is a registered trademark of V. Thai Food Product
Co., Ltd.; Twitter is a registered trademark of Twitter, Inc.; Wehani is a regis-
tered trademark of Wehah Farm, Inc. DBA Lundberg Family Farms.

10 9 8 7 6 5 4 3 2 1

CHRONICLE BOOKS LLC
680 Second Street
San Francisco, California 94107
www.chroniclebooks.com

Acknowledgments

How lucky I am to have had such a great team cheering me on. Books like this happen with the help and generosity of many people.

Enormous thanks go to Sharon and Joe Hernandez, owners of Melissa's/World Variety Produce, for giving me the opportunity to write this book. These produce pioneers founded the company in 1984. Their family-run business has become the nation's largest distributor of specialty and organic fruits and vegetables. The Melissa's brand is named after Sharon and Joe's daughter, Melissa, who—along with her husband, Aaron—takes an active role in the company.

Food writers from coast to coast rely on the information garnered from produce guru Robert Schueller, Melissa's director of public relations. He is a walking encyclopedia of produce knowledge. His talent and enthusiasm are greatly appreciated. Thanks go to Debra Cohen, Melissa's director of special projects, for her steadfast fact checking.

I am extremely grateful to nutrition experts Cheryl Forberg, RD, and David Feder, RD. Cheryl, a former nutritionist for NBC's *The Biggest Loser*, wrote the book's foreword and painstakingly did the nutritional analyses of the recipes. David Feder, a food writer and nutrition scientist, contributed the nutritional information related to each topic.

Heartfelt thanks to chef Ida Rodriguez, executive chef of Melissa's corporate kitchen, along with her very talented team, chef/kitchen director Tom Fraker and chef Raquel Perez. Chef Tom and Chef Raquel tested each and every recipe in the book.

Special thanks to editorial director Bill LeBlond and associate editor Sarah Billingsley; designer Alice Chau; photographer Angie Cao; and the rest of the editing, production, marketing, and publicity team at Chronicle Books.

Finally, of course, I would like to thank my children and my husband, Phil McCullough, for their patience and love, as well as culinarian Tillie Clements, who cooked up my first newspaper food-writing gig. Thank you to Françoise Thomas, who gave me my initial lessons in French cuisine and perseverance.

Infinite gratitude to my late parents, Harriett and Loren Young, who kept our family table filled with fresh fruits and vegetables seven days a week.

—CATHY THOMAS

Contents

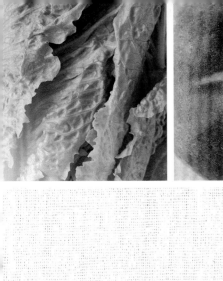
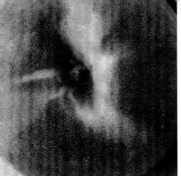

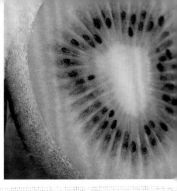

Foreword

by **CHERYL FORBERG, RD**
James Beard Award–winning chef, former nutritionist
for *The Biggest Loser*, and author of *Flavor First*

Go online or pick up a newspaper and you're almost guaranteed to read bad news about our health. In recent years, increasingly frequent headlines have tracked our nation's downward spiral—as evidenced by skyrocketing child and adult obesity rates, an uptick in type 2 diabetes, and a drop in the number of home-cooked meals we consume.

Nowhere is the reality of these statistics clearer to me than on the set of NBC's *The Biggest Loser*. Since the first episode aired in 2004, I served as the show's nutritionist and co-wrote the eating plan that produced dramatic weight-loss results for contestants and viewers alike.

The contestants who arrive at "The Ranch" (the fitness and residential facility where they begin their weight-loss journey) are morbidly obese and often face the prospect of life-threatening conditions, such as heart disease and diabetes. Almost invariably, their pre-show diets are full of empty calories—that is, foods lacking in nutrient value but packing plenty of excess fat and sugar calories. Soft drinks, drive-through meals, and processed foods are usually staples.

Naturally, as part of the guidance I gave *Biggest Loser* contestants, I urged them to eliminate these unhealthy foods from their diets. But the massive lifestyle changes they undertake wouldn't be sustainable if they only involved deprivation. Instead, one of the cornerstones of the *Biggest Loser* eating plan is to increase—that's right, increase!—consumption of

nutritious, high-quality foods. And that's where fresh fruits and vegetables come in.

I explained to contestants that fresh produce is the ultimate high-quality food, because most fruits and vegetables are:

- **LOW IN CALORIES** Fruits and vegetables typically have high water content, so eating even a small quantity delivers satisfying bulk with just a few calories.

- **HIGH IN FIBER** Many fruits and vegetables are loaded with dietary fiber, which promotes healthy digestion and nutrient absorption and helps lower the risk of diabetes, heart disease, and possibly colorectal cancer.

- **RICH IN ANTIOXIDANTS** Antioxidants protect your body against inflammation, diabetes, heart disease, cancer, and other ailments. Because they're rich in vitamins and plant nutrients called phytochemicals, fruits and vegetables pack a strong antioxidant punch.

As contestants on *The Biggest Loser* experiment with flavorful new combinations of produce and switch to a "clean eating" lifestyle, they reap the rewards on the scale, at the doctor's office, and with increased overall energy to fuel those killer workouts the show features. They realize that it's not just about the quantity of calories they consume, but the quality—both in terms of flavor and nutrient composition. They're not just counting calories; they're making every calorie count.

That's why I'm so excited about this book. *50 Best Plants on the Planet* features fifty foods that score high for nutrition density—a measurement that compares the nutrient content of food to its calories. In short, while *50 Best Plants on the Planet* isn't a weight-loss book, it's based on the same principles as the *Biggest Loser* plan, which are making every calorie count, and making the experience delicious, to boot!

When I first collaborated with Melissa's Produce almost a decade ago, I knew right away that our relationship was a match made in heaven. As a chef who'd gone on to earn a nutrition degree, I worked as a registered dietician and knew that produce plays a vital role in our diet. Not only do fresh fruits and vegetables provide plenty of vitamins, minerals, and age-defying antioxidants, but they also satisfy my culinary expectations for flavor. Fresh produce has the potential to lend dazzling color and a wide array of textures and tastes to dishes for every meal, course, and occasion—even cocktails!

In the course of my work, it's become clear that Melissa's provides a much-needed service. By delivering produce to doorsteps across America, Melissa's can help families reverse one particularly important statistic: America is skipping its vegetables. According to data from the Centers for Disease Control, in 2009 more than two-thirds of the nation's adults ate fewer than three servings of vegetables per day, with only 14 percent consuming a full five servings of produce daily.

No, produce shouldn't be a marginal afterthought—just the opposite. Because produce is nutrient dense, meaning vitamin and mineral content is high when compared with total calories, it should be the cornerstone of our diet. While no one food can deliver every essential nutrient, every fruit and vegetable featured in this book packs a powerful punch when it comes to vitamins, minerals, and fiber.

I've long been a fan of Cathy's work as a food columnist for the *Orange County Register*. Week after week, she presents fresh food ideas that put seasonal produce front and center. Her approachable style and flavorful recipes encourage experimentation with new produce—which is another reason I'm excited about this book. Not only do such standbys as grapefruit and spinach get their due on the pages that follow, but also Cathy has applied her culinary know-how to a variety of fruits and vegetables that may be new to you—from kumquats to passion fruit, and bok choy to watercress.

I hope her guidance will give you the confidence to explore! Not only will you and your family discover new fruits, vegetables, and taste sensations, but also your overall nutrition and health will benefit, too. *50 Best Plants on the Planet* will help you optimize your calories for maximum efficiency while boosting the variety of your produce repertoire. So go ahead, make every calorie count—toward better health and scrumptious flavors. Bon appétit!

"The goal is to enjoy nutrient-rich fresh fruits and vegetables to feel good and have plenty of energy and vitality—to find uncomplicated ways to savor produce at its very best."

Introduction

The jury is still out on the value of dietary supplements. Most studies point to a nutrient-rich, balanced diet that is rich in plant-based ingredients as the best way to get vitamins and minerals, fiber, and antioxidants.

Is this the end of popping vitamins pills? Probably not, but few would deny that nutrient-dense fruits and vegetables are infinitely more satisfying and delicious. Fresh produce has endless culinary potential, providing alluring tastes and textures, aromas, and colors. Because they are so naturally delectable, it doesn't take much time or effort to showcase them in mouth-watering ways.

Within the pages of this book, fifty of the most nutrient-dense fruits and vegetables are demystified in simple recipes for irresistible dishes and valuable time-saving tips, as well as easy-to-understand nutritional information. "Nutrient dense" means that the vitamin and mineral content of these foods are high when compared with total calories.

User-friendly, bold headings take you to specifics about how to buy and store each fruit or vegetable, how to quickly cook to preserve the most nutritional bling, and how to easily transform recipes that contain meat into vegetarian renditions. From arugula to watermelon, the book is arranged alphabetically to help readers quickly find topics.

This isn't a diet book. It is a guide to bettering the nutrient content and quality of the food you eat. The goal is to enjoy nutrient-rich fresh fruits and vegetables to feel good and have plenty of energy and vitality—to find uncomplicated ways to savor produce at its very best.

Melissa's/World Variety Produce, a family-run business owned by Sharon and Joe Hernandez, is the nation's leading distributor of organic and specialty produce. Founded is 1984, the company offers more than a thousand produce items and food products to retailers across the country. Consumers have grown to recognize and seek out the Melissa's® logo, a colorful emblem that spells out "Melissa's" in a red radish hue with a colorful carrot standing in for the letter "i."

For more information, visit Melissa's Produce Web site at www.melissas.com and follow Melissa's Produce on Twitter at http://twitter.com/MelissasProduce.

ARUGULA

Packed with peppery-tart attitude, arugula adds zesty flavor to a salad or soup, as well as a stir-fry or pasta. Although it's most often used as a salad green, its deep green leaves are also used like a fresh herb. Incorporated in smaller amounts, arugula should be added during the last minute of cooking. Or it can be ground raw into a delectable pesto. Either raw or cooked, it brings tasty bling to a dish.

Known as a concentrated source of folate and vitamins A and C, arugula (sometimes called "rocket") is also replete with vitamin K, necessary for bone and blood health. Vitamin K also is gaining attention for its support of nerve health in the brain, including possible protection against Alzheimer's disease.

NUTRITIONAL INFORMATION
(per 1 ounce raw, chopped)

calories 7	sodium (mg) 8	vitamin A IUs 13%
fat calories 2	total carbohydrates (g) 1	vitamin C 7%
total fat (g) 0	fiber (g) 0	calcium 4%
sat fat (g) 0	sugars (g) 1	iron.............................. 2%
cholesterol (mg) 0	protein (g) 1	

CANCER CHASER

Just one ounce of the peppery leafy green has more than a third of an adult's daily vitamin K needs. Arugula also has a plentiful complement of phytochemicals across several classes, including indoles, thiocyanates, and sulfurophanes. Not only do they have the potential to help prevent cancer, but also they have been shown to be toxic to cancer cells. The compounds also have demonstrated an ability to counter the carcinogenic effects of excess estrogen.

BUG BASHER

Other phytochemicals in arugula have shown antibacterial and antiviral action. Arugula's abundance of A and C vitamins provides beauty-from-within antioxidant actions that support skin and collagen integrity as well as eye health and healthy immune functioning. Plus, minerals such as copper, calcium, iron, and magnesium make the leafy green a true nutritional star.

AVAILABLE

Year-round

KEEP IT FRESH

Choose leaves that are bright green without any yellowing or wilting. To wash, submerge leaves in a large bowl of cold water. Gently spin the leaves dry or drain in a colander and pat dry. Wrap them in a clean kitchen towel or paper towels and store in a partially closed plastic bag. Refrigerate in the crisper drawer up to 5 days.

QUICK COOK
Serve raw or briefly cooked for the most nutritional benefit. To stir-fry, heat 2 tablespoons canola oil in a wok or large, deep skillet on high heat. When hot but not smoking, add 7 cups baby arugula leaves in quick handfuls, because the oil may splatter. Add 1 large clove garlic (minced). Stir-fry for about 30 seconds, or until the arugula is heated through and wilted. Season with a little salt and a pinch of dried red pepper flakes. Serve as is or spooned over cooked brown rice or quinoa.

try it!

SANDWICHES
Add arugula leaves to grilled cheese or BLTs.

ATOP SLIVERS OF CHEESE PIZZA
Sprinkle baby arugula leaves over steaming hot pizza so it just begins to wilt.

CLASSIC AND SIMPLE, WITH PARMESAN
Place baby arugula on a plate and top with shaved Parmesan cheese. Drizzle with a little fruity extra-virgin olive oil. Season with coarse salt and freshly ground black pepper.

Broccoli, Garbanzo, and Arugula Salad

Because it is strained, Greek-style yogurt has a thick, luxurious texture. One cup of Greek-style yogurt contains as much as 20 grams of protein. Used in salad dressing, it lends creaminess as well. In this salad, the dressing teams yogurt with sherry vinegar, Dijon mustard, and a little olive oil, plus some minced fresh mint or basil. Either fat-free or low-fat Greek-style yogurt works equally well.

Yields 8 servings

NUTRITIONAL INFORMATION
(per serving with fat-free yogurt, without optional garnishes)

calories 150	sodium (mg) 125	vitamin A IUs 90%
fat calories 40	total carbohydrates (g)... 22	vitamin C 90%
total fat (g) 4.5	fiber (g) 7	calcium 8%
sat fat (g) 0.5	sugars (g) 4	iron 15%
cholesterol (mg) 0	protein (g) 8	

DRESSING

- 2 tablespoons sherry vinegar
- 1 teaspoon Dijon mustard
- ¼ teaspoon salt
- 1½ tablespoons extra-virgin olive oil
- ¼ cup plain fat-free or low-fat Greek-style yogurt
- 2 teaspoons minced fresh mint or basil

SALAD

- 1 pound small broccoli florets
- Two 15-ounce cans garbanzo beans, drained, rinsed, drained again
- ½ small red onion, cut in half top to bottom, thinly sliced (*see Cook's Notes*)
- 1 cup thinly sliced small peeled carrots
- Freshly ground black pepper
- 3 cups baby arugula

OPTIONAL GARNISH ¾ cup finely diced Manchego or smoked mozzarella cheese

OPTIONAL GARNISH 1 pita bread, cut into narrow triangles, toasted (*see Cook's Notes*)

1. Put a large pot of salted water on high heat and bring to a boil.

2. To make the dressing: In a small bowl or a measuring cup with a handle, mix together the vinegar, mustard, and salt. Stir in the oil, then the yogurt. Stir in 1½ tablespoons water and the mint. Set aside.

3. To make the salad: Blanch the broccoli in the boiling water until tender-crisp, 3 to 4 minutes. Drain and refresh with cold water. Drain well and place in a large bowl. When the broccoli is completely cool, add the beans, onion, and carrots.

4. Add the dressing, season with pepper, and toss.

5. Divide the arugula between eight plates. Top with the broccoli mixture. If desired, scatter the cheese on top and place the pita triangles next to the salad before serving.

COOK'S NOTES If red onion is too strong for you, slice and soak it in ice water for 30 minutes. Drain and pat dry before adding to the salad.

To toast pita triangles, place them in a single layer on a rimmed baking sheet. Coat with nonstick olive oil spray. Toast in a 350-degree-F oven until lightly browned and starting to crisp.

Taste the salad at the end of step 3; if you like, add a pinch of dried red pepper flakes and gently toss again.

Spaghetti with Arugula Pesto

Raw arugula, with its assertive flavor profile, provides just-right perkiness for pesto. Here it is tossed with whole-grain spaghetti, but it is also delicious with steamed or blanched green beans or fingerling potatoes. To make larger portions, toss some blanched or roasted cauliflower with the spaghetti. To learn how to easily roast cauliflower florets, *see Cook's Note*, page 339.

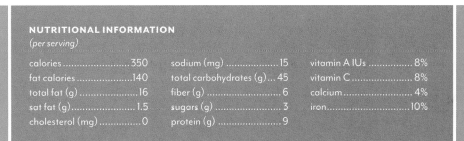

Yields 8 first-course or side-dish servings

NUTRITIONAL INFORMATION
(per serving)

calories 350	sodium (mg) 15	vitamin A IUs 8%
fat calories 140	total carbohydrates (g)... 45	vitamin C 8%
total fat (g) 16	fiber (g) 6	calcium 4%
sat fat (g).......................1.5	sugars (g) 3	iron.............................10%
cholesterol (mg) 0	protein (g) 9	

2 medium garlic cloves, peeled

½ cup toasted pine nuts
  (*see Cook's Note*)

4 cups arugula

5 tablespoons extra-virgin olive oil

2 tablespoons fresh lemon juice

Freshly ground black pepper

1 pound dry whole-grain spaghetti

Salt

GARNISH 2 Roma tomatoes, cored, seeded, diced

OPTIONAL GARNISH grated Parmesan cheese

1. Put a large pot of salted water on high heat and bring to a boil.

2. Meanwhile, with the motor running, drop the garlic into a food processor fitted with the metal blade; process until minced. Stop the machine and add the pine nuts and arugula; process until finely minced. With the motor running, add the oil in a thin stream. Scrape down the sides of the bowl. Add the lemon juice and season with pepper. Process until smooth.

3. Cook the spaghetti in the boiling water until al dente (following the package directions). Scoop out and reserve ½ cup of the cooking liquid. Drain the spaghetti. In a large bowl, toss the spaghetti and pesto. Toss in enough of the reserved cooking liquid to make the pesto a little saucy. Taste and add more salt or pepper, if needed. Divide the pasta between small shallow bowls and top with the diced tomato. Pass the Parmesan when serving, if desired.

COOK'S NOTE To toast pine nuts, place them in a small skillet on medium-high heat. Shake the handle of the skillet to keep rotating the pine nuts as they lightly toast. Watch carefully because they burn easily.

Arugula Salad with Parmesan, Fruit, and Easy Lavash Crackers

Thin sheets of lavash flatbread toasted with a little Parmesan cheese make irresistible crisp crackers to accompany this arugula-based salad. To reduce calories in this ambrosial concoction, use less fruit and/or cheese. The amounts given here are generous.

Yields 4 servings

NUTRITIONAL INFORMATION
(per serving)

calories 240	sodium (mg) 380	vitamin A IUs 15%
fat calories 120	total carbohydrates (g)... 23	vitamin C 10%
total fat (g) 13	fiber (g) 3	calcium 25%
sat fat (g) 4	sugars (g) 9	iron 8%
cholesterol (mg) 15	protein (g) 7	

Nonstick vegetable oil cooking spray

One 9-by-12-inch sheet of lavash

1 tablespoon grated Parmesan, plus 3-ounce chunk, shaved into thin strips using a peeler

8 cups baby arugula

3 tablespoons extra-virgin olive oil

2 tablespoons fresh lemon juice

Salt

Freshly ground black pepper

6 fresh figs, quartered, or 2 ripe pears, cored and cut into eighths lengthwise

1. Preheat the oven to 400 degrees F. Coat a rimmed baking sheet with nonstick spray. Place the lavash on the prepared sheet and coat it with non-stick spray. Sprinkle the Parmesan on top. Bake until crisp, 3 to 4 minutes. Remove from the oven. Cut crosswise into 8 pieces; set aside.

2. Place the arugula in a large bowl. Drizzle with the oil and toss to coat the leaves. Add the lemon juice, season with salt and pepper, and toss. Add half the Parmesan strips and toss. Divide the salad between four dinner plates. Top with the remaining strips of cheese. Place the figs around the perimeter of the salad, interspersed with pieces of lavash. Serve immediately.

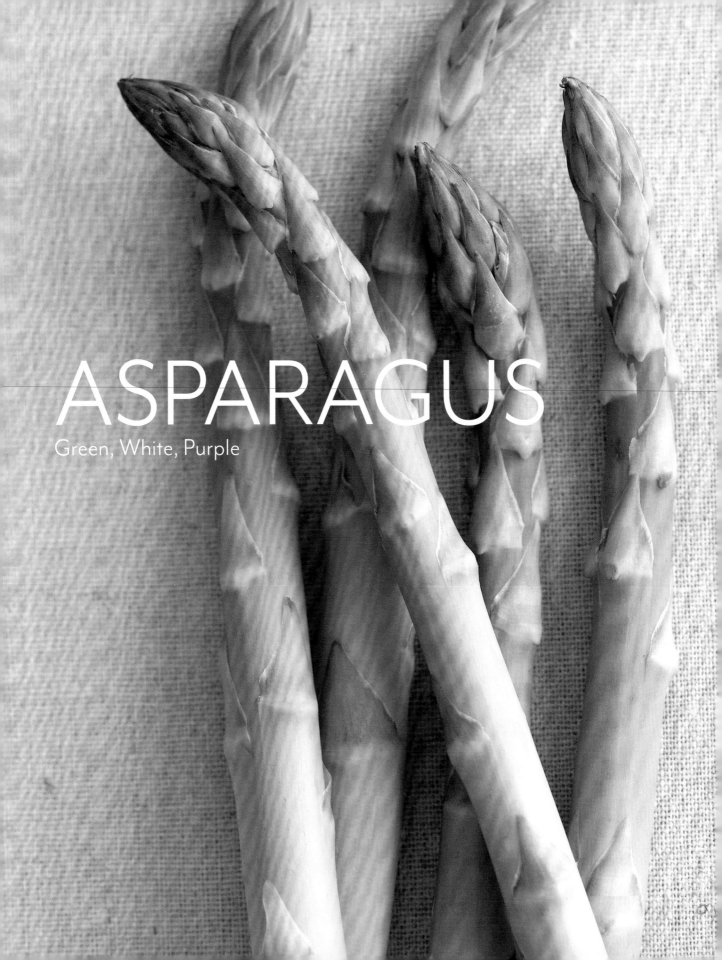

ASPARAGUS

Green, White, Purple

Asparagus has a regal appearance. Each stately stalk is topped with an imperious budlike point, a delicate crown that sits atop a lanky shoot. Sought out as a delicacy in ancient Rome and dubbed the "food of kings" by King Louis XIV of France, asparagus offers much more than an elegant appearance, more than an appealing grassy, nutty-sweet flavor profile, and more than an alluring tender texture.

It is one of the most nutrient-dense foods on the planet, leading nearly all fruits and vegetables in the healthful components it provides.

NUTRITIONAL INFORMATION
(per 1 cup raw, chopped)

calories 27	sodium (mg) 3	vitamin A IUs 20%
fat calories 1	total carbohydrates (g).... 5	vitamin C 13%
total fat (g) 0	fiber (g) 3	calcium 3%
sat fat (g)....................... 0	sugars (g) 3	iron............................. 16%
cholesterol (mg) 0	protein (g) 3	

FOLATE BONANZA
Five spears supply about 60 percent of the average daily requirement for folic acid, the essential B vitamin that helps to prevent birth defects. Folic acid also plays a key role in preventing heart disease because it helps to control homocysteine, which otherwise can promote atherosclerosis by reducing the integrity of blood vessel walls.

EYEBALL LOVE
Asparagus contains more dietary glutathione than any other fruit or vegetable. This phytochemical recycles vitamins C and E back to their active forms, and research suggests that it helps reduce cataract development in the eyes.

NATURAL DIURETIC
Asparagus contains the amino acid asparagine that promotes the formation of urine in the kidneys. Because it reduces swelling, asparagus can be useful for treating PMS-related water retention. Although it seems to be the subject of great debate, most think it is the asparagine that gives some people's urine that peculiar, post-meal smell.

ADDITIONAL BONUS
It's an excellent source of vitamins A, C, and K, as well as a good source of dietary fiber and potassium, plus an impressive source of minerals and B vitamins. Asparagus is also high in rutin, a flavonoid that is thought to have anti-inflammatory and antioxidant properties.

AVAILABLE
Year-round

KEEP IT FRESH

Choose stalks that are about the same size for even cooking. Asparagus needs to be kept cold; refrigerate, unwashed, in a plastic bag up to 3 or 4 days in the crisper drawer. Or store upright in about 1 inch of water, covered with a plastic bag. Note that folate diminishes when exposed to heat or light.

LAST-MINUTE PREP

Wash thoroughly with cold water. If the tips are sandy, dunk them in and out of a bowl of cold water to loosen the sand. Trim tough, woody ends or grasp both ends and snap at the breaking point.

QUICK COOK

Briefly cook or serve asparagus raw, unpeeled, to preserve the most nutritional benefits. Both green and purple varieties turn bright green when cooked. Whether steaming, blanching, roasting, or grilling, heat only long enough for the asparagus to become tender-crisp. White asparagus cooks very quickly, so be especially cautious not to overcook it.

try it!

STEAMED AND LIGHTLY DRESSED

Put trimmed asparagus in a covered steamer basket over boiling water for about 3 minutes or just until tender-crisp (time varies depending on width of stalks). Place on a platter and drizzle on a ginger vinaigrette (combine ¼ cup rice vinegar, 1 tablespoon agave syrup, 1 tablespoon minced unpeeled fresh ginger, 2 tablespoons vegetable oil, plus salt and freshly ground black pepper to season).

RAW IN SALADS

Thinly slice trimmed raw asparagus on the diagonal and toss into mixed green salads.

GRILLED, HERBED, AND GARNISHED

Heat the grill to medium-high heat and clean the grate. Toss trimmed asparagus with a little extra-virgin olive oil, salt, and freshly ground black pepper. Place on the grill either in a grill basket or with the stalks positioned perpendicular to the grate; grill until tender-crisp and lightly browned, shaking the basket occasionally or turning with tongs to redistribute the asparagus. Depending on the heat of the fire and width of the stalks, it will take between 5 and 8 minutes. Place the asparagus on a plate or platter and sprinkle with finely chopped fresh Italian parsley or basil. If desired, top with thin slices of peeled orange and a few very thin shavings of Parmesan cheese.

Salmon and "Noodle" Salad

The noodle shapes in this colorful salad are actually ribbons of thinly shaved zucchini. They are combined with diagonally sliced raw asparagus dressed with a citrusy vinaigrette and garnished with slivers of assertive cheese. The salad teams winningly with broiled salmon but is certainly flavorful enough to serve on its own.

Yields 6 servings

NUTRITIONAL INFORMATION
(per serving)

calories 350	sodium (mg) 230	vitamin A IUs 25%
fat calories 230	total carbohydrates (g)..... 6	vitamin C 35%
total fat (g) 25	fiber (g) 2	calcium 15%
sat fat (g) 4.5	sugars (g) 3	iron 8%
cholesterol (mg) 75	protein (g) 27	

SALMON

One 1½-pound skinless salmon fillet
    (center cut preferred, about 1 to
    1¼ inch thick)

2 teaspoons extra-virgin olive oil

¼ teaspoon coarse salt
    (kosher or sea)

¼ teaspoon freshly ground black pepper

SALAD

1 pound green or purple asparagus,
    trimmed

2 medium zucchini, trimmed

DRESSING

¼ cup extra-virgin olive oil

2 ½ tablespoons fresh lemon juice

1 tablespoon minced fresh basil or dill

GARNISHES 1 ounce pecorino cheese,
peeled into shavings; 1 lemon (preferably
Meyer), sliced

1. Adjust an oven rack to 6 to 8 inches below the broiler. Arrange a second rack in the middle of the oven. Preheat the broiler. Line a rimmed baking sheet with aluminum foil.

2. To make the salmon: Pat the fillet dry with a paper towel. Place it on the prepared baking sheet. Drizzle with the oil and season with the salt and pepper. Broil on the top rack until lightly browned on top, about 6 to 8 minutes. Turn off the broiler and set the oven to 350 degrees F. Move the salmon to the middle rack and roast until it is cooked to the desired degree of doneness, 3 to 7 minutes. Remove it from the oven and separate the salmon flesh with a fork or knife in the thickest part to take a peek; it should be just barely opaque throughout. Set aside to cool while you prepare the salad. (Note that the salmon can be served warm, but shouldn't be piping hot for this dish.)

3. To make the salad: Cut the asparagus into thin diagonal slices (leaving tips whole); place them in a bowl. Working from end to end, peel the zucchini into long, thin ribbons using a vegetable peeler or mandoline; add them to the asparagus.

4. To make the dressing: In a small bowl or glass measuring cup with a handle, combine the oil and lemon juice and season with salt and pepper. Mix well and stir in the basil. Taste and adjust the seasoning as needed. Add the dressing to the vegetables and gently toss with wooden spoons or silicone spatulas.

5. Divide the cooled salmon between six plates. Surround each portion with salad. Garnish the salad with the cheese and the salmon with the lemon. Serve.

MEATLESS ALTERNATIVE Prepare the salad without the salmon, starting with step 3. If desired, add a pinch of dried red pepper flakes to the dressing.

Gingered Brown Rice Confetti with Asparagus, Carrots, and Mint

Brown rice has a delightfully nutty taste because only the outermost layer, the hull, is removed during processing. The milling and polishing (which converts brown rice into white rice) destroys much of the vitamins B_1, B_3, and B_6. There is also a substantial loss of manganese, iron, and dietary fiber in white rice. Serve this salad as is or on a bed of caramelized onions. Or serve over cooked slices of butternut squash or atop slices of seasoned heirloom tomatoes.

Yields 8 side-dish servings

NUTRITIONAL INFORMATION
(per serving, without sesame seeds)

calories 120	sodium (mg) 740	vitamin A IUs 90%
fat calories 10	total carbohydrates (g)... 24	vitamin C 15%
total fat (g) 1	fiber (g) 4	calcium 4%
sat fat (g) 0	sugars (g) 3	iron 10%
cholesterol (mg) 0	protein (g) 4	

2¼ cups fat-free, low-sodium chicken or vegetable broth or water

1 cup long-grain brown rice (such as Texmati)

2 teaspoons coarse salt (kosher or sea)

3 medium carrots, peeled, cut into matchsticks about ¾ by ⅛ by ⅛ inches

12 to 16 ounces asparagus, trimmed, cut into 1-inch diagonal pieces, tips left whole

½ cup chopped fresh mint

3 green onions, trimmed, cut into thin slices (including half of dark green stalks)

1 tablespoon minced fresh unpeeled ginger

1 lime, zested and juiced

1 teaspoon agave syrup

Freshly ground black pepper

GARNISH lime wedges

OPTIONAL GARNISH toasted sesame seeds (*see Cook's Note*)

1. In a heavy-bottomed, medium-large saucepan (with a tight-fitting lid) bring the broth to a boil over high heat. Stir in the rice and salt. Cover, reduce the heat to low, and gently simmer for 30 minutes. Add the carrots and asparagus (no need to stir them in). Cover and cook 3 to 5 minutes more, or until the rice is tender, the vegetables are tender-crisp, and the broth is absorbed. Transfer to a large bowl; fluff gently with a fork.

2. In a small bowl or glass measuring cup with a handle, mix the mint, onions, ginger, zest, juice, and syrup; season with salt and pepper. Add to the rice mixture and gently toss. Taste and adjust the seasoning as needed. Serve with the lime wedges and top with toasted sesame seeds, if using.

COOK'S NOTE Toasted sesame seeds are sold at some supermarkets and most Asian markets. Or, if you prefer, you can toast them. Place them in a small skillet on medium-high heat. Shake the handle to redistribute the seeds, cooking until they are lightly browned. Remove from the heat and let cool.

Vegetable Patties with Asparagus, Green Beans, and Potatoes

These burger-size asparagus-spiked patties are delicious on their own or served atop a thick slice of seasoned heirloom tomato topped with a little plain Greek-style yogurt.

Yields 6 to 8 servings

NUTRITIONAL INFORMATION
(per serving, using 8 portions)

calories 100	sodium (mg) 225	vitamin A IUs 8%
fat calories 45	total carbohydrates (g).....11	vitamin C 30%
total fat (g) 5	fiber (g) 2	calcium 2%
sat fat (g) 0.5	sugars (g) 1	iron 6%
cholesterol (mg) 0	protein (g) 2	

1 pound fingerling potatoes (*see Cook's Note*), **unpeeled, cut into 2-inch crosswise slices**

Salt

3 tablespoons extra-virgin olive oil

½ cup finely chopped asparagus

½ cup finely chopped green beans

Freshly ground black pepper

¼ cup finely chopped fresh Italian parsley

¼ cup finely chopped fresh chives or dark green parts of green onions

1 teaspoon finely minced lemon zest

1 to 2 tablespoons all-purpose flour

1. Put the potatoes in a large pan or Dutch oven; cover with water and season with salt. Bring to a boil on high heat. Reduce the heat to medium and cook until the potatoes are tender, about 15 minutes. Drain well.

2. Heat 1 tablespoon of the oil in a large, deep skillet on medium-high heat. Add the asparagus and green beans and toss. Cook, stirring occasionally, until the vegetables are tender-crisp, about 2 minutes. Season with salt and pepper.

3. In a large bowl, coarsely mash the potatoes, leaving some small pieces intact. Add the asparagus, green beans, parsley, chives, and zest. Stir in 1 tablespoon flour to make the mixture dry enough to form into patties, adding more as needed.

4. Divide the mixture into six to eight ½-inch-thick patties. Heat the remaining 2 tablespoons oil in a large nonstick skillet on medium heat. Add the patties in batches, keeping them in a single layer, and cook until they are browned on one side, about 4 minutes. Carefully turn with a flexible metal spatula. Cook until they are browned and firm on the other side. Serve.

COOK'S NOTE Any fingerling variety will work except the Purple Peruvian.

BEET AND BEET GREEN

The beet's bulb is a nutritional powerhouse, as are the hearty greens that sprout above it. The earthy sweet bulbs range in color from magenta, gold, or pink to a fancy striped variety with red and white candy-cane glamour. The verdant leaves look dramatic, with roadmaps of brightly colored ribs and veining.

Beets are so good for you they border on the mystic. From root tip to leafy green, the amount of nutrition in a single beet is impressive.

NUTRITIONAL INFORMATION
(per 1 cup raw sliced red beets/per 1 cup raw beet greens)

calories 59/8	sodium (mg) 106/86	vitamin A IUs 1%/48%
fat calories 2/0	total carbohydrates (g).13/2	vitamin C 11%/19%
total fat (g) 0/0	fiber (g) 4/1	calcium.................. 2%/4%
sat fat (g).................... 0/0	sugars (g) 9/0	iron.......................... 6%/5%
cholesterol (mg) 0/0	protein (g) 2/1	

ROOT MINERALS
The beet root is high in fiber and folate, and it's also loaded with nearly every metabolically important mineral (iron, zinc, calcium, copper, magnesium, and potassium). It is one of the best sources of manganese, which is important for bone health, and is a good source of the unique antioxidant mineral selenium.

IMMUNE SUPPORT
Beet greens are high in fiber and B vitamins in addition to more concentrated values for all the minerals their underground partners deliver.

SUPER K
The greens really kick it when it comes to vitamins A and K. Just 1½ cups of steamed beet greens gives you three times the daily A you need and 1,000 percent of your K needs!

AVAILABLE
Year-round

KEEP IT FRESH
For greens, leaves should be free of discoloration and wilting. Cut them 1 inch above the bulb and swish them in a large bowl or sink of cold water. If necessary, run clean water and repeat to remove every bit of dirt or grit. Shake off the excess water and wrap them in a clean kitchen towel or paper towels, then store them in a partially closed plastic bag. Refrigerate in the crisper drawer up to 2 days.

For bulbs, they should be firm and free of soft spots. Remove all but 1 inch of the stem. Refrigerate dry and unwashed in a plastic bag in the crisper drawer up to 2 weeks.

LAST-MINUTE PREP

Wash bulbs with cold water just before use. If the greens have not been washed prior to storage, wash them thoroughly in cold water.

TO STEAM-ROAST AND PEEL BEETS

This is the less messy way to cook beets. It is a steaming method that uses the oven. Preheat the oven to 400 degrees F. Wash the beets in cold water. Wrap the wet beets three to a packet (four if they are small) in heavy-duty aluminum foil. Place the packet(s) on a rimmed baking sheet. Roast until the beets are fork tender, 30 to 60 minutes, depending on their size. When cool enough to handle, slip off the peels with your fingers.

TO COOK GREENS

Beet greens can be stir-fried, steamed, or microwaved. One tasty method quickly blanches, then sautés them (see page 34).

try it!

APPETIZER-SIZE BEET SANDWICHES

Cut large golden beets that have been steam-roasted and peeled into ¼-inch-thick slices. Season with a little salt. Cut cold log-style herbed goat cheese into thin slices (use unflavored dental floss to easily cut the cheese). Sandwich the goat cheese between two beet slices. If desired, garnish with minced parsley and serve atop thin slices of toasted baguette.

PERFECTLY PICKLED

Steam-roast seven medium-large beets. Cool, peel, and cut into ¼-inch-thick slices. Put them in a glass or ceramic bowl. In a separate bowl, whisk together 3 tablespoons seasoned rice vinegar, 2 tablespoons fresh orange or tangerine juice, 1½ teaspoons salt, and freshly ground black pepper. Add ¼ cup extra-virgin olive oil in a thin stream, whisking constantly; pour over the beets. Allow them to rest for 30 minutes before serving.

WITH TANGERINES

For a colorful salad, peel and tear into sections several tangerines. Place the sections on a large plate in a single layer. Top with sliced (steam-roasted and peeled) beets and slivers of red onion. Drizzle on a simple vinaigrette and chopped pistachios. If desired, add a little crumbled goat cheese or grated Manchego cheese.

GREENS IN MISO SOUP

Roughly chop clean beet greens. Heat miso soup in a saucepan and add the chopped beet greens. Cook just until the greens wilt. Add cubes of firm tofu.

Quinoa Tabbouleh with Beets

Far from traditional Middle-Eastern tabbouleh made with bulgur wheat, this version uses quinoa. The South American grain gives the dish an appealing nuttiness. Serve the salad in cups made with large leaves of butter lettuce. Or serve it as a bed under grilled fish or tofu.

Yields 4 servings as a side salad, 8 servings as a lettuce wrap

NUTRITIONAL INFORMATION
(per 8 servings, with lettuce)

calories 180	sodium (mg) 170	vitamin A IUs 8%
fat calories 110	total carbohydrates (g) 16	vitamin C 20%
total fat (g) 12	fiber (g) 2	calcium 4%
sat fat (g) 1.5	sugars (g) 2	iron 10%
cholesterol (mg) 0	protein (g) 4	

¾ **cup white or golden quinoa**
(*see Cook's Notes*)

⅓ **cup fresh lemon juice**

Salt

Freshly ground black pepper

⅓ **cup extra-virgin olive oil**

2 **medium beets, golden preferred, roasted, peeled, cut into ½-inch chunks**

⅔ **cup finely diced unpeeled cucumber**

½ **cup finely chopped fresh Italian parsley**

½ **medium red onion, finely diced**

⅓ **cup finely chopped fresh mint**

⅓ **cup slivered almonds, toasted**
(*see Cook's Notes*)

OPTIONAL 8 butter lettuce cups

1. In a medium saucepan, combine 1½ cups water and the quinoa. Bring to a boil on high heat. Cover and reduce the heat to medium-low. Simmer for 12 minutes. Remove from the heat and allow the pan to rest off the heat, covered, for 4 minutes. If any water remains, drain if off. Fluff the quinoa with a fork.

2. In a large bowl, season the lemon juice with salt and pepper. Add the oil and whisk to combine. Add the quinoa, beets, cucumber, parsley, onion, and mint, and gently toss. For the best flavor, allow the tabbouleh to sit for 30 to 40 minutes before serving. Taste and adjust the seasoning if needed. Sprinkle with the almonds just before serving. Spoon the tabbouleh into bowls or the lettuce cups, if using, and serve.

COOK'S NOTES If using red beets, consider using red quinoa since the beets will stain the salad red. It is sold at stores that specialize in natural foods. Cook red quinoa the same way as white.

To toast slivered almonds, place them in a single layer on a rimmed baking sheet. Bake in a 350-degree-F oven for 3 to 4 minutes, or until lightly browned. Watch carefully because nuts burn easily.

Cold Beet, Pear, and Red Bell Soup

A purée of brightly colored fruits and vegetables makes a delicious cold soup. Serve it in 2-ounce shot glasses or demitasse cups as a passed appetizer. Garnish with a sprinkling of soft crumbled cheese, such as feta or goat cheese, or top each serving with a small dollop of plain Greek-style yogurt.

Yields 12 appetizer servings

NUTRITIONAL INFORMATION
(per serving)

calories 70	sodium (mg) 105	vitamin A IUs 8%
fat calories 30	total carbohydrates (g)..... 8	vitamin C 25%
total fat (g) 3.5	fiber (g) 2	calcium 4%
sat fat (g) 1.5	sugars (g) 5	iron................................ 4%
cholesterol (mg) 5	protein (g) 2	

4 medium red beets (with 1-inch stems intact)

1 tablespoon extra-virgin olive oil

½ medium red onion, coarsely chopped

1 red bell pepper, cored and seeded, cut into 1-inch strips

1 ripe pear, peeled and cored, cut into 1-inch strips

4 cups vegetable broth

About 2 tablespoons fresh lemon juice

Salt

Freshly ground black pepper

GARNISH ¾ cup crumbled goat cheese

1. Preheat the oven to 400 degrees F. Wash the beets in cold water. Wrap the wet beets in heavy-duty aluminum foil. Place the packet on a rimmed baking sheet. Roast until the beets are fork tender, 30 to 60 minutes, depending on their size. When they are cool enough to handle, peel and coarsely chop or slice the beets.

2. In a medium pan or Dutch oven, heat the oil on medium-high heat. Add the onion and cook until it begins to soften, about 3 minutes. Add the pepper and pear; cook, stirring occasionally, for 3 minutes. Add the broth and bring to a boil. Reduce the heat to medium-low. Cover and cook for 15 minutes. Add the beets and cook for 10 minutes more, until all the produce is tender.

3. Let the soup cool slightly. Season with the lemon juice, salt, and pepper. Remove 1 cup broth from the soup and reserve. Purée the soup in batches in a blender. If it is too thick, add enough of the reserved broth to reach the desired consistency. Cover and refrigerate.

4. Taste the soup before serving. It may need more salt, pepper, and/or lemon juice, as chilling can dull those flavors. Ladle the soup into small demitasse cups or pots de crème cups. Top each serving with a sprinkling of cheese.

Beet Green Two-Step

Serve these glorious greens over cooked farro or brown rice. To add flavor and texture, add a topping such as toasted slivered almonds, chopped tomato, or crumbled goat cheese. Or toast some coarse fresh bread crumbs made from rustic whole-wheat bread and sprinkle them over the top for a tasty crunch. If you can't find beet greens, substitute mustard greens or dandelion greens.

Yields 8 side-dish servings

NUTRITIONAL INFORMATION
(per serving, without optional toppings)

calories 50	sodium (mg) 45	vitamin A IUs 24%
fat calories 45	total carbohydrates (g) 2	vitamin C 10%
total fat (g) 5	fiber (g) 1	calcium 2%
sat fat (g) 1	sugars (g) 0	iron 4%
cholesterol (mg) 0	protein (g) 1	

Salt

10 to 12 cups beet greens

3 tablespoons extra-virgin olive oil

2 medium garlic cloves, minced

½ red onion, roughly chopped

Freshly ground black pepper

1½ tablespoons red wine vinegar

OPTIONAL TOPPINGS ¼ cup slivered almonds, toasted (*see Cook's Note*); chopped fresh tomato; toasted bread crumbs; crumbled goat cheese; grated Parmesan cheese

1. Bring a large pot of salted water to a boil on high heat. Meanwhile, rinse the greens thoroughly in several changes of cold water.

2. Place a colander in the sink. Place the beet greens in the boiling water for 1 minute. Drain them in the colander and run cold water over them to stop the cooking. With your hands, squeeze out excess water and coarsely chop the greens.

3. In a large, deep skillet, heat 1½ tablespoons of the oil on medium-high heat. Add the garlic and onion; cook, stirring occasionally, until the onion softens, about 2 to 3 minutes. Do *not* brown the garlic; reduce the heat as needed. Add the greens and increase the heat to high. Season with salt and pepper. Cook for about 2 minutes more, stirring frequently, until the greens are tender.

4. In a small bowl, combine the remaining 1½ tablespoons oil and the vinegar; stir with a fork. Pour over the greens and toss. Garnish with the toppings of choice. Serve.

COOK'S NOTE To toast almonds, place them in a single layer on a rimmed baking sheet. Bake in a 350-degree-F oven for 3 to 4 minutes, or until lightly browned. Watch carefully because nuts burn easily.

BLACKBERRY

One chew and a blackberry's tiny juice sacs burst with flavor-packed goodness. The juice is a seductive blend of deep sweet-tart flavors, while the flesh that encases it is a counterpoint of gentle crunch. Both the color and taste are prized in desserts, jams, and juices. The vibrant flavors lend excitement to yogurt or cooked grains, as well as to game, pork, and grilled tofu.

Blackberries are concentrated sources of the phytochemical ellagic acid, which acts as a powerful antioxidant. Quercetin, one of the main antioxidant compounds in berries and especially prevalent in blackberries, protects against cancers. It also works best in combination with vitamin C, and blackberries coincidentally are higher in vitamin C than many other fruits.

THINK STRONG
The compounds in blackberries and other berries have demonstrated a capability to reverse defects in memory, cognition, and motor function, especially as connected with aging.

NUTRITIONAL INFORMATION
(per 1 cup raw)

calories	62	sodium (mg)	1	vitamin A IUs	6%
fat calories	6	total carbohydrates (g)	15	vitamin C	50%
total fat (g)	1	fiber (g)	8	calcium	4%
sat fat (g)	0	sugars (g)	7	iron	5%
cholesterol (mg)	0	protein (g)	2		

STONE BREAKERS
The proanthocyanadin compounds of the type found in high amounts in blackberries were shown in peer-reviewed research to lower the risk of kidney stones.

CALCIUM CONTENDERS
Blackberries also are one of the best sources of calcium among the berry family, with more than two times the amount of many other fruits. Although in recent years calcium has received a lot of attention for the function it plays in keeping the cardiovascular system healthy, it still is the most important mineral for bone health. Enjoying lots of dietary calcium can reduce and even counter osteoporosis.

AVAILABLE
Year-round

KEEP IT FRESH
Look for berries that are fragrant, without any mold or mushiness. A dark black color is best because only purple or dark red may be a sign that they were not ripe when harvested. If packaged in a container, look at the pad underneath the berries; if it looks saturated with dark juice, choose another container. Or if the berries stick together when the container is tilted, it could be a sign that there is deterioration. Store unwashed berries in a single layer in a shallow container; cover loosely with plastic wrap and refrigerate. Blackberries are perishable, so if not using within 3 or 4 days, freeze them. To freeze, place them in a single layer on a rimmed baking sheet; once frozen, transfer them to a zipper-style plastic freezer bag—push out the air, seal, and return them to the freezer. Use frozen or defrosted berries only in cooked dishes since they become mushy when frozen and thawed.

LAST-MINUTE PREP

Place in a colander and wash briefly with cold water. Drain, then place the berries on paper towels or a clean kitchen cloth to absorb more water.

QUICK COOK

For a dessert sauce, bring 2 cups frozen or fresh blackberries and ½ cup agave syrup to a boil in a medium saucepan on medium-high heat. Reduce the heat and simmer on medium-low for 1 minute. In a small bowl, combine 1 tablespoon fresh orange juice with 2 teaspoons cornstarch. Add the mixture to the berries and stir, simmering, until thickened, about 1 minute. Cool and serve over pudding, custard, ice cream, or yogurt.

try it!

GINGERED IN FRUIT SALAD

In a small saucepan, combine 2 tablespoons agave syrup with 2 tablespoons water; bring to a boil on high heat. Stir in 2 teaspoons minced fresh ginger and remove from the heat. Let cool. In a large bowl, combine the gingered syrup with 2 tablespoons fresh lemon juice. Add 10 cups of mixed fresh fruit, such as blackberries, peaches or plums (peeled, pitted, sliced), grapes, tangerine sections, cubed melon (such as cantaloupe, watermelon, or honeydew) and/or kiwi (peeled, sliced). Toss. Serve or cover and chill up to 4 hours.

IN A QUICK SPINACH SALAD

In a medium-large bowl, toss 5 cups fresh baby spinach with 2 tablespoons extra-virgin olive oil. Add 3 tablespoons balsamic vinegar, ¼ red onion (cut into thin slivers), ⅓ cup crumbled feta cheese, 1 cup halved grape tomatoes, 3 tablespoons chopped toasted walnuts, and 2 cups blackberries (fresh or thawed) and toss again.

IN SHOTS OF COLD DESSERT SOUP

In a medium pan or Dutch oven, combine 3¾ cups fresh or frozen IQF (individually quick frozen without sugar) blackberries, 2 cups water, 3 tablespoons agave syrup or maple syrup, ½ lemon (thinly sliced), 1 cinnamon stick, and 3 whole cloves. Bring to a boil on high heat; reduce the heat to medium-low and simmer for 5 minutes, mashing the berries with a potato masher or slotted spoon. Strain using a fine sieve, pressing the contents with the back of a sturdy spoon to release the juice; discard the solids. Let cool. Put the juice in a food processor with ¾ cup plain Greek-style yogurt; pulse just enough to incorporate the yogurt into the fruit mixture. Place the soup in a pitcher; cover and refrigerate until cold. Stir, then pour it into 2-ounce glasses or demitasses cups and serve topped with a small dollop of plain yogurt sweetened with honey.

Blackberry Gratin

This dessert looks something like a cobbler. The tofu-enhanced mixture browns nicely, creating a crisp surface with a berry-spiked biscuity interior. If you like, dust each serving with a little powdered sugar: Place a small amount in a fine sieve; gently shake over the top of each serving.

Yields 6 servings

NUTRITIONAL INFORMATION
(per serving)

calories ... 160	sodium (mg) ... 70	vitamin A IUs ... 6%
fat calories ... 70	total carbohydrates (g) ... 23	vitamin C ... 25%
total fat (g) ... 7	fiber (g) ... 4	calcium ... 4%
sat fat (g) ... 2	sugars (g) ... 17	iron ... 6%
cholesterol (mg) ... 30	protein (g) ... 4	

Nonstick vegetable oil cooking spray

- ⅓ cup plus 1 tablespoon sugar
- ⅓ cup pecan halves, toasted (*see Cook's Note*), at room temperature
- 2 tablespoons all-purpose flour
- ½ teaspoon ground cinnamon
- ⅛ teaspoon salt
- ⅓ cup silken firm tofu
- 1 egg
- 1 tablespoon unsalted butter, at room temperature
- 2¾ cups fresh blackberries

OPTIONAL GARNISH 6 sprigs fresh mint, powdered sugar

1. Preheat the oven to 400 degrees F. Generously coat a 1-quart gratin pan with cooking spray.

2. Put the sugar, pecans, flour, cinnamon, and salt in a food processor fitted with the metal blade; process until finely ground. Add the tofu, egg, and butter; process until puréed and smooth.

3. Put the berries in a single layer in the prepared pan. Add the batter and spread it over the berries. Bake until the gratin is set and lightly browned, 40 to 50 minutes. Let it cool for 25 to 30 minutes. If desired, dust with powdered sugar and garnish each serving with a sprig of fresh mint.

COOK'S NOTE To toast pecans, place them in a single layer on a rimmed baking sheet. Bake in a 350-degree-F oven for 4 to 5 minutes, or until lightly browned. Watch carefully because nuts burn easily.

Cherries Poached in Red Wine with Blackberries and Mint

Blackberries and fresh sweet cherries have such complementary flavor profiles. Bing (bright red to mahogany red) is the most common cherry variety in the marketplace, but others such as Rainiers (yellow with a red blush) can be substituted. The easiest and least messy way to remove the seeds is to use a cherry pitter. The gadget works something like a scissor-style paper punch with a shaft that pushes the pit out.

Yields 8 servings

NUTRITIONAL INFORMATION
(per serving)

calories 250	sodium (mg) 10	vitamin A IUs 2%
fat calories 5	total carbohydrates (g)... 47	vitamin C 20%
total fat (g) 0	fiber (g) 3	calcium 4%
sat fat (g)......................... 0	sugars (g) 41	iron............................... 4%
cholesterol (mg) 0	protein (g) 3	

2½ cups dry red wine

1 cup granulated sugar or agave syrup

Two 2-inch-wide strips orange or tangerine zest

1½ pounds fresh sweet cherries, pitted, halved

8 ounces whole fresh blackberries

OPTIONAL 2 teaspoons minced fresh mint

¾ cup plain fat-free Greek-style yogurt

1 tablespoon honey

OPTIONAL GARNISH sprigs fresh mint

1. In a large non-aluminum saucepan, combine the wine, sugar, and zest. Bring to a simmer on medium-high heat, stirring to dissolve the sugar. Add the cherries and reduce the heat to maintain a simmer until the cherries are just barely tender, about 4 to 5 minutes. Transfer everything to a bowl to cool. When it is lukewarm, add the blackberries and mint, if using. Gently toss.

2. In a small bowl, stir together the yogurt and honey until combined.

3. Divide the cherry-berry mixture into eight small bowls. Top each with a dollop of the yogurt mixture. If desired, garnish each serving with a small sprig of mint.

Breakfast Quinoa with Blackberries

The only thing difficult about quinoa is its pronunciation. Pronounced KEEN-wah, it cooks up fast and easy. Boil it in water or broth for 10 minutes. Then let it rest, covered, for another 4 minutes for al dente crunch or about 7 minutes to bring the tasty seeds to a softer state. The longer heating makes the seeds fluffier but still pleasingly chewy. The red-hued quinoa variety is called for in this breakfast treat, but the white or black varieties (or a mixture) work well, too.

Yields 5 servings

NUTRITIONAL INFORMATION
(per serving)

calories 230	sodium (mg) 15	vitamin A IUs 8%
fat calories 60	total carbohydrates (g) ... 35	vitamin C 10%
total fat (g) 7	fiber (g) 4	calcium 6%
sat fat (g) 0	sugars (g) 6	iron 15%
cholesterol (mg) 0	protein (g) 8	

1   **cup red quinoa** (*see Cook's Note*)

2   **teaspoons extra-virgin olive oil**

¼   **cup slivered almonds**

⅓   **cup diced mixed dried fruit, such as apricots, figs, peach, mango, and papaya**

2   **tablespoons maple syrup**

1   **teaspoon ground cinnamon**

¼   **cup plain fat-free Greek-style yogurt**

1   **cup fresh blackberries**

1. Put the quinoa and 2 cups water in a small saucepan. Bring to a boil on high heat. Cover and decrease the heat to medium-low. Simmer until tender and the water is absorbed, about 10 minutes. Gently stir and set off the heat, covered, for 4 minutes.

2. Meanwhile, heat the oil in a medium skillet on high heat. Add the almonds and cook on medium heat until golden, shaking the skillet to redistribute the nuts as they lightly brown, about 1½ minutes. Add the dried fruit, syrup, and cinnamon; stir and cook until heated through. Add the quinoa and gently toss.

3. Divide the quinoa mixture between five bowls. Place small scoops of yogurt in the center of each serving. Surround with the blackberries.

COOK'S NOTE In its natural state, quinoa is coated with bitter saponins. Most quinoa sold in North America has been processed to remove the coating, so it doesn't need rinsing. Check the cooking instructions on the package to see if they direct you to rinse the quinoa before cooking. If buying in bulk or if package advises rinsing, rinse quinoa in a fine-meshed strainer under running water for about 45 seconds. Shake handle rigorously to remove excess water.

BOK CHOY

Bok choy offers such an appealing mix of taste and texture. Whether a 16-inch mature or a petite 7-inch "baby" head, both stalks and leaves are delicious. The stems are celery-like, both juicy and crisp. The leaf's flavor profile varies, some weighing in with a sweet vegetal taste, others edged with peppery spice.

Choy, Chinese for "cabbage," is a major food staple throughout Asia. It has a good nutrition profile and the ability to grow throughout the year in poor soil and weather conditions.

HEART HEALTHY

The rich green leaves draw a lot of vitamins and minerals from those stressful conditions, especially calcium for bone and cardiovascular health and iron for muscle and red blood cell building. Vitamins A, C, and K are abundant, as well as folate and vitamin B_6 (pyridoxine).

NUTRITIONAL INFORMATION
(1 cup shredded, raw)

calories 10	sodium (mg) 45	vitamin A IUs 40%
fat calories 0	total carbohydrates (g)..... 2	vitamin C 50%
total fat (g) 0	fiber (g) .... less than 1	calcium..........................8%
sat fat (g)........................0	sugars (g) 0	iron...............................4%
cholesterol (mg) 0	protein (g) 1	

NERVE SUPPORT

While folate helps protect the heart and prevent neural tube defects during fetal development, vitamin B_6 helps nerve cells and red blood cells develop and function.

GLUCOSE BALANCER

It also helps keep the figure trim; the fiber in bok choy increases satiety while the B_6 helps regulate glucose production. Hormone function also relies on B_6, especially the hormones estrogen, progesterone, and testosterone. All this for only about 10 calories per cup!

AVAILABLE
Year-round

KEEP IT FRESH

Look for crisp stalks with no discoloration and bright green leaves that are not wilted. Refrigerate unwashed in perforated bags up to 5 days.

LAST-MINUTE PREP

Trim and discard a shallow slice off the base of the stalks, trimming off the tough, sometimes discolored portion but leaving the stalks attached. Most often bok choy is washed with the stalks still attached at the base, either quartered lengthwise for large bok choy, or halved for smaller bok choy. Wash in large amounts of cold water, gently swirling to expose the leaves to water. If using raw, drain well and pat dry. Often bok choy quarters or halves are steamed with plenty of water still clinging to the leaves.

QUICK COOK

Bok choy can be eaten raw, combined with mild-flavored greens in salads. For a simple cooking approach, soak 3 quartered large bok choy or 6 halved baby bok choy in large amounts of cold water. Meanwhile, heat 1½ tablespoons extra-virgin olive oil on medium-high heat in a large, deep skillet. Add 1 garlic clove (minced) and 1 tablespoon minced fresh ginger; stir-fry until they begin to soften, about 30 seconds. Drain and add the wet bok choy in an even layer. Add 1 tablespoon oyster sauce, 2 tablespoons sodium-reduced soy sauce, and 1 teaspoon Asian sesame oil. Cover and cook for 5 minutes. If desired, add a pinch of dried red pepper flakes. Gently toss. Serve with the pan sauce spooned on top.

try it!

STEAMED AND TOPPED WITH SCRAMBLED EGGS

Coarsely chop 1 large head of halved, washed bok choy. Heat 1½ tablespoons extra-virgin olive oil in a large, deep skillet on medium-high heat. Add the bok choy and season with salt and freshly ground black pepper. If the bok choy is wet from washing, you may not need to add any water, but if dry, add ⅓ cup water. Cook, stirring occasionally, until the stalks are tender and the liquid evaporates, about 10 minutes. Spoon into four shallow bowls and top each with a scrambled egg, chopped chives, and shaved Parmesan.

CREAMED OVER BAKED POTATOES

Coarsely chop 4 quartered, washed baby bok choy. Heat 1 tablespoon extra-virgin olive oil in a large, deep skillet on medium-high heat. Add the bok choy and season with salt and freshly ground black pepper. Cook for 1 minute. If the bok choy is wet from washing, you may not need to add any water, but if dry, add ¼ cup water. Cook, stirring occasionally, until the stalks are tender and the liquid evaporates, about 10 minutes. Let cool. Wring out the excess water by squeezing one handful at a time and put the bok choy in a food processor. Add ¼ cup fresh basil; process until finely chopped. Add ½ cup ricotta cheese and 3 tablespoons evaporated skim milk; pulse to combine. Heat 1 tablespoon butter or extra-virgin olive oil in a saucepan on medium heat. Add the bok choy mixture and cook, stirring occasionally, until hot. Use as a topping for baked potatoes.

WITH MISO SAUCE

Coarsely chop 4 or 5 quartered, washed baby bok choy. Heat 1 tablespoon extra-virgin olive oil in a large, deep skillet on medium-high heat. Add the bok choy and season with salt and freshly ground black pepper. Cook for 1 minute. If the bok choy is wet from washing, you may not need to add any water, but if dry, add ⅓ cup water. Cook, stirring occasionally, until the stalks are tender and the liquid evaporates, about 10 minutes. Remove from the skillet. On medium-high heat, add 1 teaspoon extra-virgin olive oil and 1 teaspoon minced fresh ginger to the skillet. Cook for 30 seconds. Stir in 1 tablespoon yellow miso, 1 tablespoon mirin (sweet rice wine), 1½ tablespoons seasoned rice vinegar, a pinch of dried red pepper flakes, and 1½ tablespoons water; stir rigorously to combine. Return the bok choy to the skillet; toss. Heat through and serve.

Arborio Rice Salad with Baby Bok Choy and Asparagus

Ringed with cooked baby bok choy, this salad makes a colorful presentation on a buffet table. It is made using Arborio rice, the plump Italian variety that is the basis of risotto. Then it's tossed with lemony vinaigrette. If desired, use only two-thirds of the dressing in the salad, offering leftover dressing on the side. For a vegetarian version, simply omit the chicken.

Yields 8 servings

NUTRITIONAL INFORMATION
(per serving, using all the vinaigrette)

calories 300	sodium (mg) 500	vitamin A IUs 60%
fat calories 100	total carbohydrates (g)...44	vitamin C 15%
total fat (g) 12	fiber (g) 4	calcium.........................4%
sat fat (g)......................1.5	sugars (g) 3	iron.................................6%
cholesterol (mg) 0	protein (g) 7	

About 1½ teaspoons canola oil

2 large garlic cloves, minced

8 to 10 baby bok choy (about 1½ pounds), halved lengthwise, soaked in cold water

1 teaspoon Asian sesame oil

DRESSING

¼ cup finely chopped fresh Italian parsley

3 tablespoons fresh lemon juice

1½ teaspoons Dijon mustard

¼ cup extra-virgin olive oil

Salt

Freshly ground black pepper

⅓ cup chopped red onion

RICE SALAD

1 teaspoon salt

2 cups raw Arborio rice

1 pound asparagus, trimmed, cut in ¼-inch pieces, leaving tips whole

OPTIONAL 8 ounces cooked boneless chicken thighs, cut into ½-inch chunks

1 ripe Roma tomato, cored, diced

½ cup slivered almonds, toasted (see Cook's Note)

1. Heat the canola oil in a large, deep skillet on medium-high heat. Add half the garlic and cook for 30 seconds (do not brown). Drain the bok choy and place it in the skillet in an even layer. Drizzle with the sesame oil and cover. Cover and cook for 4 to 5 minutes, or until the leaves wilt and the stems remain tender-crisp. Line a rimmed baking sheet with a clean kitchen towel or paper towels; add the bok choy and set aside.

2. To make the dressing: In a small bowl or measuring cup with a handle, stir together the parsley, lemon juice, remaining garlic, and mustard. Whisk in the oil in a thin stream. Season with salt and pepper and add the onion; stir to combine. Set aside.

3. To make the salad: Bring 6 cups of water to a boil in a large saucepan or Dutch oven on high heat. Add the salt and rice. Boil until the rice is almost tender, 10 to 12 minutes. Add the asparagus and cook for another 4 to 5 minutes, until the rice is cooked and the asparagus is tender-crisp. Transfer everything to a large sieve and drain. Rinse with cold water. Drain well.

4. In a large bowl, combine the rice mixture, dressing, chicken (if using), and tomatoes. Gently toss. Taste and adjust the seasonings as needed.

5. Arrange the bok choy on a large platter, placing it around the perimeter with the stems pointing toward the center. Pile the rice salad in the center. Sprinkle with the almonds and serve.

COOK'S NOTE To toast almonds, place them in a single layer on a rimmed baking sheet. Bake in a 350-degree-F oven for 3 to 4 minutes, or until lightly browned. Watch carefully because nuts burn easily.

Bok Choy and Romaine Salad

Filled with crunch and bok choy attitude, this salad is garnished with toasted sesame seeds. The seeds add rich nuttiness and aroma to the salad, qualities that are enhanced by toasting. Some Asian markets sell small skillets that are designed for toasting these tiny seeds. The petite skillets have a hinged screen attached that prevents the frisky seeds from escaping when they are heated. You can use a small, deep skillet to do the job, also.

Yields 4 servings

NUTRITIONAL INFORMATION
(per serving)

calories 110	sodium (mg) 180	vitamin A IUs 90%
fat calories 70	total carbohydrates (g).....8	vitamin C 35%
total fat (g) 8	fiber (g) 2	calcium 6%
sat fat (g) 1	sugars (g) 3	iron 8%
cholesterol (mg) 0	protein (g) 3	

DRESSING

1 ½ tablespoons rice vinegar

1 teaspoon honey, dark honey preferred

1 ½ tablespoons sodium-reduced soy sauce

2 teaspoons Asian sesame oil

SALAD

2 ½ cups ½-inch-wide strips romaine lettuce hearts

2 ½ cups ½-inch-wide strips baby bok choy

2 tablespoons coarsely chopped fresh cilantro

GARNISHES 1 tablespoon toasted sesame seeds (*see Cook's Note*); ¼ cup cashew nuts, coarsely chopped; 4 lemon wedges

OPTIONAL GARNISH coarse salt (kosher or sea)

1. To make the dressing: In a small bowl or glass measuring cup with a handle, whisk together the vinegar and honey until the honey dissolves. Whisk in the soy sauce and sesame oil.

2. To make the salad: In a large bowl, combine the romaine and bok choy. Stir the dressing; add to the bowl and toss. Add the cilantro and toss. Allow the salad to rest for 15 minutes at room temperature.

3. Divide the salad between four shallow bowls or plates. Sprinkle each with the sesame seeds and cashews. Taste and, if desired, sprinkle each salad with a tiny amount of coarse salt. Place a lemon wedge on the side of each salad and serve.

COOK'S NOTE Toasted sesame seeds are sold at some supermarkets and most Asian markets. Or, if you prefer, you can toast them. Place them in a small skillet on medium-high heat. Shake the handle to redistribute the seeds, cooking until they are lightly browned. Remove from the heat and let cool.

Bok Choy and Mushroom Soup

Simple to make, this appetizing soup is open to many variations. It calls for common white mushrooms, but fresh shiitake mushrooms would be a delicious substitution. Or add a can of drained straw mushrooms, those fungi with the alluring woodsy taste and caps that look like whimsical conical hats. And, if desired, augment each serving with a cooked potsticker dumpling.

Yields 6 servings

NUTRITIONAL INFORMATION
(per serving)

calories 90	sodium (mg) 410	vitamin A IUs 110%
fat calories 35	total carbohydrates (g).....11	vitamin C 110%
total fat (g) 4	fiber (g) 3	calcium 15%
sat fat (g)..................... 0.5	sugars (g) 6	iron............................. 10%
cholesterol (mg) 0	protein (g) 4	

8 baby bok choy or 3 to 4 large bok choy (about 1½ pounds), halved lengthwise, soaked in cold water

2 teaspoons extra-virgin olive oil

2 garlic cloves, minced

2 tablespoons minced unpeeled fresh ginger

6 cups chicken broth or vegetable broth

2 cups thinly sliced white button mushrooms

3 tablespoons sodium-reduced soy sauce

3 tablespoons seasoned rice vinegar

2 tablespoons dry sherry

1 tablespoon Asian sesame oil

1 cup sugar snap peas, strings removed

OPTIONAL ½ cup cooked edamame

Coarse salt (kosher or sea)

OPTIONAL Asian-style hot sauce, such as Sriracha

GARNISH 3 small or 4 large green onions, trimmed, thinly sliced (including dark green stalks)

1. Drain the bok choy and shake off the excess water (leaves can be wet, but it is easier to cut up if some water is removed). Cut crosswise into ½-inch slices. Coarsely chop into bite-size pieces. Set aside.

2. In a large pan or Dutch oven, heat the oil on medium-high heat. Add the garlic and ginger; stir and cook until just barely softened, about 30 seconds. Add the bok choy, broth, mushrooms, soy sauce, vinegar, sherry, and sesame oil. Bring to a boil on high heat. Reduce to medium-low and simmer for 5 minutes. Add the peas and cook until tender-crisp, about 4 minutes more. Add the edamame, if using, and simmer until heated through, about 30 seconds. Taste and, if needed, add salt. If desired, add hot sauce, starting with a small amount.

3. Ladle into soup bowls, top with the green onions, and serve.

BROCCOLI

Through a child's eyes, a broccoli floret may resemble a leafy tree. The clusters of tightly closed buds at the top look like foliage, the stalk below the image of a sturdy trunk. Eat it raw or briefly cooked, and its appealing vegetal flavor is balanced with hints of sweetness and a trace of pepper.

As green vegetables go, it's hard to beat broccoli for the amount and variety of beneficial vitamins, minerals, and phytochemicals.

NUTRITIONAL INFORMATION
(per 1 cup chopped, raw)

calories 31	sodium (mg) 30	vitamin A IUs 11%
fat calories 3	total carbohydrates (g) 6	vitamin C 135%
total fat (g) 0	fiber (g) 2	calcium 4%
sat fat (g) 0	sugars (g) 2	iron 4%
cholesterol (mg) 0	protein (g) 3	

VITAMIN POWERHOUSE
Broccoli contains lots of fiber, B vitamins (especially vitamin B_6), folate, vitamin C, and vitamin K, plus abundant minerals such as manganese, magnesium, potassium, iron, calcium, and zinc.

EYE PROTECTION
Broccoli, especially the leaves, is an outstanding source of carotenoid compounds, specifically vitamin A, zeaxanthin, and lutein. Lutein and zeaxanthin are both critical to eye health. They help protect against age-related macular degeneration, one of the most common forms of blindness, and protect against the development of cataracts.

CANCER SHIELD
As a member of the family of cruciferous or brassicae vegetables, broccoli is replete with phytochemicals called isothiocyanates, a family that comprises dozens of compounds shown to protect against cancer, especially breast and prostate cancers.

AVAILABLE
Year-round

KEEP IT FRESH
Select bunches that smell fresh and have tightly closed buds that are dark green, purplish, or deep bluish green, without yellow. Stalks should not have soft spots; they should be firm, not rubbery. Refrigerate unwashed and dry in a plastic bag in the crisper drawer up to 1 week.

LAST-MINUTE PREP

Rinse well with cold water. If the recipe calls for florets, cut high enough on the stalk so that individual florets fall from the stalk. If desired, peel the stalks and thinly slice them to use as well.

QUICK COOK

Cook broccoli only a brief amount of time, just until tender-crisp. Stalks cook quicker and are more tender if peeled before cooking (but remember there are carotenoid compounds in the leaves). Blanch, steam, sauté, or toss with a little olive oil and roast at high heat.

try it!

WITH TRIMMED-DOWN CHEESE SAUCE

Place 1 tablespoon all-purpose flour in a heavy-bottomed saucepan. Whisk in 1¼ cups evaporated fat-free milk. Place on medium-high heat. Cook, stirring constantly, until thickened and bubbly, 2 to 3 minutes. Off the heat, whisk in ⅓ cup finely shredded reduced-fat sharp Cheddar cheese. Whisk in 2½ tablespoons grated Parmesan cheese, ½ teaspoon Worcestershire sauce, and ¾ teaspoon Dijon mustard. Stir in seasoned salt; spoon over blanched or steamed broccoli. Add freshly ground black pepper, if desired.

IN COLESLAW

Grate raw (peeled if desired) broccoli stems. Add to your favorite coleslaw.

ROASTED AND CHILE-FIED

Adjust an oven rack to the middle position. Preheat the oven to 425 degrees F. On a rimmed baking sheet, toss 7 to 8 cups broccoli florets with 3 tablespoons extra-virgin olive oil. Roast for 15 minutes. In a small bowl, toss 1 garlic clove (minced) with ⅛ teaspoon dried red pepper flakes; toss with the broccoli and roast an additional 10 minutes, until deeply caramelized on the exterior and fork tender. Season with coarse salt.

Couscous with Broccoli, Basil, and Pecans

This appetizing side dish can become a main course by adding chunks of cooked chicken breast or spooning it over thin slices of grilled steak or tofu. If you like, omit the cheese and add some dried fruit, such as golden raisins or dried cranberries.

Yields 6 side-dish servings

NUTRITIONAL INFORMATION
(per serving)

calories 220	sodium (mg) 250	vitamin A IUs 30%
fat calories 110	total carbohydrates (g)... 27	vitamin C 70%
total fat (g) 12	fiber (g) 6	calcium 4%
sat fat (g) 1.5	sugars (g) 1	iron............................. 8%
cholesterol (mg) 0	protein (g) 6	

3 tablespoons extra-virgin olive oil

½ large red onion, finely diced

2½ cups coarsely chopped broccoli florets

1 cup whole-wheat couscous

1 large garlic clove, minced

1⅔ cups fat-free low-sodium vegetable broth

½ cup chopped fresh basil

⅓ cup pecans, toasted (*see Cook's Note*), finely chopped

Salt

Freshly ground black pepper

¼ cup grated Manchego or Asiago cheese

1. Heat the oil on medium-high heat in a large, deep skillet with a lid. Add the onion and cook, stirring occasionally, until it is softened and just starting to slightly brown, about 4 minutes. Add the broccoli and toss to coat with oil. Cook, stirring frequently, 6 to 7 minutes, or until it is tender-crisp.

2. Stir in the couscous; cook, stirring constantly, until the couscous begins to brown. Stir in the garlic and cook for 30 seconds. Add the broth and bring it to a boil on high heat. Cover and reduce the heat to low. Gently simmer 14 to 15 minutes, until all the liquid is absorbed.

3. Remove from the heat; stir in the basil and pecans. Season with salt and pepper. Toss. Top each serving with some grated cheese.

COOK'S NOTE To toast pecans, place them on a rimmed baking sheet in a single layer. Bake in a 350-degree-F oven for 4 to 5 minutes, or until lightly toasted. Watch carefully because nuts burn easily.

Broccoli Stalk and Garlic Soup

If you make a habit out of discarding broccoli stalks, you will change your ways once you taste this dish. Along with sliced broccoli stalks, garlic and saffron give this ambrosial soup its backbone. Slices of rustic crusty bread, slathered with a little extra-virgin olive oil and toasted, are the secret crunch under the steaming soup.

Yields 4 servings

NUTRITIONAL INFORMATION
(per serving)

calories 280	sodium (mg) 630	vitamin A IUs 45%
fat calories 100	total carbohydrates (g)...34	vitamin C 80%
total fat (g) 12	fiber (g) 3	calcium 15%
sat fat (g)......................2.5	sugars (g) 1	iron..............................15%
cholesterol (mg) 5	protein (g) 11	

3 tablespoons extra-virgin olive oil

Four ½-inch slices rustic, crusty bread, whole-wheat sourdough preferred

5 large garlic cloves, peeled and halved lengthwise

1 tablespoon paprika

½ teaspoon ground cumin

5 cups fat-free low-sodium chicken broth or vegetable broth

⅛ teaspoon ground saffron

5 stalks broccoli (florets removed and reserved for another use), peeled and cut into ¼-inch rounds

Salt

¼ cup finely chopped fresh Italian parsley

⅓ cup grated Parmesan cheese

1. Adjust an oven rack to 8 inches below the broiler and preheat the broiler. Using 1 tablespoon of the oil, brush the bread slices on both sides. Place them on a rimmed baking sheet and broil until the bread is lightly toasted. Turn and toast on the opposite side until lightly browned. Watch carefully because bread can burn easily. Set aside.

2. Heat the remaining 2 tablespoons oil in a heavy-bottomed large pan or Dutch oven on low heat. Add the garlic and cook until it is golden and softened, about 10 minutes, stirring often. Add the paprika and cumin; stir to combine and remove the pan from the stove. Tilt the pan and push the ingredients to one side; mash the garlic with a fork. Return the pan to the stove; stir in the broth and saffron. Bring to a simmer on high heat; reduce the heat to medium or medium-low and simmer for 10 minutes. Add the broccoli; simmer 10 minutes more, or until the broccoli is just barely tender. Taste and season with salt.

3. In each of four shallow soup bowls, place a toasted bread slice. Ladle soup into the bowls and top with parsley and Parmesan. Serve.

Broccoli-Tofu Stir-Fry

Soy sauce, hoisin sauce, and red pepper flakes boost the flavor profile of this quick stir-fried dish. Be sure to have all the components ready and set next to the stove before you start to cook. The mixture is delicious served over cooked brown rice, quinoa, or farro.

Yields 6 servings

NUTRITIONAL INFORMATION
(per serving, without rice)

calories 130	sodium (mg) 230	vitamin A IUs 20%
fat calories 60	total carbohydrates (g).....11	vitamin C 50%
total fat (g) 6	fiber (g) 3	calcium..........................6%
sat fat (g)........... less than 1	sugars (g) 4	iron.............................10%
cholesterol (mg) 0	protein (g) 9	

½ cup fat-free, low-sodium chicken or vegetable broth

2 tablespoons hoisin sauce

1 tablespoon sodium-reduced soy sauce

1 teaspoon cornstarch

Pinch dried red pepper flakes

1 pound extra-firm tofu

2 tablespoons sesame seeds

1 tablespoon peanut oil

½ teaspoon Asian sesame oil

Nonstick vegetable oil cooking spray

12 ounces fresh shiitake mushrooms, stems removed, cut into ¼-inch slices

2½ cups small broccoli florets, about 1½ inches long

3 green onions, cut diagonally into ¼-inch slices (including half of dark green stalks)

1 large garlic clove, minced

1. In a small bowl, combine the broth, hoisin, soy sauce, cornstarch, and pepper flakes. Stir to combine and set next to the stove.

2. Drain the tofu and pat dry with paper towels. Cut it into 1-inch cubes. In a bowl, gently toss the tofu and sesame seeds. Heat the oils in a wok or large, deep nonstick skillet on medium-high heat. Add the tofu and stir-fry until nicely browned, about 4 to 5 minutes. Transfer it to a plate.

3. Coat the skillet with nonstick spray and return it to medium-high heat. Add the mushrooms and stir-fry until they are softened, about 4 minutes. Add the broccoli and stir-fry until it is tender-crisp, about 4 minutes, adding 1 tablespoon water if the mixture seems dry. Add the onions and garlic; stir-fry for about 30 seconds. Stir the broth mixture and add it to the broccoli mixture. Cook, gently stirring, until the sauce thickens. Add tofu and gently toss. Serve spooned over brown rice, quinoa, or farro, if desired.

BRUSSELS
SPROUT

Overcooking Brussels sprouts is a culinary crime. Cooked just enough to be easily pierced with the tip of a knife, they taste delicious and smell fresh and appealing. But cooked too long, these tiny cabbage-like vegetables get mushy and take on an unpleasant sulfurous odor.

As with its *Brassica* cousins (cabbage, mustard greens, and broccoli), Brussels sprouts are cruciferous vegetables bursting with nutrition in the form of vitamins, minerals, and cancer-fighting phytochemicals.

NUTRITIONAL INFORMATION
(per 1 cup raw, chopped)

calories 38	sodium (mg) 22	vitamin A IUs 13%
fat calories 2	total carbohydrates (g).....8	vitamin C 125%
total fat (g) 0	fiber (g) 3	calcium 4%
sat fat (g)......................... 0	sugars (g) 2	iron................................. 7%
cholesterol (mg) 0	protein (g) 3	

DIGESTION AID AND ANTIOXIDANT BOOST
The fiber in sprouts helps digestion and satiety. They also contain antioxidant carotenoids, both vitamin A for skin health and regulation of gene function and lutein and zeaxanthine that contribute to eye health.

METABOLIC BOOSTER
The B vitamin content of Brussels sprouts includes a generous amount of not only folate and pyridoxine (B_6) but also thiamine and riboflavin.

Thiamine is vital to hundreds of metabolic processes in the body, not the least of which is the breakdown of sugars and the amino acid components of proteins. Riboflavin is also needed for multiple chemical reactions in every cell of the body and is especially critical to the metabolism of the key food components fat, protein, and carbohydrate. It also is important to liver function and eye health.

AVAILABLE
Year-round (available on the stalk September through March)

KEEP IT FRESH
Choose sprouts that are tightly packed without any yellowing or soft spots. For consistent cooking, select similar sizes. Refrigerate, dry and unwashed, loosely packed in a plastic bag, in the crisper drawer up to 10 days.

LAST-MINUTE PREP

Wash sprouts thoroughly with cold water; if pan-searing, pat them dry. Pull off and discard any discolored leaves. Trim off a small portion at the stem end if discolored, but be sure just to shave off only the discolored portion. The stem end needs to stay intact, and if cut too deeply, the outside leaves will fall off. Halve, slice, or leave sprouts whole. To steam them, some people like to cut a shallow X at the stem end before placing the sprouts in a steamer basket.

QUICK COOK

For any method, be sure to cook them until just barely fork tender. A combination of pan-searing and gentle steaming is a delectable approach. This technique browns the cut sides, which adds subtle sweetness. It works best with small Brussels sprouts. Cut them in half from top to bottom and toss with a little extra-virgin olive oil. Gently brown them cut-side down in a nonstick skillet with a bit of melted butter and olive oil on medium heat (or just olive oil if you prefer). Cover and gently cook until tender and beautifully browned, reducing heat if needed. Oven roasting, quick blanching, and steaming also yield ambrosial results.

SLICED AND QUICK-COOKED IN BROTH

Thinly slice about 12 ounces sprouts, cutting them lengthwise cautiously on a mandoline or with a sharp knife. Put them in a saucepan with ½ cup vegetable or chicken broth and 2 tablespoons extra-virgin olive oil. Cover and bring to a boil on high heat; reduce the heat to medium-low and simmer until they are just barely tender, 4 to 5 minutes, adding more broth if needed. Season with salt and freshly ground black pepper. Add a pinch of dried red pepper flakes and/or ½ teaspoon cider vinegar, if desired.

WITH CARROTS AND RED ONIONS

Melt 2 teaspoons butter with 2 teaspoons extra-virgin olive oil on medium-high heat in a medium skillet. Add ½ red onion (coarsely chopped) and cook until it is just starting to brown, about 3 minutes. Stir in 1 cup sliced, peeled carrots and 1 pound halved Brussels sprouts; cook until they are starting to brown, about 4 minutes, stirring occasionally. Add ¼ cup vegetable broth; cover and cook on medium-low heat until the vegetables are just barely tender, 5 to 8 minutes. Add 1 teaspoon balsamic vinegar and season with salt and freshly ground black pepper; gently toss.

WITH CHUNKS OF ROASTED YUKON GOLD POTATOES

Pan-sear and gently steam some small Brussels sprouts (see Quick Cook). Toss them with cooked unpeeled fingerling potatoes (halved lengthwise) that have been seasoned with salt and freshly ground black pepper. Drizzle with a little balsamic vinegar.

Brussels Sprouts with Asian Peanut Dressing and Rice

Tangy Asian-style peanut dressing is classically slathered on noodle salads or slaws. Here the sweet-spicy mixture dresses tender-crisp Brussels sprouts that have been seared and steamed. They sit on a bed of brown rice, adorned with slivers of red bell peppers and a sprinkling of chopped cilantro.

Yields 6 servings

NUTRITIONAL INFORMATION
(per serving)

calories 260	sodium (mg) 200	vitamin A IUs 10%
fat calories 80	total carbohydrates (g)... 37	vitamin C 110%
total fat (g) 9	fiber (g) 5	calcium 4%
sat fat (g)........................ 2	sugars (g) 4	iron............................... 4%
cholesterol (mg) 0	protein (g) 6	

11 ounces (about 20) small, tightly closed Brussels sprouts, trimmed, halved top to bottom

1½ tablespoons plus 2 teaspoons extra-virgin olive oil

Coarse salt (kosher or sea)

ASIAN PEANUT DRESSING

2 tablespoons light coconut milk

2 tablespoons fresh lime juice

1½ tablespoons peanut butter

2 teaspoons fish sauce

1 teaspoon minced jalapeño (*see Cook's Notes*)

1 teaspoon light brown sugar or dark honey

4 cups cooked brown rice (*see Cook's Notes*)

GARNISH ½ red bell pepper, cored, seeded, cut into thin strips

OPTIONAL GARNISH ¼ cup chopped fresh cilantro

1. Put the halved Brussels sprouts in a bowl; drizzle with 2 teaspoons of the oil and gently toss to lightly coat.

2. Heat the remaining 1½ tablespoons oil in a large skillet on medium heat. Place the sprouts cut-side down in a single layer (the pan shouldn't be sizzling hot, or the exteriors will overbrown before the interiors are cooked). When the sprouts begin to brown, sprinkle them with salt and cover; cook until the bottoms are nicely browned and the interiors are tender-crisp, about 5 minutes, reducing heat if necessary.

3. Meanwhile, make the dressing: In a food processor fitted with the metal blade, combine the coconut milk, lime juice, peanut butter, fish sauce, 1½ tablespoons water, the jalapeño, and sugar. Process until blended.

4. Spread the rice in an even layer on a small platter or large plate. Top with the Brussels sprouts. Scatter the bell pepper on top. Stir the dressing and drizzle it on top of the vegetables. If desired, garnish with the cilantro.

COOK'S NOTES Use caution when working with fresh chiles. Upon completion, wash your hands and work area thoroughly; do *not* touch your eyes or face.

Brown rice generally triples in volume when cooked, so cook about 1⅓ cups raw brown rice.

VEGETARIAN ALTERNATIVE Substitute soy sauce for the fish sauce.

Pan-Caramelized Brussels Sprouts with Pistachios and Dried Cherries

Sweet dried cherries and crunchy pistachios add a just-right spark to seared and steamed Brussels sprouts. If you buy roasted and salted pistachios, be cautious about adding salt to the dish. If you wish to make this dish vegan, leave out the butter and double the amount of oil in step 3.

Yields 4 to 6 side-dish servings

NUTRITIONAL INFORMATION
(per serving)

calories 110	sodium (mg) 400	vitamin A IUs 15%
fat calories 60	total carbohydrates (g).....11	vitamin C 80%
total fat (g) 6	fiber (g) 4	calcium..........................4%
sat fat (g)......................1.5	sugars (g) 4	iron.................................8%
cholesterol (mg) 5	protein (g) 3	

¼ cup coarsely chopped dried cherries

3½ teaspoons extra-virgin olive oil

14 ounces (about 25) small, tightly closed Brussels sprouts, trimmed, halved top to bottom

1½ teaspoons butter

Coarse salt (kosher or sea)

¼ cup coarsely chopped roasted pistachios

1. In a small bowl, combine ⅓ cup warm water and the cherries. Set aside.

2. Put the sprouts in a bowl; drizzle with 2 teaspoons of the oil and gently toss to lightly coat them.

3. Heat the butter and the remaining 1½ teaspoons oil in a large skillet on medium heat. When the butter melts, shake the handle of the skillet to swirl the butter with the oil. Place the sprouts cut-side down in a single layer (the pan shouldn't be sizzling hot, or the exteriors will overbrown before the interiors are cooked). When they begin to brown, sprinkle them with salt and cover; cook until the bottoms are nicely browned and the interiors are tender-crisp, about 5 minutes, reducing heat if needed.

4. Add the water and cherries to the pan; increase the heat to high. Cook until the water evaporates and the sprouts are nicely caramelized. Transfer to a platter. Scatter the pistachios on top and serve.

Orange-Glazed Oven-Roasted Brussels Sprouts

Oranges add a nice touch of sweetness to Brussels sprouts, as well as a subtle acidity. Minced zest, juice, and peeled segments team up with cornstarch to make a delicious sauce to coat these oven-roasted Brussels sprouts.

Yields 6 side-dish servings

NUTRITIONAL INFORMATION
(per serving)

calories 90	sodium (mg) 400	vitamin A IUs 15%
fat calories 35	total carbohydrates (g)....14	vitamin C 110%
total fat (g) 4	fiber (g) 4	calcium 4%
sat fat (g)......................1.5	sugars (g) 7	iron.............................. 6%
cholesterol (mg) 5	protein (g) 3	

- 1 **pound Brussels sprouts, trimmed, halved top to bottom**
- 2 **teaspoons extra-virgin olive oil**

Coarse salt (kosher or sea)

Freshly ground black pepper

- 3 **oranges, Cara Cara preferred** (*see Cook's Note*)

Orange juice (if needed)

- 1 **tablespoon unsalted butter**
- 2 **teaspoons cornstarch**

Dried red pepper flakes

1. Adjust an oven rack to the middle position. Preheat the oven to 400 degrees F. In a medium bowl, toss the Brussels sprouts with the oil; use more if necessary to very lightly coat them. Season with salt and pepper.

2. Spread them in a single layer on a rimmed baking sheet. Roast for 13 to 15 minutes, or until tender-crisp (just barely fork tender).

3. Meanwhile, remove the zest from one orange using a Microplane, or finely mince the zest. Put it in a medium bowl. Cut that orange in half and squeeze the juice into the bowl. Working over the bowl, cut the remaining two oranges into supremes (see page 230) and put them in a separate bowl. Squeeze any remaining juice from the membranes into the bowl with the zest and juice. You'll need about ⅓ cup juice, so add fresh orange juice if more is needed.

4. In a saucepan, melt the butter on medium-high heat. Stir in the cornstarch. Add the zest and orange juice and simmer until thickened, stirring constantly. The sauce should be thick enough to coat the back of a spoon.

5. In a large bowl, gently toss together the Brussels sprouts, orange segments, and sauce. Season with a pinch of pepper flakes. Taste and adjust the seasoning as needed.

COOK'S NOTE Blood oranges or navel oranges also work well.

CABBAGE
Common Green, Red (Purple)

With its spicy-sweet flavor profile and toothsome texture, cabbage is wonderful served raw or cooked for a short time without using much liquid. It is often bargain-basement priced, especially considering that only the central core goes to waste. Store it properly and it will last for 2 weeks in the refrigerator, standing ready for use in a wide range of hot and cold dishes.

Although not as high in vitamin and mineral content as its *Brassica* cousins (Brussels sprouts, bok choy, broccoli, and mustard greens), cabbage still is big on vitamins A, C, and K as well as fiber and the sulforaphane and isothiocyanate group of phytochemicals.

ANTIOXIDANT BANK
Powerful antioxidants that have been shown to protect against cancers of the breast, colon, and prostate make cabbage an outstanding ultra-low-calorie food that is hearty and filling.

NUTRITIONAL INFORMATION
(per 1 cup raw, chopped)

calories 22	sodium (mg) 16	vitamin A IUs 2%
fat calories 1	total carbohydrates (g).....5	vitamin C 54%
total fat (g) 0	fiber (g) 2	calcium 4%
sat fat (g).........................0	sugars (g) 3	iron...............................2%
cholesterol (mg) 0	protein (g) 1	

CHOLESTEROL CLEARANCE
Glucosinolates and isothiocyanates in cabbage help reduce cholesterol levels in the blood. When pickled in the form of kimchee, cabbage nurtures powerful probiotic bacteria that help digestion and fat metabolism and boost immune function. And red cabbage adds a rich dose of cancer-protective anthocyanin antioxidants to the health complement.

INFLAMMATION REDUCER
Isoflavones and kaempferol, two flavonoid-class compounds in cabbage, reduce inflammation and help regulate insulin for more even blood glucose levels, a boon for people with pre-diabetes or type 2 diabetes.

AVAILABLE
Year-round

KEEP IT FRESH
Look for heads that are tightly closed, without discoloration or soft spots, and those that seem heavy for their size, with crisp leaves. Refrigerate them, dry and unwashed, in a plastic bag in the crisper drawer up to 2 weeks.

LAST-MINUTE PREP
Remove the first layer of leaves if they are discolored or wilted. Wash the exterior with cold water. Cut the cabbage into quarters from top to bottom, then cut away and discard the solid white core. To shred, place the flat side on a cutting surface and cut crosswise into narrow shreds.

QUICK COOK

Stir-fry, braise, or steam cabbage. To stir-fry, core and shred ½ head. Heat 1½ tablespoons vegetable or canola oil in a wok or large, deep skillet on high heat; swirl to coat the pan. Add 1 large garlic clove (minced) and stir-fry for 20 seconds. Add the cabbage and stir-fry for about 2 minutes; add 2 to 3 tablespoons vegetable broth. Cook, stirring occasionally, until the broth evaporates and the cabbage starts to brown and is cooked through. Season with salt and freshly ground black pepper.

try it!

BRAISED WITH APPLES

If cooking red cabbage, include acid in the cooking liquid to prevent discoloration (it turns an unpleasant blue hue). In a large, deep skillet, heat 2 tablespoons extra-virgin olive oil on medium-high heat. Add 1 large garlic clove (minced) and cook until it softens, about 40 seconds. Add 6 cups cored and shredded red cabbage, ½ cup apple juice, 1 teaspoon cider vinegar, 1 cored (unpeeled) Fuji or Gala apple (cut into ¾-inch chunks), ¾ teaspoon caraway seeds, and season with salt and freshly ground black pepper. Toss and bring it to a simmer. Decrease the heat to medium, cover, and cook for about 15 minutes, or until just tender. Uncover and cook on medium-high heat until the liquid evaporates. Taste and add more cider vinegar, if desired.

WITH A LIGHTER DRESSING FOR COLESLAW

Instead of just mayonnaise, use a combination of light mayonnaise and plain nonfat yogurt. Use up leftover coleslaw in sandwiches along with cold meat or grilled eggplant.

WITH SOME MEXICAN INGREDIENTS IN COLESLAW

Augment slaw with peeled and grated jícama, chopped cilantro, minced jalapeño, and fresh lime juice. If desired, garnish with toasted pumpkin seeds (see page 257).

Cabbage and Farro Soup with Pistou

Farro is an ancient grain that is said to have fed the Roman soldiers. It has a delightful chewy texture and nutty flavor. Most farro is sold semi-peeled (semi-pearled). If the package doesn't designate it as "semi-pearled," look at the cooking directions. If it says that it cooks in about 20 minutes, that's the ticket. *Pistou* is the French version of pesto, a mixture of crushed fresh basil, garlic, cheese, and olive oil that is most often used as a garnish atop soup.

Yields 12 servings

NUTRITIONAL INFORMATION
(per serving)

calories 220	sodium (mg) 690	vitamin A IUs 80%
fat calories 90	total carbohydrates (g)... 25	vitamin C 30%
total fat (g) 10	fiber (g) 6	calcium.......................15%
sat fat (g)..................... 2.5	sugars (g) 5	iron.............................10%
cholesterol (mg) 5	protein (g) 9	

1 cup semi-pearled farro

1½ tablespoons canola or vegetable oil

2 medium-large onions, coarsely chopped

4 medium carrots, peeled, coarsely chopped

1 medium fennel bulb, trimmed, halved, cored, and thinly sliced

1 large garlic clove, minced

1 *bouquet garni* (2 sprigs fresh thyme plus 2 bay leaves, tied in a double layer of cheesecloth and secured with cotton string)

One 14½-ounce can diced tomatoes with juice

3 quarts fat-free, low-sodium chicken or vegetable broth

2½ cups cored, coarsely chopped green cabbage

One 15-ounce can garbanzo beans, drained, rinsed

Coarse salt (kosher or sea)

Freshly ground black pepper

PISTOU

3 medium garlic cloves, peeled

3 cups (packed) fresh basil leaves

½ teaspoon coarse salt

5 tablespoons extra-virgin olive oil

⅔ cup grated Parmesan cheese

1. Put the farro in a medium bowl and cover it with cold water to 1 inch above the surface of the farro. Set aside.

2. In a 4- to 6-quart saucepan or Dutch oven, heat the oil over medium-high heat. Add the onions, carrots, and fennel. Cook, stirring occasionally, until they are softened but not browned, 6 to 10 minutes. Add the garlic and cook 1 additional minute.

3. Drain the farro and add it to the pan. Add the *bouquet garni*, the tomatoes with juice, and broth. Bring them to a boil on high heat; reduce the heat to medium-low and simmer for 15 minutes. Add the cabbage and simmer until the farro is tender, about 15 minutes. Add the beans; season with salt and pepper. Cook for 1 additional minute.

4. To make the pistou: With the motor running, add the garlic through the feed tube of a food processor fitted with the metal blade. Once the garlic is minced, add the basil and salt; process until it is finely chopped, scraping down the sides as needed. With the motor running, add the oil in a thin stream. Add the cheese and process just until mixed. Place the pistou in a serving bowl.

5. Ladle the soup into bowls. Place a small spoonful of pistou atop each serving. Pass the remaining pistou for additional topping, as desired.

Slaw-Topped Fried Green Tomatoes

The tart-sweet vegetal taste of fried green tomatoes creates the perfect accompaniment for raisin-enhanced coleslaw. The slaw is lean—dressed with a neutral oil and lime juice—lending just-right simplicity to allow the crunchy coating on the tomatoes to shine through. The shape of the tomatoes will determine how many are needed. If they are wide without much height, additional tomatoes may be needed.

Yields 8 servings

NUTRITIONAL INFORMATION
(per serving)

calories 160	sodium (mg) 40	vitamin A IUs 10%
fat calories 70	total carbohydrates (g)...20	vitamin C 60%
total fat (g) 8	fiber (g) 3	calcium 4%
sat fat (g)........................1	sugars (g) 12	iron...............................6%
cholesterol (mg) 25	protein (g) 3	

SLAW

- ½ cup golden raisins
- 2 tablespoons canola oil or vegetable oil
- 2 tablespoons fresh lime juice

Coarse salt (kosher or sea)

Freshly ground black pepper

- 3 cups cored, shredded green cabbage
- 2 cups cored, shredded red cabbage
- ¾ cup chopped fresh cilantro

FRIED TOMATOES

About 1¼ pounds medium-large or large green tomatoes, enough to make eight ½-inch slices

- ½ cup cornmeal
- 1 large egg
- 2 tablespoons canola oil or vegetable oil

1. To make the slaw: Put the raisins in a small bowl; cover with hot water and set aside.

2. In a large bowl, whisk together the oil and lime juice; season with salt and pepper. Add the green and red cabbage and cilantro. Toss and set aside.

3. To make the tomatoes: Slice off the stem end of each tomato (the top ¼ inch). Cut the tomatoes into ½-inch-thick crosswise slices and drain them on paper towels. In a shallow pan or pie plate, season the cornmeal with salt and pepper. In a separate bowl, beat the egg and 1 tablespoon water with a fork.

4. Heat the oil in a large nonstick skillet on medium-high heat. Meanwhile, dip each tomato slice in the egg mixture, coating both sides, then in the cornmeal mixture, covering both sides. Fry the coated slices on both sides until nicely browned (you will probably need to work in two batches).

5. Divide the tomatoes between eight plates. Drain the raisins and add them to the slaw; toss and spoon it over the warm tomatoes. Serve immediately.

Cabbage with Rotini and Cannellini Beans

To speed up the cooking process, the cabbage quickly cooks in the boiling water that is then used to cook the pasta. This twofer technique means that only one Dutch oven–sized pan is needed to prepare the dish. Instead of the Parmesan garnish, you can sprinkle the mixture with some chopped fresh basil or mint.

Yields 6 servings

NUTRITIONAL INFORMATION
(per serving)

calories 330	sodium (mg) 310	vitamin A IUs 15%
fat calories 60	total carbohydrates (g)... 53	vitamin C 70%
total fat (g) 7	fiber (g) 14	calcium 15%
sat fat (g) 1	sugars (g) 8	iron 30%
cholesterol (mg) 9	protein (g) 14	

½ teaspoon salt

2½ cups cored, coarsely chopped green cabbage

8 ounces dry whole-grain or multi-grain rotini

1½ tablespoons extra-virgin olive oil

2 large or 3 small leeks, trimmed, halved, washed, thinly sliced

1 large celery stalk with leaves, chopped

1 medium carrot, peeled, diced

2 sprigs fresh thyme

⅓ cup dry white wine

1¼ cups fat-free low-sodium vegetable or chicken broth

Two 15-ounce cans cannellini beans, drained, not rinsed

Freshly ground black pepper

⅛ teaspoon dried red pepper flakes

GARNISH grated Parmesan cheese

1. In a 4- to 6-quart pan or Dutch oven, bring water to boil on high heat. Add the salt and cabbage; cook until the cabbage is tender-crisp, about 3 to 4 minutes. Using a slotted spoon, transfer the cabbage to a bowl. Bring the water back to a boil. Add the pasta and boil until it is al dente (following the package directions), about 8 minutes. Drain.

2. Return the empty pan to medium heat; add the oil. Add the leeks, celery, carrot, and thyme. Cook, stirring occasionally, until the vegetables are tender, about 6 minutes. Add the wine and increase the heat to medium-high. Cook until most of the wine disappears.

3. Remove from the heat and cautiously add the broth (it may splatter at first), beans, and cabbage. Toss and return the pot to the heat; cook until everything is heated through, about 4 minutes. Remove thyme sprigs. Add the pasta and gently toss. Season with pepper and the pepper flakes. Spoon into shallow bowls and top with Parmesan.

CACTUS LEAF

also Cactus Paddle, Nopales

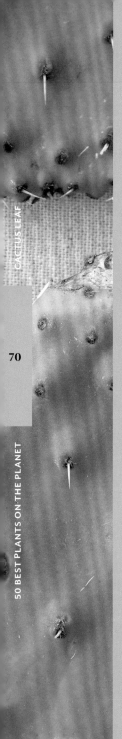

Cooked cactus leaves have the appealing texture of blanched green beans. A green bean taste dominates, but with a little green bell pepper and lemon juice thrown into the mix. Before cooking, these fleshy paddles need to have their thorns removed. Some vendors sell them with their thorns stripped away, but have a careful look to make sure that the barb removal has been thorough before cooking them.

PHENOL-PACKED

Cactus leaves contain a number of phenolic compounds in concentrations almost as rich as some berries. These natural antioxidant and anti-inflammatory chemicals demonstrate the ability to fight cancer and vascular disease.

NUTRITIONAL INFORMATION
(per 1 cup raw, sliced)

calories 20	sodium (mg) 25	vitamin A IUs 10%
fat calories 0	total carbohydrates (g) 4	vitamin C 25%
total fat (g) 0	fiber (g) 3	calcium 20%
sat fat (g) 0	sugars (g) .... less than 1	iron 4%
cholesterol (mg) 0	protein (g) 2	

LOWER TRIGLYCERIDES

Phytochemicals in cactus were shown in placebo-controlled research to work up to five times better than the control in helping lower blood triglyceride levels and countering metabolic syndrome linked to cardiovascular disease.

HAIR OF THE DOG

A study at Tulane University showed that cactus can actually help reduce the symptoms of overindulgence in alcoholic beverages. While the idea is not to endorse drinking to excess, for the occasional overenthusiastic celebrant, compounds in cactus reduce the headache severity, nausea, and dry mouth typical of hangovers.

BONE STRENGTHENER

Cactus contains isorhamnetin and kaempferol, the flavonoid phytochemicals that exhibit strong anti-osteoporosis benefits, according to studies conducted at the Chengdu Institute of Biology in China. Kaempferol has exhibited pain-relief abilities, too.

AVAILABLE

Year-round

KEEP IT FRESH

Avoid leaves that are limp or wrinkled; fresh leaves should be somewhat rigid. Look for leaves that are about 8 inches long; smaller leaves don't provide enough flesh, while larger leaves are sometimes tough. Whole leaves can be sealed in plastic wrap and refrigerated up to 1 week. Some markets sell ¼- to ½-inch-wide prepared strips in plastic bags; cooked or raw, they can be frozen, well sealed, up to 3 months.

LAST-MINUTE PREP

To remove barbs, wear gloves to protect your hands. Trim off the edge around the perimeter of the leaf. Cut or scrape off the thorns from both sides, or peel the leaves with a swivel-bladed vegetable peeler. Rinse the paddles thoroughly with cold water to remove the sticky fluid and loose thorns. Use them right away or pat dry, cover with plastic wrap, and refrigerate up to 2 days.

QUICK COOK

Simmering strips of cactus leaf creates a slimy substance. Grill or roast them to mitigate the slime factor. Roast strips in a 375-degree-F oven on a rimmed baking sheet for about 18 minutes, or until limp and tender. Or to grill, brush whole leaves with canola oil. Sprinkle with coarse salt and grill them over medium coals until limp, turning frequently, for 4 to 9 minutes (grilling times vary depending on size of leaf and degree of heat). Or cut trimmed, oiled, and salted leaves into ½- to ¾-inch-wide strips and grill them on a grill pan atop the stove or in a grill basket or grill rack (sometimes called a "grill screen") on the barbecue grill. Perforated grill baskets and grill racks are specifically designed to grill atop the grate. Cook until grill marks form and the strips are limp, about 5 minutes.

try it!

IN BLACK BEAN SOUP

In a large saucepan, simmer 1 cup undrained fresh salsa on medium heat for 3 minutes. Drain and rinse two 15-ounce cans black beans; add to the salsa. Add 2½ cups vegetable broth and ¼ teaspoon ground cumin; simmer, covered, for 15 minutes. Purée half the soup; add the puréed mixture back to the pan. Stir in ½ cup coarsely chopped grilled cactus leaf strips; reheat. Serve hot, topping each serving with a dollop of plain Greek-style yogurt and a spoonful of drained fresh salsa. Sprinkle with chopped cilantro, if desired.

IN TACO SALAD OR ENCHILADAS

Toss grilled strips of cactus leaf into taco salad or use them as part of the vegetable filling in vegetarian enchiladas.

AS AN OMELET FILLING

Chop grilled strips of cactus leaf and use them as a filling in omelets along with sliced green onions and crumbled queso fresco or goat cheese.

Roasted Cactus Leaves with Sautéed Potatoes, Corn, and Cabbage

Grilled strips of cactus leaves add a subtle edge of smokiness to this vegetable skillet dish. To turn it into an entrée, add a can of drained and rinsed pinto beans before adding the cabbage and corn. Or cook one or two strips of turkey or pork bacon until crisp; drain on a paper towel and crumble a little atop each serving.

Yields 8 side-dish servings

NUTRITIONAL INFORMATION
(per serving)

calories	100	sodium (mg)	260	vitamin A IUs	6%
fat calories	45	total carbohydrates (g)	12	vitamin C	15%
total fat (g)	5	fiber (g)	2	calcium	8%
sat fat (g)	1	sugars (g)	2	iron	4%
cholesterol (mg)	15	protein (g)	3		

2 cups ½-inch strips cleaned raw cactus leaves

3 tablespoons extra-virgin olive oil

Coarse salt (kosher or sea)

Freshly ground black pepper

1½ tablespoons seasoned rice vinegar

1 tablespoon chopped fresh cilantro

8 ounces skin-on Yukon Gold or Baby Dutch Yellow potatoes, cut into ¼-inch dice

1 small sweet onion, such as Maui, coarsely chopped

1½ cups shredded green cabbage

2 ears corn, kernels cut off cobs (about 1¼ cups)

¼ cup crumbled queso fresco or grated pepper Jack cheese

1. Preheat a grill to medium-high heat.

2. In a bowl, toss together the cactus with 1½ tablespoons of the oil. Season with salt and pepper. Spread the mixture in a grill basket. Do not wash the bowl. Grill until the vegetables are slightly charred and softened, about 5 minutes. Return them to the bowl and toss with the vinegar and cilantro. Place them on a platter and cover with aluminum foil.

3. Heat the remaining 1½ tablespoons oil in a large, deep skillet on medium-high heat. Add the potatoes and onion; cook, stirring occasionally, until the potatoes are tender and nicely browned, about 5 minutes. Season with salt and pepper. Add the cabbage and corn. Cook until the cabbage is tender-crisp and limp, 3 to 4 minutes. Uncover the cactus leaves and spoon the potato-cabbage mixture on top. Top with the cheese and serve hot.

Brown Rice Salad with Roasted Cactus Leaves and Tortilla Strips

Instead of potato salad, show off this side dish at an outdoor gathering, picnic, or potluck. Be sure to add the crisp little tortilla chips and radish slices just before serving.

Yields 6 servings

NUTRITIONAL INFORMATION
(per serving)

calories 200	sodium (mg) 45	vitamin A IUs 20%
fat calories 70	total carbohydrates (g)...29	vitamin C 30%
total fat (g) 8	fiber (g) 2	calcium 2%
sat fat (g).........................1	sugars (g) 2	iron..............................6%
cholesterol (mg) 0	protein (g) 4	

¾ cup uncooked long-grain brown rice

2 corn tortillas

2 cups ½-inch strips cleaned raw cactus leaves

3 tablespoons extra-virgin olive oil

1 small red bell pepper, cored, seeded, finely diced

1 ear corn, kernels cut off cob (¾ to 1 cup)

1 medium jalapeño, seeds and ribs discarded, minced

1½ tablespoons cider vinegar

1 tablespoon chopped fresh cilantro

1 tablespoon chopped fresh Italian parsley

1 garlic clove, minced

Coarse salt (kosher or sea)

Freshly ground black pepper

6 romaine leaves

OPTIONAL GARNISH ¼ cup sliced radishes

1. Cook the rice according to the package directions. Spread it out on a rimmed baking sheet to cool.

2. Preheat the oven to 375 degrees F. Cut the tortillas into ¼-inch strips. Place them on a rimmed baking sheet in a single layer. Bake on the middle oven rack until crisp and lightly browned, 10 to 11 minutes. Set aside to cool.

3. Preheat the grill to medium-high heat. In a large bowl, toss the cactus with 1½ tablespoons of the oil. Spread the mixture in a grill basket or on a grill rack. Do not wash the bowl. Grill until the cactus is slightly charred and softened, about 5 minutes. Return them to the bowl.

4. Add the remaining 1½ tablespoons oil, the bell pepper, corn, jalapeño, vinegar, cilantro, parsley, and garlic; stir to combine. Add the rice; toss. Season with salt and pepper; toss.

5. Spoon the salad into the romaine leaves. Top with the tortilla strips and the radishes, if desired.

Open-Faced Grilled Cactus Leaf and Pepper Jack Sandwiches

Using a knife and fork to eat an open-faced sandwich doesn't diminish the joy, especially if two elements are in play. A sandwich with only one piece of bread requires bread that is really tasty to start; brushing it with a wee bit of olive oil and toasting gives it more flavor and appealing crunchiness. Second, the topping must be delicious and have interesting contrasting textures. These open-faced beauties fit the bill.

Yields 4 servings

NUTRITIONAL INFORMATION
(per serving)

calories 260	sodium (mg) 340	vitamin A IUs 6%
fat calories 150	total carbohydrates (g)....18	vitamin C 2%
total fat (g) 17	fiber (g) 2	calcium 25%
sat fat (g)........................7	sugars (g) 4	iron..............................6%
cholesterol (mg) 25	protein (g) 10	

2 cups ½-inch strips cleaned raw cactus leaves

½ medium red onion, thinly sliced

2 tablespoons extra-virgin olive oil

Coarse salt (kosher or sea)

Freshly ground black pepper

1½ tablespoons seasoned rice vinegar

1 tablespoon chopped fresh cilantro

4 slices rustic whole-grain bread, about ⅜ inch thick

1 garlic clove, peeled

8 ounces pepper Jack cheese, thinly sliced

1. Preheat a grill to medium-high heat.

2. In a bowl, toss together the cactus, onion, and 1½ tablespoons of the oil. Season with salt and pepper. Spread the mixture in a grill basket or on a grill pan. Do not wash the bowl. Grill until the vegetables are slightly charred and softened, about 5 minutes. Return them to the bowl and toss with the vinegar and cilantro.

3. Brush one side of each piece of bread with the remaining ½ tablespoon oil. Grill the bread, oiled-side down, until golden. Rub the browned sides with the garlic. Place the bread toasted-side up and top with the cactus-onion mixture and cheese. Place on the grill and close the lid. Grill just long enough to melt the cheese, about 1 minute; watch carefully because bread burns easily. Serve hot.

CACTUS PEAR

also Prickly Pear

The prickly skinned fruit of the opuntia cactus are filled at their core with seeds. Those edible seeds vary in their rigidity; some are soft and only slightly crisp, while others are hard and too much of a challenge to chew. The skin and flesh can be either green or magenta, with a taste that is similar to watermelon—juicy with a floral scent.

As with their parent plants, cactus pears contain an array of plant chemicals that help the body ward off disease and dysfunction. In addition to antioxidants and fiber, the healthful chemicals are thought to help prevent cell death and cancer-cell development. The magenta-red variety, which has an abundance of anthocyanins and proanthocyanins, has a high ORAC (oxygen radical absorbance capacity) value.

NUTRITIONAL INFORMATION
(per 1 cup raw red cactus pear, chopped)

calories 61	sodium (mg) 7	vitamin A IUs 1%
fat calories 6	total carbohydrates (g)....14	vitamin C 35%
total fat (g) 1	fiber (g) 5	calcium 8%
sat fat (g)........................ 0	sugars (g) .... less than 1	iron............................... 2%
cholesterol (mg) 0	protein (g) 1	

SPIKE IMMUNITY
The types of anthocyanins in cactus pears help improve immunity. They also improve the function of the infection-fighting white blood cells.

THIN AS A CACTUS
The anti-inflammatory factors in cactus pears have demonstrated promise for being effective against the type of inflammation response now associated with obesity. And they are a good source of vitamin C.

AVAILABLE
Year-round

KEEP IT FRESH
The fruit should give to gentle pressure but shouldn't be mushy. If it is too firm, ripen at room temperature for a few days. Ripe fruit, dry and unwashed, can be refrigerated up to 6 days.

LAST-MINUTE PREP

Wear gloves to protect your hands from barbs. To peel, cut off both ends; using a small knife, make shallow lengthwise cuts about 3 inches apart. Starting at one end, grasp the peel between a gloved thumb and knife, pull off the skin, and discard it. The seeds may be soft enough to eat, but often they are hard and the fruit needs to be strained. If you know in advance that you will be straining the fruit, you don't need to peel it; cut it in half from top to bottom and scoop out the flesh with a spoon (discard peel). To make strained purée, coarsely chop the peeled fruit. Place a medium-mesh strainer over a bowl and press the chopped fruit through the strainer using the back of a large spoon (discard seeds and residue left in the strainer). The purée can be frozen.

QUICK COOK

Most often consumed raw, cactus pears are delicious in a cooked dessert sauce. Combine 2 cups strained purée and ¼ cup agave syrup in a small saucepan. Cook on medium heat, stirring frequently, until the mixture reduces to 1 cup. Let cool. Stir together ¾ cup raw strained purée, 1 tablespoon fresh lime juice, and ¼ teaspoon ground cinnamon. Spoon the sauce over oatmeal or chill it and serve atop frozen yogurt or ice cream.

try it!

IN AGUA FRESCA

Peel and quarter 4 to 5 cactus pears. Put them in a blender with 2 cups water and ½ cup agave syrup; whirl until smooth. Pour through a sieve into a large pitcher, pressing down the pulp in the sieve. Discard the seeds and residue. Stir in water to taste, about 4 to 6 cups. Taste and adjust as needed, adding more agave syrup or a little fresh lime juice to suit your taste. Serve over ice.

IN VINAIGRETTE

Combine ½ cup strained purée, ¼ cup extra-virgin olive oil, and 3 tablespoons balsamic vinegar, and season with garlic salt; whisk to combine. Spoon over grilled shrimp, sliced grilled pork tenderloin, or grilled peaches or nectarines.

IN A MARGARITA

In a blender, combine 4 ounces tequila blanco, 2 ounces orange liqueur, 3 ounces strained cactus purée (magenta variety preferred), 1 ounce fresh lime juice, and 1 cup ice. Cover and whirl until slushy. Garnish with a lime slice.

Grown-Up South-of-the-Border Fruit Salad

In very moderate amounts, tequila, lime juice, and agave syrup give this fruit salad luscious appeal. If possible, make it 3 or 4 hours in advance, then cover and refrigerate. The chilling time will give the fruit a chance to absorb the cocktail-style flavors.

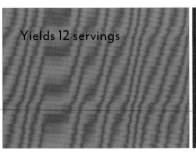

Yields 12 servings

NUTRITIONAL INFORMATION
(per serving)

calories 60	sodium (mg) 10	vitamin A IUs 30%
fat calories 0	total carbohydrates (g)....15	vitamin C 60%
total fat (g) 0	fiber (g) 2	calcium 2%
sat fat (g).........................0	sugars (g) 12	iron.................................2%
cholesterol (mg) 0	protein (g) 1	

½ cantaloupe or casaba melon, cubed or scooped into balls (about 3 cups)

½ pineapple, peeled, cored, cubed (about 2½ cups)

1½ cups cubed seedless watermelon

1 mango, peeled, seeded, cubed (about 1¼ cups)

2 cactus pears, peeled, halved lengthwise, cut crosswise into ½-inch slices (if large, hard seeds are present, remove them with the tip of a small knife)

8 strawberries, halved if small, quartered if large

2 tablespoons agave syrup

1 tablespoon tequila

1 lime, zested and juiced

1 tablespoon minced fresh mint

OPTIONAL GARNISH coarse sea salt, such as fleur de sel

1. Gently toss the fruits together in a large glass or ceramic bowl.

2. In a small bowl or a glass measuring cup with a handle, stir together 2 tablespoons water, the syrup, tequila, lime zest and juice, and mint. Pour over the fruit and gently toss. Cover and chill up to 4 hours. Serve as is, or top each serving with a pinch of sea salt.

Cactus Pear Sorbet

If possible, use the magenta variety of cactus pears to produce an eye-popping crimson-colored sorbet. Serve it accompanied with crisp cookies, or shave bittersweet chocolate on top. Fresh berries, such as raspberries or pomegranate seeds, also make a delectable garnish. Allow the sorbet to freeze for several hours (or up to 1 week), then let it sit in the refrigerator for 20 minutes to soften slightly before serving.

Yields 8 servings

NUTRITIONAL INFORMATION
(per serving)

calories 160	sodium (mg) 10	vitamin A IUs 2%
fat calories 10	total carbohydrates (g)....41	vitamin C 40%
total fat (g) 1	fiber (g) 6	calcium............10%
sat fat (g)............0	sugars (g) 25	iron............2%
cholesterol (mg) 0	protein (g) 1	

8 cactus pears (about 3 pounds), magenta preferred

¾ cup agave syrup

2 tablespoons unsweetened pomegranate juice or cranberry juice

2 tablespoons fresh lime juice

OPTIONAL GARNISH ⅓ cup fresh raspberries or pomegranate seeds (arils); shaved dark chocolate

1. Wear rubber gloves to protect your hands. Cut each cactus pear in half lengthwise. Scoop out the pulp with a small spoon and force it through a medium-mesh strainer (discard seeds left in strainer) with the back of a large wooden spoon into a bowl.

2. Place the pulp in a blender with the syrup and juices; whirl to combine. Freeze in an ice-cream machine according to the manufacturer's directions.

3. Transfer the sorbet to a container with a tight lid. Cover and freeze for at least 5 hours before serving or up to 1 week. Place in the refrigerator for 20 minutes before serving to soften slightly. Scoop into eight small bowls. If desired, top with raspberries, pomegranate seeds, and/or shaved dark chocolate.

French Toast with Cactus Pear Mojo

Mojo? Absolutely. A mojo, used to describe self-confidence and charm, perfectly describes this lovely fruit-based sauce. It is spooned here over fat-reduced French toast, but would also find an appealing home atop pancakes or waffles. Or spike it with a pinch of dried red pepper flakes and spoon it over goat cheese; serve the mojo-enhanced cheese with crackers or sturdy corn tortilla chips.

Yields 8 servings

NUTRITIONAL INFORMATION
(per serving)

calories 170	sodium (mg) 180	vitamin A IUs 2%
fat calories 30	total carbohydrates (g)... 29	vitamin C 20%
total fat (g) 3	fiber (g) 6	calcium 15%
sat fat (g) 1	sugars (g) 7	iron 8%
cholesterol (mg) 25	protein (g) 7	

TOPPING

- 4 cactus pears (about 1½ pounds)
- 1½ tablespoons agave syrup
- 1½ tablespoons low-sugar raspberry preserves

FRENCH TOAST

- ¾ cup 1% milk
- 2 egg whites
- 1 egg
- ¾ teaspoon ground cinnamon
- ½ teaspoon vanilla extract
- 2 teaspoons soft tub margarine or butter
- 8 slices whole-wheat bread
  (*see Cook's Note*)

1. To make the topping: Wear rubber gloves to protect your hands. Cut each cactus pear in half lengthwise. Scoop out the pulp with a small spoon and force it through a medium-mesh strainer (discard seeds left in strainer) with the back of a large wooden spoon into a bowl. Put the strained pulp in a blender. Add the syrup and preserves; whirl to combine. Set aside.

2. To make the French toast: Whisk together the milk, egg whites, egg, cinnamon, and vanilla in a pie plate or shallow bowl. Melt 1 teaspoon of the margarine in a large, nonstick skillet on medium-high heat. Dip half of the bread slices, one at a time, in the egg mixture, turning to coat both sides. Place them in the skillet, and cook 6 to 8 minutes, or until lightly browned on both sides. Repeat with the remaining margarine, bread slices, and egg mixture.

3. Serve the hot French toast topped with the cactus pear mojo.

COOK'S NOTE For more generously coated French toast, use 6 slices of bread.

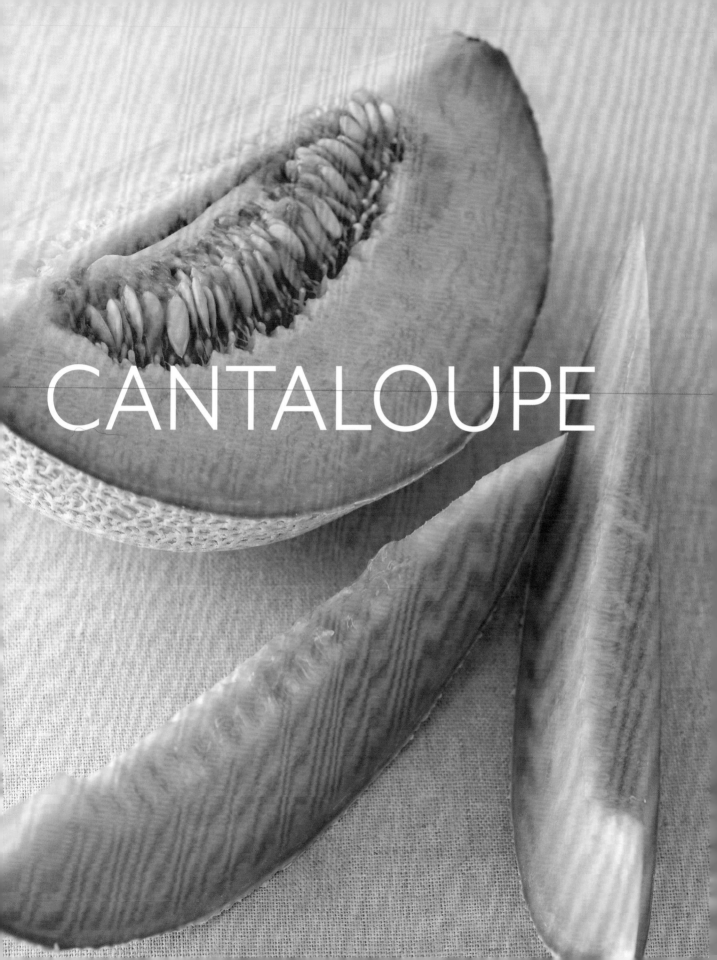

CANTALOUPE

Cantaloupe has an alluring fragrance that is powerfully sweet yet pleasantly musky. The dense texture of its salmon-orange flesh is rich in aromatic juices. Classic Italian recipes call for wrapping cantaloupe wedges in unctuous prosciutto, pairing sweet with salty. But there are a myriad of ways to serve it, in everything from salads to soups to smoothies.

Like their cousins squash and cucumbers, cantaloupes are loaded with vitamins (especially A and C), minerals, fiber, and phytochemicals. Plus, a third of its natural sugars are in the form of glucose, which provides energy for the brain and body.

NUTRITIONAL INFORMATION
(per 1 cup raw, diced)

calories 53	sodium (mg) 25	vitamin A IUs 120%
fat calories 2	total carbohydrates (g)....14	vitamin C 108%
total fat (g) 0	fiber (g) 1	calcium 2%
sat fat (g).........................0	sugars (g) 12	iron................................ 2%
cholesterol (mg) 0	protein (g) 1	

SCRUBBING THE WALLS
Polyphenolic antioxidants in cantaloupe help protect the endothelial cells—those that line the blood vessels. Damaging these cells can promote scarring and plaque buildup, which can lead to cardiovascular disease and myocardial infarction.

BREAST CANCER PROTECTION
A recent Chinese cancer study found that cantaloupe, as part of an overall increased consumption of fruits, significantly reduced the risk of breast cancer in women. In addition, it is exceptionally high in vitamins A and C.

BLOOD PRESSURE BALANCE
Researchers in the Netherlands found cantaloupe to be a particularly effective diuretic. By helping the body express excess fluid, cantaloupe acts to balance blood pressure and reduce the probability of chronic hypertension. This in turn aids kidney function and the excretion of toxins.

AVAILABLE
Year-round

KEEP IT FRESH
Select melons that feel heavy for their size and have a light golden color between the webbing. They should be fragrant when ripe and give slightly at their blossom end. Avoid those with cracks or spongy textures. If unripe, store whole at room temperature for up to 4 days. Once cut, refrigerate, well sealed, up to 3 days.

LAST-MINUTE PREP (OR UP TO 3 DAYS AHEAD)

Wash with cold water. To cut into rind-on wedges or halves or when scooping into balls, cut a melon in half through the equator; scoop out the seeds and strings with a spoon, and slice into wedges. To cut into rind-free wedges or cubes, place each seeded half cut-side down on a cutting board and cut off the rind in strips from top to bottom, following the contour of the melon, then cut into wedges.

try it!

IN DESSERT SAUCE

In a food processor, whirl 2 cups 1-inch pieces of ripe cantaloupe with 3 tablespoons agave syrup and 1 tablespoon orange liqueur until puréed. Drizzle over slices of fresh pineapple and top with a little chopped fresh cilantro or mint.

WITH A ROSEMARY MARINADE

Thinly slice cantaloupe and put it in a glass or ceramic bowl. Combine 2 tablespoons water with 1 teaspoon honey and 1½ teaspoons finely chopped fresh rosemary. Drizzle over the cantaloupe. Cover and chill 2 to 4 hours.

IN A BCT

Instead of lettuce, place a thin slice of cantaloupe in bacon and tomato sandwiches (best on toasted bread) for a sweet/salty combo.

Cantaloupe-Nectarine Smoothie

If you don't like itty-bitty pieces of skin in your smoothie, peel the nectarine before cutting it into wedges and freezing. Each serving provides 100 percent of the daily recommended amount of vitamin C, making this delicious drink a great way to start the day.

Yields 2 servings

NUTRITIONAL INFORMATION
(per serving)

calories 160	sodium (mg) 75	vitamin A IUs 80%
fat calories 5	total carbohydrates (g).....31	vitamin C 100%
total fat (g) 0	fiber (g) 2	calcium 15%
sat fat (g)........................0	sugars (g) 27	iron.............................2%
cholesterol (mg) 0	protein (g) 10	

- 1 large nectarine, cut into ½-inch wedges
- 1½ cups 1-inch chunks seeded, peeled cantaloupe
- ⅔ cup plain fat-free Greek-style yogurt
- 2 tablespoons nonfat dry milk
- 1 tablespoon frozen orange juice concentrate
- 1½ teaspoons honey
- ½ teaspoon vanilla extract

1. Put the nectarine wedges in an airtight container and freeze overnight.

2. The next morning, put the frozen nectarine wedges in a blender. Add the cantaloupe, yogurt, dry milk, juice concentrate, honey, and vanilla. Blend until smooth. Pour into two glasses and serve.

Cantaloupe with Indian-Spiced Yogurt

Lovers of garam masala, the Indian-inspired blend of fragrant spices, will favor this honey-edged dish. The sweet curried yogurt sauce is made vibrant with the spice blend, a concoction that often contains pepper, cloves, mace, cumin, cinnamon, cardamom, nutmeg, star anise, and coriander seeds.

Yields 6 servings

NUTRITIONAL INFORMATION
(per serving)

calories 70	sodium (mg) 35	vitamin A IUs 90%
fat calories 0	total carbohydrates (g)....14	vitamin C 80%
total fat (g) 0	fiber (g) 1	calcium 4%
sat fat (g)........................ 0	sugars (g) 13	iron.............................. 2%
cholesterol (mg) 0	protein (g) 4	

1   cup plain, fat-free Greek-style yogurt

2   teaspoons fresh lime juice

1½ teaspoons dark honey

1   teaspoon minced lime zest

1   teaspoon garam masala

1   large chilled cantaloupe, peeled, cut into bite-size chunks

GARNISH 1 tablespoon finely chopped fresh mint

1. In a small bowl or glass measuring cup with a handle, combine the yogurt, juice, honey, zest, and garam masala; stir to combine. Cover and refrigerate for 20 minutes.

2. Divide the melon chunks between six bowls. Spoon about 2 tablespoons of sauce over each serving. Top with the mint and serve.

Cantaloupe and Fig Salad

Green-skinned, fresh Kadota figs add a colorful element to this delectable fruit-based dish. Kadotas have a shorter season than many other fig varieties; generally they are only available from August to October. Other fresh fig varieties are available from July to November and can be substituted for Kadotas in this recipe.

Yields 10 servings

NUTRITIONAL INFORMATION
(per serving)

calories 210	sodium (mg) 200	vitamin A IUs 60%
fat calories 60	total carbohydrates (g)... 37	vitamin C 50%
total fat (g) 7	fiber (g) 3	calcium 4%
sat fat (g) 1	sugars (g) 32	iron 4%
cholesterol (mg) 0	protein (g) 2	

FIGS

- ½ cup dry sherry
- ½ cup honey
- 12 whole fresh ripe figs, Kadota variety preferred, stemmed

DRESSING

- 2 tablespoons fresh lime juice
- ½ teaspoon coarse salt (kosher or sea)
- ½ teaspoon cracked black pepper
- 2 tablespoons honey
- ¼ cup extra-virgin olive oil
- 1 tablespoon minced fresh mint

SALAD

- 1 large cantaloupe, peeled, seeded, cut into very thin wedges

GARNISH 3 tablespoons coarsely chopped pistachio nuts, salted if desired

1. To make the figs: Combine the sherry and honey in a large saucepan. Bring to a simmer on medium-low heat. Remove from the heat and add the figs; gently toss with a rubber spatula. Let them cool to room temperature.

2. To make the dressing: In a small bowl or glass measuring cup with a handle, whisk together the lime juice, salt, and pepper until the salt dissolves. Add 1 tablespoon hot water and the honey; whisk to combine. Whisk in the oil in a thin stream. Add the mint and stir to combine.

3. To make the salad: Arrange the cantaloupe wedges slightly overlapping on a rimmed platter. Arrange the figs on the platter. Stir the dressing and spoon it over the fruit, adding just enough to lightly coat. Scatter the pistachios on top.

CASABA MELON

Casaba melons are golden on the outside, often with some dramatic green streaks. The shape of these 3- to 5-pound melons can best be described as a rounded oval. Inside, the flesh is honeydew green and delicately sweet with mild cucumber overtones.

They join their cantaloupe cousins in being rich sources of vitamins A and C, plus folate, minerals, and fiber.

NUTRITIONAL INFORMATION
(per 1 cup raw, cubed)

calories 48	sodium (mg) 15	vitamin A IUs 0%
fat calories 1	total carbohydrates (g).....11	vitamin C 62%
total fat (g) 0	fiber (g) 2	calcium 2%
sat fat (g).........................0	sugars (g) 10	iron................................3%
cholesterol (mg) 0	protein (g) 2	

LOW-CAL REFRESHER
Among summer melons, casabas are super low in calories at fewer than 50 per 5 ounces of fruit. But in that 50-calorie packet there is two-thirds of the daily recommended vitamin C requirement.

IMMUNI-C
Vitamin C not only helps immunity as an antioxidant but also is a key co-factor in several metabolic functions connected to the immune response. It aids the production of white blood cells and cytokines (proteins that modify the immune process); it also helps phagocytes to do their job "eating up" toxins and invading organisms.

BEAUTY BUILDER
Vitamin C also is important for the production of collagen and slowing the development of wrinkles. But in addition, casaba melons are good sources of the mineral copper, which is needed to form connective tissue, keeping skin taut and healthy.

IRON BOOSTER
The copper in casabas also plays a critical function in allowing the body to metabolize and use iron, necessary for healthy red blood cells and to keep energy levels up.

AVAILABLE
May to September

KEEP IT FRESH

Look for melons that feel heavy for their size and give ever so slightly to pressure at the blossom end. Avoid those with cracks or bruises. If unripe, leave them at room temperature for 1 to 4 days. Once cut, refrigerate, well sealed, up to 3 days.

LAST-MINUTE PREP

Wash with cold water. To cut into rind-on wedges or halves or when scooping into balls, cut melons in half through the equator; scoop out the seeds and strings with a spoon. To cut into rind-free wedges or cubes, cut off a small slice at blossom and root ends, then cut the melon in half through the equator and scrape out the seeds and strings. Place the cut-side (equator) down on a cutting board and cut off the rind in strips from top to bottom, following the contour of the melon. Cover and refrigerate for up to 3 days.

try it!

IN AN EASY GREEK-STYLE SALAD

Cut casaba melon into ½-inch chunks. Combine about 3 cups casaba chunks with 1 teaspoon fresh lime juice and 1 tablespoon minced fresh mint. Place the salad in shallow bowls and divide 8 pitted kalamata olives (cut into lengthwise slivers) and about 2 ounces feta cheese (cut into ½-inch dice) between the servings.

IN GREEN TEA SMOOTHIE

Brew 1 cup strong green tea. Cool and freeze it in an ice-cube tray. In a blender, combine the green tea ice cubes, 2 cups cubed casaba melon, ⅓ cup plain fat-free Greek-style yogurt, ½ cup cubed fresh pineapple, and 1 teaspoon agave syrup. Whirl for 3 to 4 minutes. Taste and add more agave syrup if needed.

IN WHITE SANGRIA

Use a melon baller to scoop about 1½ cups casaba melon balls; place them in a pitcher with ¼ cup agave syrup and toss to coat. Let stand 15 minutes. Add one 750-milliliter bottle chilled Sauvignon Blanc, 1 tablespoon brandy, and 1 tablespoon orange liqueur, such as Grand Marnier; stir. Pour the sangria into eight highball glasses, making sure that each glass gets some melon balls. Add ice and top it off with sparkling water. Garnish each with a thin lime slice.

Casaba, Cantaloupe, and Strawberry Compote

Compotes make such delectable yet practical desserts. They can be prepared 6 hours in advance and refrigerated. In this version, orange juice and zest offer a jolt of citrus that pairs beautifully with the melons and berries. If you like, garnish each serving with a sprig of fresh peppermint or spearmint.

Yields 6 servings

NUTRITIONAL INFORMATION
(per serving)

calories 70	sodium (mg) 15	vitamin A IUs 50%
fat calories 0	total carbohydrates (g) 18	vitamin C 80%
total fat (g) 0	fiber (g) 1	calcium 2%
sat fat (g) 0	sugars (g) 16	iron 2%
cholesterol (mg) 0	protein (g) 1	

3 tablespoons honey

3 tablespoons fresh orange juice

1½ tablespoons minced orange zest

2 cups 1-inch chunks peeled ripe casaba

1 cup hulled strawberries, quartered

1 cup 1-inch chunks peeled ripe cantaloupe

OPTIONAL crisp cookies for serving

1. In a large nonreactive bowl such as glass or ceramic, whisk together the honey, juice, and zest. Add the casaba, strawberries, and cantaloupe; gently toss.

2. Cover and refrigerate until chilled, or up to 6 hours. Serve the compote in small stemmed bowls accompanied by cookies if desired.

Casaba Crostini

In the heart of summer, choose fragrant casaba melons to use in these simple crostini appetizers. For picnics, provide guests with all the components, then let them assemble their own to suit their taste. They are also delicious served as part of a brunch menu.

Yields about 18 servings

NUTRITIONAL INFORMATION
(per serving)

calories 130	sodium (mg) 300	vitamin A IUs 20%
fat calories 30	total carbohydrates (g)....21	vitamin C 15%
total fat (g) 3.5	fiber (g) 1	calcium.........................4%
sat fat (g).....................1.5	sugars (g) 3	iron...............................8%
cholesterol (mg) 5	protein (g) 5	

½ large French baguette

2 tablespoons olive oil

TOPPING

1 medium hothouse cucumber, peeled, cut into ¼-inch dice (*see Cook's Note*)

3 cups ¼-inch dice peeled ripe casaba

1 tablespoon minced fresh mint or basil

Seasoned salt

Freshly ground black pepper

3 ounces herbed goat cheese (about ½ cup)

1. Preheat the oven to 350 degrees F. Cut the baguette into ¼-inch-thick crosswise slices; brush each with oil. Place them on a rimmed baking sheet in a single layer. Toast the slices in the oven until golden brown, turning halfway through, about 10 minutes total.

2. Meanwhile, prepare the topping: In a medium bowl, combine the cucumber, casaba, and mint; season with salt and pepper. Toss. Taste and adjust the seasoning as needed.

3. Spread the goat cheese on the crostini and top each with a small spoonful of casaba mixture. Serve.

COOK'S NOTE Hothouse (English) cucumbers are the long variety that are sealed in plastic wrap. They are generally seedless. If you substitute common cucumbers, cut them in half lengthwise and use a spoon to remove the seeds.

Sliced Casaba and Watermelon Platter with Lime-Mint Syrup

If you buy a "mini" watermelon that weighs about 4 to 5 pounds, you can get prettier wedges or slices than if you buy a chunk of a larger melon. Either way, it will taste delicious. This presentation requires a fork and a knife. If you prefer, remove the rind from the melons before you start step 2.

Yields 10 servings

NUTRITIONAL INFORMATION
(per serving)

calories 90	sodium (mg) 15	vitamin A IUs 10%
fat calories 5	total carbohydrates (g)... 23	vitamin C 80%
total fat (g) 0	fiber (g) 2	calcium 2%
sat fat (g)........................0	sugars (g) 20	iron.............................. 4%
cholesterol (mg) 0	protein (g) 2	

3 tablespoons agave syrup

¼ cup fresh lime juice

2 teaspoons minced lime zest

1 medium casaba melon
(about 3 ½ pounds)

1 "mini" watermelon
(about 4 pounds)

2 ½ tablespoons finely chopped
fresh mint

OPTIONAL GARNISH coarse salt
(kosher or sea)

1. In a small bowl, whisk together the syrup and 3 tablespoons hot water. Add the lime juice and minced zest. Stir to combine. Cover and refrigerate.

2. To make wedges, cut the melons in half through the equator and remove the rind and seeds. Put the halves cut-side down on a cutting board and cut them into ½- to ¾-inch-thick slices. Arrange the wedges on a large, rimmed platter slightly overlapping, alternating casaba and watermelon. Cover and refrigerate until thoroughly chilled, 4 to 8 hours.

3. Stir the mint into the chilled lime mixture. Pour it over the melons and serve. If desired, sprinkle with a bit of coarse salt.

CHARD

Green, Rainbow, Swiss

Chard's glossy, deep green leaves ruffle around its sturdy stalks. The color of the puckered lush leaf is the same from one chard variety to the next. It's the color of ribs and veins that varies. Green chard has a white stalk and veining; Swiss chard has crimson. Rainbow chard offers ribs and veins in a variety of colors: some orange, others pink, purple, or gold.

As with its fellow leafy greens, chard gives a blast of vitamins A, C, and K to support skin and eye health as well as protect against cancer and heart disease.

NUTRITIONAL INFORMATION
(per 1 cup chopped, raw)

calories 7	sodium (mg) 77	vitamin A IUs 44%
fat calories 1	total carbohydrates (g) 1	vitamin C 18%
total fat (g) 0	fiber (g) 1	calcium 2%
sat fat (g) 0	sugars (g) 0	iron 4%
cholesterol (mg) 0	protein (g) 1	

BABY'S BEST
Chard is one of the best sources of folate, important for heart health and to prevent neural tube defects in developing fetuses.

IRON MAN
Just 1 cup of chard presents one-fifth of your day's iron requirement, which is needed to build blood and keep your tissues oxygenated. Twice your daily A and more than seven times your daily K (also for bones, blood, and immunity) are in that single cup, too.

MINERAL LODE
Minerals abound in chard: calcium (for your heart, nerve function, and of course bones and teeth); more than one-third of your magnesium needs (critical to enzymatic function, energy production, and gene expression); and almost one-third of your daily manganese and potassium.

AVAILABLE
Year-round

KEEP IT FRESH
Buy chard with a fresh scent, without wilted or discolored leaves. Rinse it in a tub of cold water, gently swishing the leaves around to remove any dirt or grit; repeat if necessary until the water is clear. Shake to remove excess water. Wrap the leaves in a clean kitchen towel or paper towels and place them in a partially closed plastic bag. Refrigerate them in the crisper drawer up to 3 days.

LAST-MINUTE PREP

Most recipes just call for chard's leafy greens. The thick central stalks (ribs) are usually removed before use. The stalks can be discarded or composted, or they can be coarsely chopped and added to soups or stews. Or quickly blanch and use them in gratins, frittatas, or stir-fries. To remove the stalks, cut around them with a knife. Or use your hand by cupping the fingers and thumb around the stem below the leaf; holding the stem with the opposite hand, scrape the leaf from the stem. Stack several leaves together and coarsely chop.

QUICK COOK

Chard can be cut across into thin ribbons and eaten raw in salads, but most often it is cooked. To steam, place the leaves (central stalks removed) in a steamer basket and cook, covered, over boiling water about 3 minutes, or until wilted and tender. Or bring a large pot of water to a boil. Remove the thick central stalks and wash the leaves thoroughly in cold water (if not already washed) and, if desired, stack the leaves and cut them coarsely into bite-size pieces. Put them in the boiling water and briefly cook until they are just barely limp and tender. Drain them in a colander for 2 to 3 minutes. Toss the leaves with coarse salt, freshly ground black pepper, and a little extra-virgin olive oil. If desired, add a squeeze of fresh lemon juice or a little cider vinegar.

try it!

ON BRUSCHETTA

Heat 2 tablespoons extra-virgin olive oil in a 4- or 6-quart saucepan on medium-high heat. Add 3 thinly sliced garlic cloves; cook for 30 seconds. Add 1½ pounds chard (thick central stalks removed and discarded, leaves washed and coarsely chopped, still damp, about 10 to 11 cups). Toss, cover and cook, stirring occasionally, until the chard is wilted, about 4 to 5 minutes. Uncover and cook until the liquid has evaporated. Add ¼ cup dried currants and 2 tablespoons toasted pine nuts, and season with salt and freshly ground black pepper. Place spoonfuls of warm chard mixture on toasted baguette slices and serve.

IN TACOS

Combine browned, crisp chunks of roasted potatoes with cooked chopped chard. Season with hot sauce and serve it as a filling for warm corn tortillas. Top with chopped tomato and chopped cilantro.

SHREDDED IN SALAD

Toss 2 cups shredded chard leaves (without ribs) with 2 cups shredded romaine lettuce and ⅓ cup dried cherries or dried cranberries. Toss with just enough extra-virgin olive oil to lightly coat the leaves. Add enough fresh lemon juice to give the mixture a little acidity (about 2 teaspoons) and season with garlic salt. Toss. If desired, top each serving with 2 slices ripe avocado or a few toasted whole almonds.

Butter Bean and Chard Slumgullion

"Slumgullion" is an old fashioned term used to describe an inexpensive stew or hash. Most often it refers to a meat-based dish, but here it gives verbal charm to a vegetarian concoction that showcases butter beans and chard. Many supermarkets stock canned butter beans. Italian markets label them *"fagioli bianchi di Spagna."*

Yields 8 main-course servings

NUTRITIONAL INFORMATION
(per serving)

calories 150	sodium (mg) 135	vitamin A IUs 80%
fat calories 50	total carbohydrates (g) ... 20	vitamin C 45%
total fat (g) 5	fiber (g) 5	calcium 6%
sat fat (g) 1	sugars (g) 3	iron 15%
cholesterol (mg) 0	protein (g) 6	

- 3 tablespoons extra-virgin olive oil
- 2 large leeks (white and pale green parts only), halved lengthwise and cut crosswise into ¼-inch slices
- 1 pound chard, thick central ribs removed and discarded, leaves washed and coarsely chopped, about 8 cups
- Two 14-ounce cans butter beans, undrained
- ⅛ teaspoon dried red pepper flakes
- Coarse salt (kosher or sea)

In a 6-quart pan or Dutch oven, heat the oil on medium-high heat. Add the leeks and cook, stirring occasionally, until they are softened and just starting to brown, about 6 to 8 minutes. Add the chard and toss; cover and cook, stirring occasionally, until the chard is wilted, about 5 minutes. Add the beans (with liquid) and pepper flakes. Gently stir to combine. Season with salt, if needed. Cook until the beans are heated through. Serve in bowls.

Grilled Mozzarella-Stuffed Chard with Black Rice

Grilling bundles of chard-wrapped fresh mozzarella creates an alluring crunchy exterior and creamy interior spiked with olives, sun-dried tomatoes, and fresh thyme. The packets are served atop Chinese black rice, sometimes labeled "forbidden rice." Its taste and texture make it a pleasing partner, but you can substitute long-grain brown rice or brown basmati rice, following the package directions.

Yields 6 servings

NUTRITIONAL INFORMATION
(per serving)

calories 230	sodium (mg) 260	vitamin A IUs 15%
fat calories 100	total carbohydrates (g)... 26	vitamin C 15%
total fat (g) 11	fiber (g) 3	calcium 4%
sat fat (g) 4	sugars (g) 1	iron................................4%
cholesterol (mg) 25	protein (g) 8	

Coarse salt (kosher or sea)

6 to 8 large chard leaves, thick ribs removed and discarded, leaves washed (*see Cook's Note*)

1 cup Chinese black rice, rinsed with cold water

One 6- to 8-ounce sphere fresh mozzarella, cut into 6 crosswise slices

2 tablespoons chopped pitted black olives, such as kalamata or niçoise

2 tablespoons chopped oil-packed sun-dried tomatoes, drained

1 tablespoon chopped fresh thyme

1/8 teaspoon dried red pepper flakes

About 1 tablespoon extra-virgin olive oil

Canola oil or vegetable oil for oiling barbecue grate

1. Preheat a grill for indirect medium heat (with a gas grill, light only one side; with charcoal, arrange coals along two sides, leaving an area in the center without any coals).

2. Bring 2 cups salted water to boil in a 5- to 6-quart saucepan or Dutch oven on high heat. Using tongs, dip each chard leaf in the boiling water just to make it limp enough to be flexible, about 15 seconds. Drain the leaves in a colander and refresh with cold running water. Drain again and pat dry.

3. Add the rice to the boiling water (there should be about 1¾ cups). Once the water returns to a boil, skim off any foam that forms on the surface. Cover and reduce the heat to low. Gently simmer until the rice is tender, 30 to 35 minutes. Drain off any remaining water. Season with salt, if needed.

4. Meanwhile, flatten out a chard leaf shiny-side down on a paper towel, overlapping the portion where the rib was removed to make a solid sheet. If necessary, patch any flimsy portion with part of an additional chard leaf. Place a mozzarella slice in the center and top it with some olives, tomatoes, thyme, pepper flakes, and salt. Fold over the bottom, top, and sides to enclose the cheese. Put it seam-side down on a plate. Repeat with the remaining chard, making five more packets. Brush with olive oil.

5. Clean the grill grate and lightly oil it. Grill the packets, cautiously turning once, until they are thoroughly heated and the chard is a little crisp, about 3 to 4 minutes on each side. Serve atop the rice.

COOK'S NOTE Remove the chard's central rib by cutting out just the lower thick part of the stalk, leaving the leaf attached at the top.

Fettuccine with Chard and Baby Heirloom Tomatoes

Chard and pasta are a classic duo in Italian cuisine. This version utilizes a tasty salad-like tomato concoction, both in the sauce and as a garnish. If desired, beet greens, dandelion leaves, or spinach can be substituted for the chard.

Yields 10 first-course servings

NUTRITIONAL INFORMATION
(per serving)

calories 250	sodium (mg) 370	vitamin A IUs 90%
fat calories 60	total carbohydrates (g)... 39	vitamin C 30%
total fat (g) 7	fiber (g) 6	calcium 15%
sat fat (g) 2	sugars (g) 3	iron 15%
cholesterol (mg) 5	protein (g) 10	

2 cups baby heirloom tomatoes or cherry tomatoes, halved

⅓ cup finely chopped fresh Italian parsley

2 teaspoons champagne vinegar or sherry vinegar

Coarse salt (kosher or sea)

Freshly ground black pepper

3 tablespoons extra-virgin olive oil

4 large garlic cloves, thinly sliced

1½ pounds chard, thick central ribs removed and discarded, leaves washed and coarsely chopped, about 10 to 11 cups

2 tablespoons tomato paste

About ½ teaspoon dried red pepper flakes

1 pound dry multi-grain or whole-wheat fettuccine

½ cup grated Parmesan cheese

1. In a medium bowl, toss the tomatoes with the parsley and vinegar; season with salt and pepper. Set aside.

2. Put a large pot of salted water on high heat and bring it to a boil. Meanwhile, in a large, deep skillet or Dutch oven, heat the oil on medium-high heat. Add the garlic and cook for 20 to 30 seconds to soften but not brown the garlic. Add the chard and toss. Cover and cook, stirring occasionally, until the chard is heated through and wilted, about 5 minutes. Add ¾ cup hot water, the tomato paste, and pepper flakes; stir to combine. Add the fresh tomato mixture, reserving ⅓ cup for garnish. Bring it to a boil; cover and reduce the heat to medium-low. Simmer gently for 12 to 14 minutes.

3. Meanwhile, cook the fettuccine in the boiling salted water until it is al dente (following the package directions). Drain, reserving 1 cup of the cooking water. Add the fettuccine to the chard mixture and gently toss. If needed, add enough of the reserved cooking water to make a creamy consistency. Off heat, add the cheese and gently toss. Taste and adjust the seasoning as needed.

4. Place the mixture in individual shallow bowls and top with the reserved tomato mixture. Serve immediately.

CHILE

Anaheim, Habañero, Jalapeño,
Pasilla or Poblano, Red Fresno, Serrano

Capsaicin is that incendiary compound in chiles that creates the sensation of heat. Turns out that it is part of what makes chiles so healthful as well. Active compounds in chiles called capsinoids help the immune system, keep blood vessels clear, lower blood pressure, and even counteract ulcer pain by decreasing acid and promoting healing in the lining of the stomach.

The amount of capsaicin varies in chile varieties. Pharmacist Wilbur Scoville developed a system for measuring a pepper's power. The system notes the parts per million and converts them into Scoville units. Here's the scorecard for fresh chiles: Anaheim (500 to 2,500), habañero (100,000 to 200,000), jalapeño (3,000 to 12,000), poblano—often referred to as pasilla—(1,000 to 3,000), red Fresno (3,000 to 12,000), serrano (15,000 to 20,000).

NUTRITIONAL INFORMATION
(per 1 cup raw jalapeño, sliced)

calories ... 27	sodium (mg) ... 1	vitamin A IUs ... 14%
fat calories ... 5	total carbohydrates (g) ... 6	vitamin C ... 66%
total fat (g) ... 1	fiber (g) ... 3	calcium ... 1%
sat fat (g) ... 0	sugars (g) ... 3	iron ... 4%
cholesterol (mg) ... 0	protein (g) ... 1	

ANTIMICROBIAL
Capsaicin in the diet demonstrates an ability to kill the salmonella microbe in animal studies. This means eating peppers with your meal could help stop these dangerous bacteria dead in their tracks should they happen to make their way into your meal.

VIRUS KILLER
Studies of capsaicin demonstrate its knack for interfering with the transcription action of viruses that allows them to replicate as they take over the body's cells. Similar actions of chile phytochemicals are believed to help stop the proliferation of the types of aberrant cells that occur in tumors.

PAIN FOR PAIN
Chile burn is a good hurt; it actually kills pain outside and inside. As a common soother for sore joints and muscles from arthritis or even a vigorous workout, capsaicin is a popular topical analgesic. But it also helps relieve pain from the inside by stimulating the release of neuropeptides associated with pain relief and inflammation reduction.

AVAILABLE
Year-round

KEEP IT FRESH
Select fresh chiles that are firm and glossy without soft spots or shriveling. Occasionally a jalapeño has a scar crack at the stem end, which doesn't affect freshness, but other varieties should be crack-free. Refrigerate unwashed, loosely wrapped in paper towels inside a partially closed plastic bag, up to 8 days.

LAST-MINUTE PREP

Wash with cold water. Use caution when cutting fresh chiles. Upon completion, wash your hands and work surface thoroughly. Do *not* touch your face or eyes. Cooks with delicate skin should use gloves when working with fresh chiles, especially when working with those that rank high on the Scoville scale. Remove the stem. Many cooks like to remove the seeds and veins to reduce the burn, while others consider this a travesty and prefer the natural "heat," using fewer chiles to make adjustments. To remove the seeds and veins, cut stemmed chiles into lengthwise quarters; cut out veins and seeds, then cut into desired shapes.

QUICK COOK

Chiles are often combined with other ingredients and eaten raw. When cooked, they are often sautéed, grilled, roasted, or broiled. To roast small chiles, put them in a heavy dry skillet (not nonstick, cast iron preferred) or grill pan on medium heat; turn when sporadic dark areas appear and the chiles are slightly softened, and repeat on the opposite sides. Small chiles are generally not peeled. To roast larger chiles, use a barbecue, gas flame, or grill pan; turn with tongs when sporadic dark areas appear and the chiles are slightly softened, and repeat on the opposite sides. Place them in a plastic bag or kitchen towel and let them sit for 5 minutes to steam; peel and seed.

try it!

IN SALSA VERDE

Adjust an oven rack to 4 to 5 inches below the broiler element. Preheat the broiler. Place 6 tomatillos (husked, rinsed, wiped clean if needed) and 1 serrano chile on a rimmed baking sheet. Broil until blackened in spots and blistered, about 5 minutes. Turn over and roast the other sides, 3 to 4 minutes more, or until blistered and soft. Let them cool on the baking sheet; remove the seeds from the chile. Put everything in a blender, including the juices. Add ¼ cup chopped fresh cilantro and ¼ cup water; blend to a coarse purée. Place the puréed mixture in a nonreactive bowl. Add ¼ cup chopped onion and season with salt.

WITH SPAGHETTI SQUASH

Cook spaghetti squash by cutting it in half lengthwise; place it cut-side down on a rimmed baking sheet coated with cooking spray and pierce the skin in several places. Bake in a 375-degree-F oven until tender, about 45 minutes. When cool enough to handle, rake the spaghetti-like strands into a bowl. Top with Grilled Tomato Salsa (page 108).

IN A CREAMY LEMON SAUCE

Bring 1 quart chicken or vegetable broth to a boil in a large saucepan. Add ⅓ cup long-grain brown rice and ½ seeded serrano chile (minced); reduce the heat to medium-low and simmer until the rice is tender, about 18 minutes. Cautiously transfer about 1¾ cups of the mixture to a blender. Add 12 ounces silken tofu (cubed), ¼ cup fresh lemon juice, and ½ teaspoon ground turmeric. Whirl until smooth, holding down the lid of the blender with a pot holder. Whisk the blended mixture into the remaining sauce. Reheat and spoon over grilled chicken breasts or thighs, or grilled eggplant slices.

Bean Tostadas with Cabbage Escabeche

Escabeche is a Latin American cabbage slaw with plenty of pizzazz. Served atop tacos, tostadas, or nachos, it adds not only the spicy punch of chiles but also the sweetness of carrots and fresh herbs. Make it at least 2 hours (or up to 4 days) ahead and refrigerate it in an airtight container.

Yields 8 servings

NUTRITIONAL INFORMATION
(per serving)

calories 210	sodium (mg) 420	vitamin A IUs 70%
fat calories 70	total carbohydrates (g) ... 29	vitamin C 60%
total fat (g) 7	fiber (g) 7	calcium 15%
sat fat (g)..................... 2.5	sugars (g) 6	iron............................. 15%
cholesterol (mg) 15	protein (g) 9	

CABBAGE ESCABECHE

7 to 8 cups shredded green cabbage

2 carrots, peeled and shredded

2 jalapeños, stemmed and seeded, cut into thin lengthwise slivers

⅔ cup finely chopped fresh Italian parsley

⅓ cup finely chopped fresh cilantro

1 cup apple cider vinegar

1 tablespoon kosher salt

1 tablespoon sugar or agave syrup

TOSTADAS

8 corn tortillas

2 tablespoons canola oil or vegetable oil

One 16-ounce can lard-free refried beans

½ cup plain fat-free Greek-style yogurt

2 teaspoons fresh lime juice

¾ cup crumbled queso fresco or feta cheese

1. To make the escabeche: In a large nonreactive bowl, combine the cabbage, carrots, jalapeños, parsley, and cilantro. Toss. Add the vinegar, salt, and sugar and toss well. Cover with plastic wrap and refrigerate for 2 hours. Drain well in a colander. It can be used at this point or refrigerated airtight in a zipper-style plastic bag up to 2 days. Before using on tostadas, drain it again in a colander.

2. To make the tostadas: Adjust the oven racks to the lower and upper third positions and preheat the oven to 450 degrees F. Brush the tortillas with the oil on both sides and arrange on two baking sheets in single layers. Bake until nicely browned, monitoring the progress, 10 to 12 minutes, rotating the sheets halfway through baking.

3. Heat the beans in a small saucepan over medium heat.

4. Combine the yogurt and lime juice in a small bowl. Spread warm beans over the toasted tortillas and top with the cheese. Place a generous amount of escabeche atop each tostada and place a dollop of topping on each.

Chicken and Toasted Bulgur Salad with Corn and Arugula

It can be tricky to judge the degree of spicy-hotness contained within chiles. When looking at the Scoville units for each variety, you see that the amount of capsaicin varies. Without tasting them, you don't know exactly how much heat they are going to pack. To be on the safe side, start by using half of the suggested amount in a recipe, then add more to suit your taste. Serrano chiles are generally much hotter than jalapeños, so when substituting them, use a smaller amount.

Yields 6 servings

NUTRITIONAL INFORMATION
(per serving)

calories 280	sodium (mg) 270	vitamin A IUs 10%
fat calories 80	total carbohydrates (g)...24	vitamin C 20%
total fat (g) 9	fiber (g) 5	calcium 4%
sat fat (g).....................1.5	sugars (g) 2	iron.............................10%
cholesterol (mg) 60	protein (g) 28	

⅔ cup coarsely ground bulgur (number 3 grind; see page 200)

½ teaspoon salt

3 tablespoons extra-virgin olive oil

4 ears corn, kernels cut off (about 2½ cups)

1 small red onion, coarsely chopped

Freshly ground black pepper

4 boneless, skinless chicken breasts (about 5 ounces each)

2 ripe Roma tomatoes, cored, diced

½ cup chopped fresh cilantro

3 tablespoons fresh lime juice

1 jalapeño or ½ serrano chile, seeds and veins removed, minced

¼ teaspoon cayenne pepper

3 cups baby arugula

1. In a large heavy-bottomed skillet, toast the bulgur over medium-high heat, stirring occasionally, for 5 to 7 minutes, or until it makes popping sounds and is browned lightly. Transfer it to a bowl and let it cool slightly.

2. In a medium saucepan, bring 1⅓ cups water and the salt to a boil and stir in the bulgur. Cover and reduce the heat to low. Simmer for 10 to 15 minutes, or until tender. Drain if all the water is not absorbed. Transfer to a bowl; fluff with a fork.

3. Heat 1 tablespoon of the oil in a large, deep skillet on medium-high heat. Add the corn and onion; season with salt and pepper. Cook, stirring occasionally, until the onion softens, about 5 minutes. Add it to the bulgur.

4. Season the chicken with salt and pepper. In the same skillet, heat 1 tablespoon more of the oil on medium-high heat. Add the chicken in a single layer. Brown well on both sides; reduce the heat, and cook until it is opaque through, about 5 minutes on each side, turning down the heat if the chicken starts to brown too much. Place the chicken on a plate; set aside.

5. Add the tomatoes, cilantro, lime juice, chile, cayenne, and remaining 1 tablespoon oil to the bulgur mixture. Taste and adjust the seasoning as needed.

6. Divide the arugula between six plates. Top the arugula with the bulgur mixture. Cut the chicken crosswise into ¼-inch slices. Divide it between the plates, fanning it out so the slices overlap slightly.

COOK'S NOTE A drizzle of optional lime oil is delicious atop the chicken. To make it, combine 1 tablespoon extra-virgin olive oil with 1 tablespoon fresh lime juice and ¼ teaspoon salt.

Grilled Tomato Salsa

Grilling fresh tomatoes brings out their natural sweetness. The easiest way to accomplish this is to cut them in half through the equator, gently toss them with a little extra-virgin olive oil, and cook them on a hot grill pan. The grill pan does double duty in this recipe because it is also used to cook halved fresh poblano chiles. Note that poblanos are often labeled "pasilla" on the West Coast. The salsa is particularly appealing teamed with grilled lamb patties, grilled fish, or a butter lettuce salad.

Yields about 3 cups

NUTRITIONAL INFORMATION
(per 1/4 cup)

calories 80	sodium (mg) 105	vitamin A IUs 15%
fat calories 60	total carbohydrates (g).....5	vitamin C 20%
total fat (g) 6	fiber (g) 1	calcium 2%
sat fat (g) 1	sugars (g) 2	iron............................... 4%
cholesterol (mg) 0	protein (g) 1	

- 5 medium, ripe heirloom tomatoes, halved crosswise through the equator
- 2 poblano chiles, halved lengthwise, seeds and veins removed
- 1/3 cup extra-virgin olive oil
- 2 limes, juiced
- 2 teaspoons sherry or champagne vinegar
- 3/4 teaspoon ground cumin
- Coarse salt (kosher or sea)
- Freshly ground black pepper
- 3 green onions, white and light green portions finely chopped
- 2 tablespoons chopped fresh cilantro
- 2 tablespoons chopped fresh mint

1. Heat a grill pan on medium-high heat. In a large bowl, gently toss together the tomatoes and chiles with 1½ tablespoons of the oil. Spread the vegetables on the pan and grill for 3 to 5 minutes on each side, until marked from the grill. Place them on a large plate or rimmed baking sheet and let them cool.

2. Coarsely chop the tomatoes and chiles and put them in a nonreactive bowl along with any juices. Add the remaining oil, the lime juice, vinegar, and cumin and season with salt and pepper. Stir in the onions, cilantro, and mint. Gently toss. Taste and adjust the seasoning as needed.

CHRYSANTHEMUM LEAF

also Tung Ho

Edible chrysanthemum leaves have an alluring scent—a mix of distinct chrysanthemum floral aromas mixed with subtle pine-like accents. Smaller, less mature leaves make a unique salad served raw, while quick cooking better suits larger leaves.

For millennia, this edible member of the chrysanthemum family has been used as a salad green in Asia and the Middle East. And for good reason: It's high in antioxidants, minerals, and vitamins, especially the antioxidant vitamins A and C.

NUTRITIONAL INFORMATION
(per 1 cup raw, chopped)

calories 12	sodium (mg) 60	vitamin A IUs 19%
fat calories 2	total carbohydrates (g).....2	vitamin C 1%
total fat (g) 0	fiber (g) 2	calcium.........................6%
sat fat (g)........................0	sugars (g) ....less than 1	iron.............................7%
cholesterol (mg) 0	protein (g) 2	

POTASSIUM POWER
Gram per gram, chrysanthemum has more potassium than nearly any food plant. Potassium is responsible for maintaining energy balance at the cellular level and is needed for muscle control.

HEARTS AND MINDS
Potassium's importance in muscle action is especially critical for the unique muscle cells of the heart. Potassium is also a fundamental element in creating the electric charge that keeps the heart pumping and the nerves functioning. The brain, too, needs adequate potassium for its trillions of nerve endings.

TOTAL PROTECTION
Chrysanthemum leaves are super sources of antioxidants that help protect cells from hazardous and carcinogenic elements. Another important phytochemical group in the greens is the monoterpene family of phytochemicals. These have been shown to help protect against breast and liver cancers.

AVAILABLE
Year-round

KEEP IT FRESH
Look for chrysanthemum leaves at Asian markets with large, fresh produce sections. Choose leaves without discoloration or soft spots. Don't be alarmed if they are droopy; that's to be expected. To store, untie the bundle and refrigerate, unwashed, wrapped in a slightly moist kitchen towel or paper towel and placed in a partially closed plastic bag. Use within 3 days.

LAST-MINUTE PREP

Cut off a small portion of the stems at the root end and discard. Submerge the leaves in cold water; drain in a colander and shake dry. Many dishes call for only the leaves; cut or tear them from the stems. However, the stems can be cut into 1-inch pieces and used in soups or stir-fries.

QUICK COOK

Chrysanthemum leaves can be eaten raw or steamed, briefly blanched, or stir-fried. If using in soups or stir-fries, add during the last 1 to 2 minutes of cooking. To steam, cut the leaves into 2-inch lengths. Steam in a basket over (but not touching) simmering water. Cover for 1 to 3 minutes, or until just barely tender. Cooking times vary depending on whether you use tender young leaves or more mature leaves. If desired, top with a small drizzle of dressing made with ¼ cup seasoned rice vinegar, 3 tablespoons soy sauce, and 1 teaspoon Asian (roasted) sesame oil.

try it!

WITH ROASTED CARROTS

Preheat the oven to 425 degrees F. Peel and halve lengthwise 1 pound carrots; put them on a rimmed baking sheet with 5 unpeeled garlic cloves. Drizzle with 1 tablespoon extra-virgin olive oil and toss. Season with coarse salt and pepper. Roast for 30 minutes, tossing after 20 minutes, until tender. Sprinkle with ⅓ cup finely chopped fresh chrysanthemum leaves.

IN A SALAD MIX

Combine equal parts bite-size lettuce leaves, baby spinach, and young (small) fresh chrysanthemum leaves.

IN CHOP SUEY

Add a generous handful of coarsely chopped young fresh chrysanthemum leaves to your favorite chop suey or stir fry, making sure to add it during the last 1 to 2 minutes of cooking.

Sautéed Chrysanthemum Leaves with Grilled Tofu

An Asian-inspired marinade lends sweet and spicy flavors to this stir-fried mixture of baby spinach and chrysanthemum leaves. The marinade does double duty—acting as the stir-fry sauce after marinating the tofu.

Yields 4 first-course or 2 entrée servings

NUTRITIONAL INFORMATION
(per serving)

calories 170	sodium (mg) 900	vitamin A IUs 70%
fat calories 100	total carbohydrates (g).....9	vitamin C 30%
total fat (g) 11	fiber (g) 2	calcium 10%
sat fat (g) 1.5	sugars (g) 3	iron..............................20%
cholesterol (mg) 0	protein (g) 10	

14 ounces firm tofu, drained

MARINADE

⅓ cup sodium-reduced soy sauce

2 tablespoons vegetable oil, plus extra for grill pan

2 teaspoons minced unpeeled fresh ginger

1½ teaspoons maple syrup

1 teaspoon Asian (roasted) sesame oil

1 garlic clove, minced

½ teaspoon hot sauce, such as Sriracha

4 cups (packed) baby spinach (about 6 ounces)

2 cups (loosely packed) bite-size pieces torn chrysanthemum leaves

1. Cut the tofu crosswise into 6 slices. Layer several paper towels on a rimmed baking sheet and arrange the tofu slices in a single layer. Top with three layers of paper towels and arrange a second baking sheet on top; place object(s) on top to weight it, such as a bottle of wine or two cans. Let it rest for 25 to 30 minutes for the tofu to fully drain.

2. To make the marinade: In a glass baking dish or casserole, stir to combine the soy sauce, 1 tablespoon of the vegetable oil, the ginger, syrup, sesame oil, garlic, and hot sauce. Add the tofu in a single layer and marinate it for 20 minutes, turning occasionally.

3. Heat a lightly oiled well-seasoned ridged grill pan over medium-high heat until hot but not smoking. Use a slotted spoon or spatula to lift the tofu from the marinade and place it on the grill pan (reserve the marinade). Cook until heated through and grill marks appear, cautiously turning once, about 3 minutes on each side.

4. Meanwhile, heat the remaining 1 tablespoon vegetable oil in a wok or large deep skillet on high heat. Add the spinach and chrysanthemum leaves; stir-fry until almost wilted, about 45 seconds. Add the reserved marinade; continue to stir-fry until the leaves are completely wilted and piping hot.

5. Divide the greens and sauce between serving plates. Top with the tofu and serve.

Chrysanthemum and Butter Lettuce Salad with Carrot-Ginger Dressing

Salad greens with assertive flavors are enhanced by the fruitiness of dried cherries or cranberries. A dressing that complements the mix with a touch of spicy sweetness is a welcome addition. This carrot-ginger dressing brings the honeyed taste of puréed carrots and maple syrup to the salad, along with the lively peppery edge of fresh ginger.

Yields 4 servings

NUTRITIONAL INFORMATION
(per serving, using all the dressing)

calories 140	sodium (mg) 40	vitamin A IUs 100%
fat calories 60	total carbohydrates (g)....19	vitamin C 8%
total fat (g) 7	fiber (g) 3	calcium 6%
sat fat (g)........................1	sugars (g) 14	iron................................8%
cholesterol (mg) 0	protein (g) 2	

DRESSING

1 large carrot, peeled, thinly sliced

1 teaspoon chopped unpeeled fresh ginger

2 tablespoons maple syrup or agave syrup

2 tablespoons extra-virgin olive oil

1½ tablespoons unseasoned rice vinegar

SALAD

4 cups bite-size pieces torn butter or Bibb lettuce

1½ cups bite-size pieces torn chrysanthemum leaves

½ medium red onion, cut into thin slivers

¼ cup dried cherries

1. To make the dressing: Put the carrot and ginger in a food processor. Process until the carrot is minced. Add the syrup, oil, and vinegar and process until smooth; set aside.

2. To make the salad: Combine the lettuce, chrysanthemum leaves, onions, and cherries in a large bowl. Stir the dressing. Add enough dressing to generously coat the leaves and toss.

Thai-Style Carrot Soup with Chrysanthemum Leaves

Only a modest amount of dried red pepper flakes is used in this flavorful soup. Be sure to taste it after it is puréed and adjust the spice level to suit your taste, adding a little hot sauce if you like. When the chopped chrysanthemum leaves are sprinkled on the warm soup, they release their lovely floral smell.

Yields 8 servings

NUTRITIONAL INFORMATION
(per serving)

calories 120	sodium (mg) 580	vitamin A IUs 160%
fat calories 50	total carbohydrates (g)....15	vitamin C 10%
total fat (g) 5	fiber (g) 3	calcium 8%
sat fat (g).......................1.5	sugars (g) 9	iron..............................6%
cholesterol (mg) 0	protein (g) 5	

- 1 tablespoon olive oil
- 1 pound carrots, peeled and coarsely chopped
- 1 large yellow onion, chopped
- 2 stalks celery, chopped
- 2 garlic cloves, chopped
- 3 tablespoons chopped unpeeled fresh ginger
- 3½ cups fat-free, low-sodium chicken or vegetable broth
- 1 cup light coconut milk
- ⅓ cup fat-free evaporated milk
- 3 tablespoons fresh lime juice
- 2 tablespoons creamy peanut butter
- 2 tablespoons brown sugar or maple syrup
- 2 teaspoons seasoned rice vinegar
- 1½ tablespoons fish sauce
- 1 teaspoon Asian (roasted) sesame oil
- ½ teaspoon ground coriander
- ½ teaspoon ground turmeric
- ¼ teaspoon dried red pepper flakes
- Salt
- Freshly ground black pepper
- ½ cup finely chopped fresh chrysanthemum leaves

1. In a large pan or Dutch oven, heat the olive oil over medium-high heat. Add the carrots, onion, celery, garlic, and ginger; cook for 5 to 6 minutes, stirring occasionally, until the onion is translucent. Add the broth, coconut milk, evaporated milk, lime juice, peanut butter, sugar, vinegar, fish sauce, sesame oil, coriander, turmeric, and pepper flakes; bring to a boil. Cover, reduce the heat, and simmer for 25 to 30 minutes, until the carrots are very tender. Remove from the heat.

2. Using a ladle, remove 1 cup of the broth and set aside. Process the remaining soup in batches in a food processor or blender until smooth; hold the lid down with a pot holder if using a blender. Taste and season with salt and pepper. If the soup is too thick, stir in all or some of the reserved broth.

3. If making it ahead, refrigerate, covered, for up to 24 hours. Gently simmer on low heat until reheated. Ladle into soup bowls. Garnish each serving with chopped chrysanthemum leaves.

VEGETARIAN ALTERNATIVE Omit the fish sauce and substitute soy sauce.

CILANTRO

Cilantro is an essential herb in many cuisines with a spicy sizzle. With its sharp, almost lemony flavor and peppery aroma, cilantro offers a cooling balance to the heat of chiles and spices. Although its fernlike leaves look fragile, it has an assertive taste that is extremely versatile. With its astringent flavor that some liken to a mix of parsley and citrus peel, cilantro is delicious in mild-mannered dishes as well: scattered atop sliced tropical fruit, tossed into green salads, or stirred into soups just before serving.

It is sometimes called Chinese parsley or coriander.

Cilantro was more familiar to Americans as a Mexican garnish until Thai and Vietnamese cuisines hit it big in the United States. A steaming rich bowl of pho, Vietnamese noodle soup, is typically accompanied by a pile of leafy herbs that includes cilantro.

NUTRITIONAL INFORMATION
(per 1/4 cup raw)

calories 1	sodium (mg) 2	vitamin A IUs 5%
fat calories 0	total carbohydrates (g).....0	vitamin C 2%
total fat (g) 0	fiber (g) 0	calcium 0%
sat fat (g)..........................0	sugars (g) 0	iron................................0%
cholesterol (mg) 0	protein (g) 0	

CONCENTRATED GOODNESS
Cilantro is a concentrated powerhouse of antioxidants and vitamins, ounce for ounce containing more nutrition than many other leafy greens. It contains not only folate and vitamins A and K but also a number of B vitamins.

ANCIENT WISDOM
Cilantro's use has been traced back more than eight thousand years, and it has a history as one of the most ancient herbal medicines, used as a blood cleanser, an antianxiety booster, and an aid to digestion.

BACTERIA BEATER
Chemical compounds found in its leaves have shown strong antibacterial activity against such dangerous microbes as salmonella.

INSULIN TRIGGER
Cilantro was recently shown to have an ability to trigger insulin release by leveling blood sugar, helping to mitigate the symptoms of diabetes.

AVAILABLE
Year-round

KEEP IT FRESH
Look for fresh-smelling, bright green leaves without any discoloration or mold. Rinse cilantro in a large bowl of cold water. Drain it well in a colander, wrap it (with some water still clinging to the leaves) in paper towels or a clean kitchen towel, and place it in a plastic bag; refrigerate it in the crisper drawer up to 5 days.

LAST-MINUTE PREP

Most recipes call for using only the leaves and thin, tender portion of the stems that are at the top; in that case, discard lower portion of stems. But some recipes specify to include the large stems and sometimes the roots as well (though it is difficult to find root-on cilantro in the marketplace).

QUICK COOK

Cilantro is most often used raw, but can be added to cooked dishes during the last few minutes of cooking.

try it!

ON SCRAMBLED EGGS

In a nonstick skillet on medium-high heat, cook some chopped red onion and strips of corn tortillas in a little extra-virgin olive oil until the onion is transparent. Beat eggs or egg whites with salt and pepper; add them to the onion mixture. Reduce the heat to medium-low. Stir frequently until the eggs are cooked but still moist. Garnish with chopped cilantro and, if desired, fresh tomato salsa.

IN MIXED GREEN SALAD

Combine baby lettuces, sliced radishes, tomatoes, and a handful of small fresh cilantro sprigs. Toss with a simple vinaigrette dressing (add a little hot pepper sauce to spice up the dressing if you like) and, if desired, a little diced ripe avocado.

IN FLAVORED BUTTER

In a food processor fitted with the metal blade, and with the motor running, drop in 1 large garlic clove and 1 tablespoon coarsely chopped fresh ginger. Add a thin slice of fresh jalapeño and a handful of fresh cilantro. Process until finely chopped. Add ½ cup cold butter (cut into 6 pieces); process until smooth. Place the mixture on a piece of waxed paper and roll it into a cylinder; place it in a sealable container and refrigerate or freeze. Use a small pat on top of steamed vegetables, broiled fish, or chicken. The butter will melt and drizzle over the top to create a simple sauce.

Chicken Breasts with Pineapple Chutney and Cilantro

Cilantro adds an essential spark to fruit-based chutneys and salsas. Boned and skinned chicken breasts take an irresistible turnaround from bland to bliss when served with this cilantro-spiked sweet-and-sour pineapple chutney. The chutney cooks on the stovetop while the chicken bakes in the oven.

Yields 4 servings

NUTRITIONAL INFORMATION
(per serving)

calories 210	sodium (mg) 190	vitamin A IUs 2%
fat calories 50	total carbohydrates (g)....14	vitamin C 50%
total fat (g) 6	fiber (g) 2	calcium 4%
sat fat (g) 1	sugars (g) 9	iron 8%
cholesterol (mg) 65	protein (g) 24	

1   tablespoon plus 2 teaspoons extra-virgin olive oil

1   medium red onion, diced

½   medium fennel bulb, trimmed, cored, diced

1¼   cups diced, cored, peeled fresh pineapple

1   cup fat-free, low-sodium chicken or vegetable broth

½   cup cider vinegar

2   tablespoons minced unpeeled fresh ginger

1½   tablespoons brown sugar

½   teaspoon ground cinnamon

OPTIONAL minced zest of 1 orange

4   boneless, skinless chicken breasts (about 4 to 5 ounces each)

Salt and freshly ground black pepper

GARNISH ½ cup roughly chopped fresh cilantro

OPTIONAL GARNISH pomegranate arils (seeds)

1. Adjust an oven rack to the middle position and preheat the oven to 350 degrees F.

2. In a large, heavy-bottomed saucepan, heat 1 tablespoon of the oil on medium-high heat. Add the onion and cook until it is softened and starting to brown, 5 to 8 minutes, stirring occasionally. Add the fennel; cook until it is starting to soften, about 4 minutes, stirring occasionally.

3. Add the pineapple, broth, vinegar, ginger, sugar, cinnamon, and orange zest, if using. Bring to a boil; reduce the heat to medium-low and simmer for 20 minutes, or until the mixture slightly thickens and the pineapple is soft.

4. Meanwhile, place the chicken in a single layer in a small roasting pan. Drizzle with the remaining 2 teaspoons oil. Season with salt and pepper. Roast until the chicken is cooked through, about 35 to 40 minutes.

5. Remove the chicken and let it rest for 5 minutes. Cut each breast into ½-inch crosswise slices. Fan each breast on a dinner plate. Spoon some pineapple chutney over the top of each. Sprinkle with the cilantro and, if desired, the pomegranate arils. Serve.

MEATLESS ALTERNATIVE Instead of chicken, serve the sauce spooned over wild rice or a mixture of different rice varieties or farro.

Soba Noodles with Cucumbers, Shrimp, and Miso-Cilantro Sauce

This cilantro sauce takes on a pleasing deep earthiness with the addition of white miso, a thick paste most often made by fermenting soybeans (but rice or barley can also be used). Look for white miso in vacuum-sealed packages or plastic tubs in the refrigerated case at natural food stores, Asian markets, and many supermarkets. Occasionally it is sold in glass jars.

Yields 4 servings

NUTRITIONAL INFORMATION
(per serving)

calories 390	sodium (mg) 570	vitamin A IUs 8%
fat calories 25	total carbohydrates (g)...75	vitamin C 10%
total fat (g) 2.5	fiber (g) 6	calcium.........................4%
sat fat (g)........................0	sugars (g) 8	iron.............................15%
cholesterol (mg) 55	protein (g) 19	

1 medium garlic clove, peeled

1-inch piece fresh ginger, unpeeled, thinly sliced crosswise

1 cup packed fresh cilantro leaves

¼ cup white miso or yellow miso
(*see Cook's Note*)

2½ tablespoons rice vinegar

½ teaspoon Asian hot sauce, such as Sriracha

Salt

12 ounces dry soba noodles

3 green onions, cut into thin crosswise slices (including half of dark green stalks)

½ large unpeeled hothouse cucumber, cut in half lengthwise, cut into thin crosswise slices

4 ounces cooked, shelled, deveined shrimp, halved lengthwise

GARNISH lime wedges

1. In a food processor fitted with the metal blade, with the machine running, add the garlic and ginger and mince. Add the cilantro and pulse until it is chopped. Add the miso, vinegar, and hot sauce. Process until everything is blended, scraping down the sides if needed. Set aside.

2. Bring a large pot of salted water to a boil on high heat. Add the noodles. Cook until they are al dente (following the package directions). Drain and rinse the noodles with cold water. Drain well, shaking the colander to remove as much water as possible.

3. In a large bowl, combine the noodles and miso mixture. Add the onions, cucumber, and shrimp. Toss gently. Taste and adjust the seasoning as needed. Serve with the lime wedges.

MEATLESS ALTERNATIVE Omit the shrimp.

COOK'S NOTE Miso is often classified by color. In general, dark red miso (really a reddish brown) is aged longer than white or light yellow miso and has a heartier, stronger flavor and fragrance. Light miso and yellow miso have a milder flavor and more delicate aroma.

Warm Quinoa Salad with Cilantro and Black Beans

Mixing quinoa with cilantro and black beans makes a salad that is delicious either warm or at room temperature. If you like, substitute other cheeses for the feta, such as tiny cubes of Parmesan or crumbled goat cheese. Or if you prefer to omit the cheese, top the dish with diced avocado.

Yields 6 servings

NUTRITIONAL INFORMATION
(per serving)

calories 260	sodium (mg) 500	vitamin A IUs 45%
fat calories 30	total carbohydrates (g)...44	vitamin C 140%
total fat (g) 6	fiber (g) 7	calcium.......................10%
sat fat (g).....................1.5	sugars (g) 6	iron............................. 25%
cholesterol (mg) 5	protein (g) 10	

1 tablespoon vegetable oil or extra-virgin olive oil

1 medium-large red onion, coarsely chopped

1 red bell pepper, cored, seeded, diced

1 yellow bell pepper, cored, seeded, diced

1 cup dry white quinoa

1½ teaspoons smoked paprika (*pimentón*)

¾ teaspoon ground cumin

½ teaspoon chili powder

½ teaspoon salt

One 15-ounce can black beans, rinsed, drained well

½ cup chopped fresh cilantro

4 cups baby spinach

¼ cup crumbled feta cheese

GARNISH 1 papaya, seeded, peeled, cut into lengthwise slices; 6 lime wedges

1. In a medium saucepan, heat the oil on medium heat. Add the onion and bell peppers. Cook, stirring occasionally, until the vegetables begin to soften, about 5 minutes. Add the quinoa, paprika, cumin, chili powder, and salt; stir to combine.

2. Add 1½ cups water and increase the heat to high. Bring it to a boil. Cover and reduce the heat to medium-low. Simmer, covered, until the quinoa is almost softened and most of the water is absorbed, about 15 minutes. Add the beans and half the cilantro; cook until they are heated through, uncovered, and no water remains, about 3 to 4 minutes.

3. Place the spinach on a platter or divide it between six plates. Top it with the quinoa mixture. Scatter the feta on top. Garnish with the papaya, reserved cilantro, and lime wedges.

DANDELION
GREEN

With their deep green hue and zigzag ragged edges, dandelion greens have interesting bitter notes, a quality that increases the bigger they grow. Use them raw to add balance to a dish that needs a spark of bitterness, or briefly blanch them to tone down some of their assertive character.

Small leaves make welcome partners teamed with baby greens in mixed green salads, especially if the dressing is a little sweet. On their own, toss with a squeeze of lemon juice, minced garlic, and high-quality extra-virgin olive oil; use the tangle of greens as an accompaniment to pork-based delicacies or sunny-side up eggs.

LIVER CLEANSER
Dandelion roots and leaves have centuries of anecdotal support for liver health, and researchers are finding the facts to back it up. One recent study showed that chemical components in dandelion greens (sesquiterpenes, anthocyanidins, and anthocyanins) arrest the development of fibrous tissue in the liver, preventing certain types of tumors from growing.

NUTRITIONAL INFORMATION
(per 1/2 cup raw, chopped)

calories 25	sodium (mg) 42	vitamin A IUs 112%
fat calories 3	total carbohydrates (g)..... 5	vitamin C 32%
total fat (g) 0	fiber (g) 2	calcium 10%
sat fat (g) 0	sugars (g) 0	iron 9%
cholesterol (mg) 0	protein (g) 1	

TOXIN FLUSHER
Their powerful diuretic capacity makes dandelion greens just dandy when it comes to helping the kidneys do their job and filter out various toxins from both internal and external sources.

WEIGHT AND CHOLESTEROL MANAGEMENT
Thousands of studies over the past half century have demonstrated the ability of dietary fiber to help bind to and express cholesterol from the blood, thereby reducing arterial plaque buildup and thus protecting the cardiovascular system. It also acts on the system that controls the flow of food from the stomach into the G.I. tract, increasing the rate of gastric emptying. This helps control the amount of calories, especially from glucose, absorbed by the body.

AVAILABLE
Year-round

KEEP IT FRESH
Leaves should smell fresh and be bright green—free of wilting, soft spots, or discoloration. Refrigerate them unwashed, up to 1 day in a plastic bag. Or, for longer storage, wash before refrigeration. Pinch off the stems at the base of the leaf before washing. Swish the leaves in a large bowl or tub of cold water. Repeat if necessary until the water is clean and free of grit. Drain in a colander. Wrap in a clean towel or paper towels and place them in a partially closed plastic bag. Refrigerate in the crisper drawer up to 3 days.

LAST-MINUTE PREP
If stored unwashed, wash as directed above.

QUICK COOK

Remove tough lower stems from 3 pounds of clean dandelion greens; stack the leaves and cut them crosswise into 2-inch pieces. Place a Dutch oven or medium pan with about 4 cups water and a good pinch of salt on high heat; bring to a boil and add the greens. Cook until the leaves are tender, about 8 minutes. Drain in a colander and refresh with cold water. Drain well, pressing out the excess water (they can be refrigerated airtight at this point if desired). Heat 3 tablespoons extra-virgin olive oil in a large, deep skillet on medium-high heat. Add 2 garlic cloves (minced) and a pinch of dried red pepper flakes. Stir for 30 seconds (do not brown the garlic). Add the greens and cook until heated through, about 4 minutes. Taste; add fresh lemon juice and/or salt as needed.

try it!

STIR-FRIED WITH DRIED CHERRIES

Cut 1 pound clean and trimmed dandelion greens into bite-size pieces. Heat 1 tablespoon extra-virgin olive oil in a large, deep skillet on medium-high heat. Add 1 garlic clove (minced) and cook for 20 seconds. Add the greens; cook, stirring frequently, for 2 minutes. Add ¼ cup dried cherries; cook, stirring frequently, until the greens wilt and are tender-crisp, about 2 more minutes. Season with fresh lemon juice, salt, and pepper.

RAW WITH HONEY-SPIKED DRESSING

Combine bite-size pieces of Bibb or butter lettuce and coarsely chopped dandelion greens. Whisk 1 tablespoon honey with 2 teaspoons hot water; add 1 tablespoon fresh lemon juice and 1 tablespoon extra-virgin olive oil. Season with garlic salt and whisk to combine. Add enough dressing to lightly coat the leaves. Garnish each serving with cored, sliced (unpeeled) Fuji or Gala apples.

ON FLATBREAD WITH CARAMELIZED ONIONS AND FIGS

Preheat the oven to 400 degrees F. Heat 1 tablespoon extra-virgin olive oil in a medium skillet on medium-high heat; tilt the pan to distribute it over the surface. Add 2 medium onions (halved, thinly sliced) and stir. When the onions start to brown, reduce the heat to medium-low. Spread the onions out evenly over the pan and cook, stirring occasionally. After 8 minutes, sprinkle some salt over the onions. Allow them to cook until they are richly browned, watching closely to prevent burning. Cut two 9-by-12-inch sheets of lavash lengthwise into 3-inch rectangles. Coat 2 rimmed baking sheets with nonstick olive oil spray. Cut 8 fresh figs into ¼-inch crosswise slices. Coarsely chop a good handful of clean dandelion greens. Top each lavash with caramelized onion, fig slices, and dandelion greens. Drizzle with olive oil and top with a few shaved pieces of fontina or Asiago cheese. Bake until the lavash is crisp and the cheese melts, 2 to 4 minutes. Cut each lavash into 2-inch pieces and serve.

Crisp Quinoa-Coated Chicken Breasts with Sautéed Dandelion Greens

Sauté chicken coated with cooked quinoa and the exterior becomes beautifully crisp, much crunchier than a bread crumb veneer. The crunchy coating is a welcome contrast to the creamy greens.

Yields 4 servings

NUTRITIONAL INFORMATION
(per serving)

calories 430	sodium (mg) 560	vitamin A IUs 35%
fat calories 130	total carbohydrates (g)...40	vitamin C 15%
total fat (g) 14	fiber (g) 3	calcium.........................8%
sat fat (g).....................2.5	sugars (g) 1	iron.............................25%
cholesterol (mg) 155	protein (g) 34	

1 cup uncooked white quinoa

¼ teaspoon salt

1½ tablespoons minced unpeeled fresh ginger

⅓ cup finely diced sweet onion, such as Maui or Walla Walla

2 tablespoons chopped fresh Italian parsley

2 teaspoons minced lemon zest (reserve juice)

Freshly ground black pepper

⅓ cup all-purpose flour

2 eggs

4 tablespoons extra-virgin olive oil

4 boneless, skinless chicken breasts (4 to 5 ounces each; *see Cook's Note*)

1 cup (packed) bite-size pieces dandelion greens

1. Put the quinoa in a strainer and rinse it with cold water. Shake the handle to remove the excess water. Bring 1¼ cups water to a boil in a medium saucepan. Add the quinoa and salt. Reduce the heat to low and cover; simmer for 10 minutes, or until all the water is absorbed. Stir in the ginger and cover. Remove from the heat and let sit, covered, for 10 minutes. Stir in the onion, parsley, and zest, and season with salt and pepper.

2. Spread the quinoa mixture on a rimmed plate or pie plate. Put the flour on a separate rimmed plate or pie plate. Put the eggs on a third rimmed plate or pie plate; lightly beat them with a fork.

3. Heat 3 tablespoons of the oil in a large, deep nonstick skillet on medium heat. Dip one chicken breast in the flour to lightly coat, then in the eggs, then in the quinoa mixture, pressing the quinoa to help it stick to the surface. Put the chicken in the skillet. Repeat with the remaining chicken breasts. Cook for 6 to 8 minutes, or until the surfaces are richly browned; turn with a wide spatula. Reduce the heat to medium-low. If the pan is dry, add a little more oil.

4. Add the greens, placing them around and between the chicken. Cook until the chicken is thoroughly opaque (the internal temperature should be 165 degrees F), about 6 to 7 minutes more. Taste the greens; if desired, season with fresh lemon juice. Serve the chicken with the dandelion greens on the side.

COOK'S NOTE If using larger chicken breasts, use two skillets, cooking two breasts per skillet. Most likely the larger breasts will need 1 or 2 minutes more of cooking.

MEATLESS ALTERNATIVE Prepare the quinoa mixture as directed in step 1. Heat 2 tablespoon extra-virgin olive oil in a large, deep skillet on medium-high heat. Add the quinoa mixture and stir-fry until it starts to lightly brown and begins to get crisp. Add 2 teaspoons additional oil and the dandelion greens. Cook, stirring frequently, until the greens wilt. Taste and adjust the seasoning as needed, adding some fresh lemon juice if desired.

Wheat Berries with Dandelion Greens and Blue Cheese

Wheat berries are whole kernels of wheat that have the bran still intact. Use either red or white wheat berries in this recipe; they have similar flavors and the same chewy texture. Look for wheat berries at natural food stores or in supermarkets with large natural food specialty sections. Serve this dandelion green–enriched side dish warm.

Yields 8 side-dish servings

NUTRITIONAL INFORMATION
(per serving)

calories 160	sodium (mg) 140	vitamin A IUs 15%
fat calories 70	total carbohydrates (g)....18	vitamin C 4%
total fat (g) 8	fiber (g) 4	calcium 6%
sat fat (g).....................2	sugars (g) 0	iron.............................6%
cholesterol (mg) 5	protein (g) 6	

1 cup uncooked wheat berries
(*see Cook's Note*)

⅛ teaspoon salt

1½ tablespoons extra-virgin olive oil

⅓ cup coarsely chopped walnuts

¾ cup coarsely chopped dandelion greens

⅓ cup chopped pitted green olives

Freshly ground black pepper

1 tablespoon red wine vinegar

½ cup crumbled blue cheese

1 tablespoon minced fresh basil

1. Put the wheat berries in a medium saucepan with 3 cups water and the salt. Bring them to a boil on high heat; cover and reduce the heat to medium-low. Simmer, covered, for 50 to 60 minutes, or until a few berries have burst and the grains are tender. Check from time to time to make sure there is water in the pan during cooking; add more if needed. Drain well.

2. Heat the oil in a large, deep skillet on medium-high heat. Add the walnuts and stir to coat them with oil; cook until they are lightly browned, about 2 minutes, stirring frequently. Watch carefully because nuts burn easily; turn down the heat if necessary to prevent overbrowning.

3. Add the wheat berries, greens, and olives. Season with salt and pepper. Cook, stirring frequently, for 2 minutes. Add the vinegar and remove from the heat. Stir in ¼ cup of the cheese and the basil. Top with the remaining cheese and serve.

COOK'S NOTE If you wish, cook a larger amount of wheat berries. Use leftover cooked wheat berries in vegetable-based soups, such as minestrone, or in cold grain-based salads dressed with citrus vinaigrette.

Dandelion Greens with Buttermilk Mashed Potatoes

If you prefer to eliminate the oil, rather than sautéing dandelion leaves, gently steam them until they wilt and are piping hot. And if you like, vary the recipe by using yellow-fleshed (tan-skinned) sweet potatoes in place of russet or Yukon Gold. The sweet potatoes may take less time; be sure to cook them just until they are fork tender.

Yields 6 to 8 servings

NUTRITIONAL INFORMATION
(per 8 servings)

calories 130	sodium (mg) 160	vitamin A IUs 120%
fat calories 50	total carbohydrates (g)....18	vitamin C 60%
total fat (g) 6	fiber (g) 4	calcium 15%
sat fat (g)........................2	sugars (g) 2	iron.............................10%
cholesterol (mg) 5	protein (g) 3	

1⅓ pounds russet or Yukon Gold potatoes, peeled, cut into 1½-inch chunks

Salt

2 tablespoons extra-virgin olive oil

1 pound dandelion leaves, small ones left whole, large ones torn into 2-inch pieces

Garlic salt

2 tablespoons 2 milk, plus more if needed

3 tablespoons low-fat buttermilk

1½ tablespoons unsalted butter or soft tub margarine

Freshly ground black pepper

GARNISH 6 to 8 lemon wedges

1. Put the potatoes in a Dutch oven or medium pan. Add cold water to come 1 inch above the potatoes and a pinch of salt. Bring them to a boil on high heat. Reduce the heat to medium-high and simmer uncovered until they are fork tender, about 10 to 14 minutes.

2. Meanwhile, in a large, deep skillet, heat the oil on medium-high heat. Add the dandelion leaves and stir-fry until wilted. Season with garlic salt.

3. Drain the potatoes well. Return them to the pan over the heat for 1 to 2 minutes to dry out the potatoes. Remove from the heat and add the milk and buttermilk. Mash them with a potato masher. If they are too thick, add a little more milk. Add the butter and stir to combine. Season with salt and pepper.

4. Spread the potatoes in the middle of a medium platter. Surround them with the dandelion greens. Garnish the platter with the lemon wedges and serve.

ENDIVE

Belgian, Curly

Belgian endive, compacted in torpedo-shaped heads about 6 inches long, has a subtle hint of bitterness. Both the pale green and burgundy red varieties are delicious raw or cooked.

The jagged, frilly edged leaves of curly endive are much larger and grow in loose bushy heads. The deep green leaves have a flavor profile with straightforward bitterness. The assertive taste is tamed by cooking. The cooked and chopped leaves are often paired with unctuous meats, such as bacon or short ribs, or rich soups that showcase starchy legumes, potatoes, or grains.

Both curly and Belgian endive are part of the chicory family. Refreshing and cleansing, they clear the palate and help digestion.

NUTRITIONAL INFORMATION FOR BELGIAN ENDIVE/CURLY ENDIVE
(per 1 cup raw, chopped)

Calories 9/8	sodium (mg) 0/10	vitamin A IUs 0%/22%
fat calories 0/0	total carbohydrates (g).1/34	vitamin C 2%/6%
total fat (g) 0/0	fiber (g) 1/2	calcium 1%/2%
sat fat (g)....................0/0	sugars (g) 0/0	iron...........................1%/2%
cholesterol (mg) 0/0	protein (g) 1/0	

MOOD BOOSTER
Endive contains flavonoid glycoside compounds, which are phytochemicals with multiple functions. In a recent study at the University of Copenhagen, they were described as being inhibitors of monoamine oxidase, thus acting as antidepressants.

PARKINSON'S FIGHTER
The flavonoids in endive also have shown an ability to help improve Parkinson's symptoms, reduce inflammation, and protect against injuries to the central nervous system.

INNER BEAUTY
Low in calories, endive is high in vitamins A, C, and E—antioxidant vitamins that protect cells from damage while preserving skin health. And they're loaded with iron and calcium to keep blood oxygenated and the heart and bones strong.

MULTIPURPOSE BENEFACTOR
Endive and its relatives contain another flavonoid called kaempferol, which studies have shown to possess analgesic and antimicrobial qualities and help reduce symptoms of diabetes, osteoporosis, and allergies. Belgian endive is a good blood cleanser, too, containing chicoric acid, which has demonstrated an ability to help cells called phagocytes, key components of the immune system that devour harmful pathogens and detritus.

AVAILABLE
Year-round

KEEP IT FRESH
For Belgian endive, look for firm, crisp, compact heads without browned edges. Refrigerate them unwashed and loose in a plastic bag for up to 5 days. Longer storage can increase bitterness. For curly endive, look for heads that are crisp without wilting. Refrigerate them unwashed and loosely wrapped in a plastic bag for up to 5 days.

LAST-MINUTE PREP FOR BELGIAN ENDIVE

Just before serving or cooking, pull off and discard any browned leaves. Wash with cold water. If using it whole, trim off a very small portion at the root end. If using individual leaves as canapé boats, trim off the root end deep enough so the leaves can be separated.

LAST-MINUTE PREP FOR CURLY ENDIVE

Trim the root end and separate the leaves. Rinse them in a tub of cold water; drain well. Cut off the stems with a small sharp knife to separate the leafy portion. Discard or compost the stems. Coarsely chop the leaves.

QUICK COOK FOR BELGIAN ENDIVE

This variety is most often eaten raw, in salads along with milder greens or as canapé boats to hold fillings. It can also be gently braised. Trim and cut 4 heads in half lengthwise. Heat 2 tablespoons extra-virgin olive oil in a large nonstick skillet on medium-high heat. Put the endive in a single layer, cut-side down; cook until they are lightly browned, 4 to 5 minutes. Add ¼ cup vegetable broth and ¼ cup dry white wine, and season with salt and freshly ground black pepper. Cover and decrease the temperature to low. Braise until the endive is tender, about 10 minutes, adding more broth if needed. Serve topped with a squeeze of fresh lemon juice and either finely chopped fresh parsley or fresh tarragon.

QUICK COOK FOR CURLY ENDIVE

In a 6-quart pan or Dutch oven, bring about 2 quarts water to boil on high heat. Add 1 teaspoon salt and 2 pounds stemmed, coarsely chopped curly endive. Cover and cook until it is tender, about 5 to 6 minutes. Drain the endive in a colander; refresh with cold water. Press out excess water with the back of a spoon, or when it is cool enough to handle, squeeze out the excess water in handfuls. Season with salt and pepper; serve with lemon wedges or vinaigrette.

CURLY ENDIVE GRILLED

Quarter 1 head lengthwise; shake off the excess water and set the head aside on towels to drain. Heat a grill to medium-high heat and clean the grate. Brush the endive with olive oil and season it with coarse salt and freshly ground black pepper. Grill, turning occasionally, until the endive is nicely browned and tender, about 10 minutes. Top with vinaigrette, if desired.

BELGIAN ENDIVE SALAD WITH TANGERINE DRESSING

In a blender, whirl 1 tangerine (peeled, pulled into sections), 1 medium garlic clove (peeled), 2 teaspoons balsamic vinegar, and 1 tablespoon extra-virgin olive oil; season with salt. In a large bowl, toss 2 cups cooked, shelled edamame with 4 heads Belgian endive (cut into 1-inch crosswise slices), ¼ medium red onion (cut into narrow slivers), and ¼ cup crumbled goat cheese. Add enough dressing to generously coat the leaves. Toss; taste and adjust the seasoning as needed.

CURLY ENDIVE TOPPED WITH BRAISED LEEKS

Preheat the oven to 350 degrees F. Trim 1 pound leeks, cutting off the roots and dark-green stalks. Cut the white and light-green portions in half lengthwise and wash; pat dry and cut them crosswise into thirds. Coat the bottom of a small baking dish with 1 tablespoon extra-virgin olive oil; arrange the leeks in a single layer cut-side down. Push 3 large garlic cloves (cut into lengthwise thirds) between the leeks. Drizzle with 2 tablespoons vegetable broth and 1 tablespoon extra-virgin olive oil; season with salt and freshly ground black pepper. Bake until the leeks are tender and lightly browned, about 35 to 40 minutes, adding more broth if needed. Serve over blanched curly endive (see Quick Cook for Curly Endive). If desired, top with toasted pine nuts.

Endive, Peas, and Sugar Snap Peas with Fresh Shiitake Mushrooms

In this beautiful green mélange of vegetables, sliced Belgian endive is gently braised with sugar snap peas and English green peas. Shiitake mushrooms add a welcome meatiness to the dish, and it can be finished with a smidgen of butter or margarine.

Yields 6 side-dish servings

NUTRITIONAL INFORMATION
(per serving)

calories ...80	sodium (mg) ...200	vitamin A IUs ...10%
fat calories ...15	total carbohydrates (g) ...12	vitamin C ...40%
total fat (g) ...2	fiber (g) ...5	calcium ...4%
sat fat (g) ...0	sugars (g) ...4	iron ...6%
cholesterol (mg) ...0	protein (g) ...4	

1 cup sugar snap peas, strings removed

2 teaspoons extra-virgin olive oil

1 cup thinly sliced fresh shiitake mushrooms (stems removed)

2 medium heads Belgian endive, halved lengthwise, cut crosswise into ½-inch slices

2 cups frozen petite English green peas

Coarse salt (kosher or sea)

Freshly ground black pepper

OPTIONAL 2 teaspoons butter or soft tub margarine

1. In a large saucepan, bring about 3 cups water to a boil on high heat. Add the sugar snap peas and cook until they are tender-crisp, 2 to 3 minutes. Drain and refresh with cold water; drain again and set aside.

2. Heat the oil on medium-high heat in a large deep skillet. Add the mushrooms and endive; toss, then cover and cook for 1 minute. Uncover; add 1 tablespoon water, and continue to cook until the mushrooms are softened and the liquid evaporates, about 3 to 4 minutes. Add the frozen peas and season with salt and pepper; gently toss. Cook uncovered until the peas are heated through, about 2 minutes. Add the sugar snap peas and gently toss. Cook until the sugar snap peas are hot. If desired, add the butter or margarine; gently toss and serve.

Lentil Soup with Curly Endive

This hearty lentil soup tastes even better the day after it is prepared, so, if possible, make it a day in advance through step 3 and refrigerate it. Add the endive, vinegar, and Canadian bacon, if using, and reheat gently on medium heat; cook until the endive is tender. The bitter bite of curly endive adds a just-right sharpness to balance the earthy lentils.

Yields 8 servings

NUTRITIONAL INFORMATION
(per serving, without Canadian bacon)

calories 160	sodium (mg) 260	vitamin A IUs 90%
fat calories 30	total carbohydrates (g)... 24	vitamin C....................20%
total fat (g) 3	fiber (g) 5	calcium........................6%
sat fat (g)........................0	sugars (g) 5	iron................................15%
cholesterol (mg) 0	protein (g) 7	

1½ tablespoons extra-virgin olive oil

3 medium carrots, peeled, coarsely chopped

1 large yellow onion, finely chopped

2 large garlic cloves, minced

One 14½-ounce can diced tomatoes, drained

1½ teaspoons minced fresh thyme

1 bay leaf

1¼ cups (7 ounces) dry lentils (green or brown), rinsed, picked over (to remove any debris)

Salt

Freshly ground black pepper

5 cups fat-free low-sodium vegetable or chicken broth

½ cup dry white wine

1¼ cups coarsely chopped curly endive

OPTIONAL ¼ cup coarsely chopped Canadian bacon

2 teaspoons balsamic vinegar

OPTIONAL GARNISH 8 very thin lemon slices

OPTIONAL GARNISH bottled hot sauce

1. In a 4- to 6-quart pan or Dutch oven, heat the oil on medium-high heat. Add the carrots and onion; cook until the onion softens, 3 to 4 minutes, stirring occasionally. Add the garlic and cook for 30 seconds. Add the tomatoes, thyme, and bay leaf; cook for 2 minutes.

2. Add the lentils and season with salt and pepper. Bring them to a simmer. Reduce the heat to medium-low, cover, and simmer for 10 minutes. Uncover and increase the heat to medium-high. Add the broth, wine, and 2 cups water. Bring to a simmer; reduce the heat to medium-low. Simmer, partially covered, until the lentils are tender, about 30 minutes. Fish out the bay leaf and discard it.

3. Using a ladle, transfer 2 cups of the soup to a food processor or blender. Process until it is smooth and return to the soup. You can complete the soup to this point, then cool and refrigerate it until the next day. Before finishing it, rewarm over medium heat.

4. Add the endive and the Canadian bacon, if using. Bring to a simmer on medium-low heat and cook until the endive softens, about 4 minutes. Stir in the vinegar. Taste and adjust the seasoning if needed.

5. Ladle the soup into bowls and, if desired, top each serving with a very thin slice of lemon. Pass bottled hot sauce as an optional addition.

Endive Boats with Green Olive, Parsley, and Walnut Salad

If you aren't a fan of feta, use finely diced Parmesan instead in these tasty canapés. Or if you prefer to omit the cheese altogether, substitute finely diced red bell pepper. Pomegranate molasses adds a lovely sweet-sour spark to this dish. It is sold at Middle Eastern markets and many natural food stores. If it is unavailable, substitute balsamic vinegar.

Yields about 24 appetizers

NUTRITIONAL INFORMATION
(per appetizer)

calories 30	sodium (mg) 60	vitamin A IUs 8%
fat calories 25	total carbohydrates (g) 2	vitamin C 10%
total fat (g) 3	fiber (g) 1	calcium 2%
sat fat (g) 0	sugars (g) 0	iron 2%
cholesterol (mg) 0	protein (g) 1	

2 cups coarsely chopped fresh Italian parsley

1 cup coarsely chopped pitted green olives

2 green onions, thinly sliced (including half of dark green stalks)

¼ cup toasted walnut pieces, coarsely chopped (*see Cook's Note*)

¼ cup crumbled feta cheese

2 teaspoons fresh lemon juice

1 teaspoon pomegranate molasses or balsamic vinegar

Salt

Freshly ground black pepper

2 tablespoons extra-virgin olive oil

24 endive leaves

OPTIONAL GARNISH ¼ cup pomegranate arils (seeds)

1. In a medium bowl, combine the parsley, olives, onions, walnuts, and feta. Toss.

2. In a small bowl or glass measuring cup with a handle, stir together the juice and molasses and season with salt and pepper. Whisk in the oil. Taste and adjust the seasoning. Pour the dressing over the onion-parsley mixture; toss.

3. Arrange the endive leaves on a large platter, preferably round, placing them like the spokes of a wheel, with the pointed ends facing the edge of the plate. Fill the leaves half full with the parsley mixture. If desired, scatter the pomegranate arils on top and serve.

COOK'S NOTE To toast walnut pieces, place them in a single layer on a rimmed baking sheet. Bake in a 350-degree-F oven for 3 to 4 minutes, or until lightly browned. Watch carefully because nuts burn easily. Let them cool before coarsely chopping and using in the salad.

GAI LAN

also Chinese Broccoli

It's understandable why gai lan is one of the most popular vegetables at Asian restaurants around the globe. Also called "Chinese broccoli," gai lan has appealing crunch and a flavor profile that can be addictive. The stalk, leaves, and the clusters of tightly packed buds have a delectable balance of sweet and peppery flavors. It is a taste that is somewhat reminiscent of rapini, but the bitterness is much more subdued, with a more evident sweetness.

One cup of cooked gai lan weighs in at only 19 calories, so you can eat 20 cups for the same caloric price as a single cheeseburger.

NUTRITIONAL INFORMATION
(per 1 cup cooked, chopped)

calories 19	sodium (mg) 6	vitamin A IUs 29%
fat calories 5	total carbohydrates (g).....3	vitamin C 41%
total fat (g) 1	fiber (g) 2	calcium 9%
sat fat (g).........................0	sugars (g) 1	iron...............................3%
cholesterol (mg) 0	protein (g) 1	

VITAMIN TRIO
As with all leafy greens, gai lan contains the triumvirate of vitamins A, C, and K while providing a good dose of needed minerals such as potassium, manganese, iron, and calcium. And, of course, being a leafy green, it's replete with folate and fiber.

VEGGIE OMEGAS
Gai lan is a good plant source of omega-3 fatty acids, almost one-third more than common broccoli. Decades of research comprising thousands of studies show that omega-3s help brain and nerve development in fetuses and children, reduce the risk of heart disease and certain types of cancer, and act as an important bulwark against memory and cognitive disorders, including Alzheimer's disease and depression.

AVAILABLE
Year-round

KEEP IT FRESH
Look for gai lan that smells fresh, with tightly closed buds rather than open flowers. The leaves should be bright green without any wilting, and the stalks should be crisp and firm, without soft spots or discoloration. Refrigerate them unwashed, wrapped in paper towels in the crisper drawer, up to 7 days.

LAST-MINUTE PREP

Wash thoroughly with cold water. Trim off the bottom of the stalks, making a shallow cut about ⅜ inch from the bottom edge. Generally gai lan is cut into manageable pieces 1 to 2 inches long but can be served whole.

QUICK COOK

Bring a large pot of salted water to boil on high heat. Cut the gai lan into 2-inch pieces and add them to the water. Blanch until they are tender-crisp, about 3 to 4 minutes. Drain and refresh with cold water; drain again. If desired, serve the gai lan topped with oyster sauce. You can thin the sauce with a splash of seasoned rice vinegar, vegetable broth, and dried red pepper flakes.

try it!

IN NOODLE SOUP

Add bite-size pieces of gai lan to your favorite noodle soup. Either cook it in the soup's broth or blanch it until tender-crisp before adding it in the last minute of cooking.

AS A DIPPER

Serve tender-crisp blanched gai lan as a dipper for a yogurt-based dip. Stir together ¾ cup plain fat-free Greek-style yogurt with 1 tablespoon minced unpeeled ginger, 1½ teaspoons sodium-reduced soy sauce, ½ teaspoon Asian sesame oil, 1 teaspoon balsamic vinegar, and a drop or two Asian hot sauce.

WITH LEMON VINAIGRETTE AND SESAME SEEDS

Blanch 1 pound gai lan (cut into 1-inch pieces) until tender-crisp. Prepare a dressing by whisking 1 tablespoon fresh lemon juice with salt and freshly ground black pepper. Whisk in 2 tablespoons extra-virgin olive oil. Toss with the gai lan. Top with toasted sesame seeds.

Gai Lan and Cauliflower Frittata

If you prefer, bring down the calorie count of this delicious frittata by making 8 to 10 smaller servings instead of 6. Serve those smaller wedges of warm frittata on beds of fresh baby spinach. The frittata's warmth will partially wilt the greens, giving them an appealing texture and aroma.

Yields 6 servings

NUTRITIONAL INFORMATION
(per serving)

calories 240	sodium (mg) 710	vitamin A IUs 25%
fat calories 140	total carbohydrates (g).....5	vitamin C 70%
total fat (g) 16	fiber (g) 1	calcium......................25%
sat fat (g)........................6	sugars (g) 2	iron.............................10%
cholesterol (mg) 275	protein (g) 20	

Nonstick olive oil cooking spray

- 4 ounces Canadian bacon, roughly chopped
- 7 eggs plus 2 egg whites
- 1 cup grated Parmesan cheese
- ⅓ cup whole milk
- 3 tablespoons chopped fresh parsley

Freshly ground black pepper

- 1 tablespoon butter
- 1 tablespoons extra-virgin olive oil
- 1½ cups small cauliflower florets
- 4 ounces gai lan, cut into ½-inch pieces
- 2 large garlic cloves, minced

1. Coat a 10-inch ovenproof nonstick skillet with nonstick spray. Add the bacon and place it on medium-high heat. Cook, stirring occasionally, until the bacon is lightly browned. Remove the bacon and set aside.

2. In a large bowl, whisk together the eggs, egg whites, Parmesan, milk, and parsley, and season with pepper.

3. In the same skillet used for the bacon, add the butter and oil. Place the pan on medium-high heat. Add the cauliflower; cook, stirring occasionally, for 5 minutes. Add the gai lan and cook until tender-crisp, about 8 minutes. Add the garlic and cook for 30 seconds. Stir the bacon into the egg mixture. Pour the egg mixture into the skillet. Reduce the temperature to low. Cover and cook until the frittata is almost set, 15 to 20 minutes. Meanwhile, adjust an oven rack 6 to 8 inches below the broiler element. Preheat the broiler.

4. Place the pan under the broiler and heat until the frittata is nicely browned and completely set, about 2 to 3 minutes. Watch carefully. Remember that the handle of the skillet is hot when removing it from the oven. Run a silicone spatula around the edge of the frittata to loosen it. Slide it onto a platter or cutting board. Cut it into wedges and serve.

MEATLESS ALTERNATIVE Omit the Canadian bacon, and start the recipe with step 2.

Gai Lan, Tofu, and Ginger Soup

Tamari is a dark, thick soy sauce that adds an earthy punch. Here it boosts the flavor of a ginger-scented broth. To bump up the flavor even more, add a dash of Asian-style hot sauce to the bubbling broth.

Yields 8 servings

NUTRITIONAL INFORMATION
(per serving)

calories 50	sodium (mg) 210	vitamin A IUs 35%
fat calories 5	total carbohydrates (g)..... 7	vitamin C 15%
total fat (g) 1	fiber (g) 2	calcium 6%
sat fat (g) 0	sugars (g) 4	iron 6%
cholesterol (mg) 0	protein (g) 3	

1 large yellow onion, coarsely chopped

1 medium carrot, peeled, coarsely chopped

OPTIONAL 1 medium kohlrabi, trimmed, peeled, cut into ½-inch slices, coarsely chopped

1½ tablespoons minced unpeeled fresh ginger

8 cups fat-free low-sodium vegetable broth

5 to 6 ounces gai lan, cut into ½-inch pieces

1 teaspoon tamari

OPTIONAL Asian hot sauce, such as Sriracha

Coarse salt (kosher or sea)

9 ounces firm tofu, cut into ½-inch cubes

3 green onions, trimmed, cut into thin slices (including dark green stalks)

GARNISH 1½ tablespoons minced fresh cilantro

1. In a medium saucepan, combine the onion, carrot, and kohlrabi, if using. Add the ginger and broth; bring them to a boil on high heat. Reduce the heat to medium and simmer for 15 minutes.

2. Add the gai lan and simmer until it is tender-crisp, about 8 to 10 minutes. Stir in the tamari. Taste and, if desired, add a drop or two of Asian hot sauce and salt.

3. Divide the tofu and green onions between eight small soup bowls. Ladle in the piping hot soup. Garnish with the cilantro.

Gai Lan Salad with Baby Greens and Dried Mango

Toasted or candied walnuts make a perfectly crunchy optional garnish for this tasty salad. If you prefer, use sweetened dried cranberries or sweet cherries instead of dried mango. The dressing needs a little sweetness for flavor balance; if desired, use maple syrup or agave syrup in place of honey.

Yields 6 servings

NUTRITIONAL INFORMATION
(per serving, without walnuts)

calories 120	sodium (mg) 35	vitamin A IUs 80%
fat calories 25	total carbohydrates (g)... 23	vitamin C 45%
total fat (g) 3	fiber (g) 4	calcium.....................10%
sat fat (g)...................... 0	sugars (g) 16	iron..............................8%
cholesterol (mg) 0	protein (g) 2	

1¼ pounds gai lan, cut into 1-inch pieces

¼ cup red wine vinegar

2½ tablespoons honey

Salt

Freshly ground black pepper

1 tablespoon extra-virgin olive oil

1 large garlic clove, minced

½ medium red onion, thinly sliced

¼ cup coarsely chopped dried mango

1 tablespoon minced fresh cilantro

5 to 6 cups mixed baby lettuces

OPTIONAL GARNISH ¼ cup toasted walnut pieces (*see Cook's Note*)

1. In a large saucepan, bring 3 to 4 cups water to a boil on high heat. Add the gai lan and cook until it is tender-crisp, 3 to 4 minutes. Drain it in a colander in the sink. Refresh with cold water and drain again.

2. In a large bowl, whisk together the vinegar and honey and season with salt and pepper. Whisk in the oil and garlic. Stir in the onion, mango, and cilantro; set aside for 15 minutes.

3. Add the gai lan to the dressing and toss. Add the lettuce and toss. Taste and adjust the seasoning as needed. Divide the salad between six plates. If desired, garnish with the toasted walnuts. Serve.

COOK'S NOTE To toast walnuts, place them in a single layer on a rimmed baking sheet. Bake in 350-degree-F oven for 4 to 5 minutes, or until lightly browned. Watch carefully because nuts burn easily.

GOOSEBERRY
Common Gooseberries

Don't confuse common gooseberries with cape gooseberries, those pumpkin-orange orbs with papery coverings that look something like Chinese lanterns. Common gooseberries are husk-free and spherical, usually about the size of blueberries. They are most commonly a grape-green hue, but they can also be either white or shades of red. Minute seeds hide at the core, but they are so tender that they are generally only detectable when cut open and examined.

The lemon-like taste and scent is slightly musky, a flavor profile that lends itself to dishes that benefit from tart edges. Delicious in pies and compotes, gooseberries are a welcome addition to relishes, sauces, and jams.

These tart berries package lots of fiber in just a few calories; 1 cup has about 6 grams of fiber and only 66 calories.

NUTRITIONAL INFORMATION
(per 1 cup raw)

calories 66	sodium (mg) 2	vitamin A IUs 9%
fat calories 7	total carbohydrates (g) 15	vitamin C 69%
total fat (g) 1	fiber (g) 6	calcium 4%
sat fat (g) 0	sugars (g) 0	iron 3%
cholesterol (mg) 0	protein (g) 1	

DIABETES DAMPENER
Gooseberries possess powerful phytochemical compounds that can help regulate blood sugar balance. They also provide a number of minerals, including iron, potassium, calcium, and especially copper and manganese.

ENERGIZING IONS
The copper in gooseberries is critical to a number of functions, especially energy production, helping metabolize oxygen and scavenging oxygen radicals. Copper also is a crucial component in the cell's natural batteries; mitochondria utilize it to make the key energy currency, ATP. Both manganese and copper help regulate the production and metabolism of the neurotransmitters (such as norepinephrine and adrenaline).

BEAUTY CHARGER
Minerals in gooseberries help the body build functioning connective tissue, especially collagen and elastin. Healthy connective tissue means that skin stays firm and youthful longer.

AVAILABLE
March to May

KEEP IT FRESH

Look for berries that are free of shriveling or discoloration; avoid those that are mushy or wet. Gooseberries should have a small portion of stem left intact and, at the bottom, a small browned blossom. Refrigerate untrimmed and dry up to 2 weeks; do not wash them before storing.

LAST-MINUTE PREP

Place gooseberries in a colander and rinse them with cold water. The easiest way to trim the stem and blossom ends is by snipping them off using clean kitchen scissors.

QUICK COOK

Place 1 cup trimmed gooseberries in a small saucepan with 1 teaspoon agave syrup and 1 table-spoon water. Bring them to a boil on medium-high heat; reduce the heat to medium and gently boil until the berries start to burst, about 3 minutes. Let them cool. Spoon the sauce over yogurt or pudding, or use as part of fruit compote.

IN SYRUP ON PANCAKES

Put 1 cup trimmed gooseberries in a small saucepan with ⅔ cup maple syrup on high heat. When it is vigorously bubbling at the edge of the pan, reduce the heat to medium and simmer for 3 minutes, stirring occasionally, or until some gooseberries start to burst. Serve warm.

IN A FOOL

To make this tangy British dessert, combine 1 cup trimmed gooseberries with 2 nectarines (peeled and sliced), 2 tablespoons water, and 2 tablespoons agave syrup over medium heat until the gooseberries start to burst, about 8 minutes. Let the mixture cool. Whip ⅓ cup cream until soft peaks form. Fold the whipped cream into ½ cup plain Greek-style yogurt. Fold in the cooled fruit. Refrigerate until serving.

IN A PURÉED SAUCE WITH FISH

In a medium skillet, heat 2 teaspoons canola oil on medium-high heat. Add ½ sweet onion (chopped); cook until tender, about 3 minutes. Add 1 cup trimmed gooseberries, 1 teaspoon agave syrup, and 1 tablespoon water. Cook, stirring occasionally, about 3 minutes, or until some gooseberries start to burst, adding more water if needed. Purée in a food processor; season with salt and pepper. Spoon 1 to 2 tablespoons of sauce on a plate next to cooked fish.

Chicken Salad with Gooseberries, Plums, and Blue Cheese

Blue-veined cheeses vary in creaminess, saltiness, and, well, funkiness. For this tasty vinaigrette, use the blue cheese you most prefer. Whichever variety you choose will bring a delightfully sharp edge to the vinaigrette. The dressing brings out the best in the gooseberries and plums.

Yields 6 servings

NUTRITIONAL INFORMATION
(per serving)

calories 160	sodium (mg) 160	vitamin A IUs 30%
fat calories 90	total carbohydrates (g).....6	vitamin C....................10%
total fat (g) 10	fiber (g) 2	calcium........................6%
sat fat (g)........................2	sugars (g) 2	iron................................6%
cholesterol (mg) 30	protein (g) 12	

3 boneless, skinless chicken breasts (about 4 ounces each)

Nonstick vegetable oil cooking spray

Coarse salt (kosher or sea)

Freshly ground black pepper

3 tablespoons extra-virgin olive oil

1/3 cup crumbled blue cheese

1½ tablespoons chopped fresh chives or dark green onion stalks

1 tablespoon balsamic vinegar

Garlic salt

2 medium heads Bibb or butter lettuce (about 12 ounces)

¾ cup gooseberries, trimmed

¼ cup walnut pieces, toasted (see Cook's Note)

2 ripe (but not squishy) plums, cut into wedges

1. Use the bottom of a saucepan or mallet to pound the chicken breasts between sheets of plastic wrap to ¼ inch thick. Coat the chicken with cooking spray on both sides and season with salt and pepper. Heat a grill pan on medium-high heat. Put the chicken on the pan and cook until it is opaque, about 3 to 4 minutes on each side. Set the chicken aside to cool while preparing the dressing.

2. In a small bowl or glass measuring cup with a handle, combine the oil and cheese. Use a fork to press half of the cheese against the bowl to mash it into the oil. Stir in the chives and vinegar and season with garlic salt.

3. Gently tear the lettuce into bite-size pieces and put them in a large bowl. Cut the cooled chicken into ½-inch crosswise slices. Add the chicken, gooseberries, walnuts, and dressing to the lettuce. Gently toss and divide between six plates. Top with the plum wedges.

COOK'S NOTE To toast walnuts, place them in a single layer on rimmed baking sheet. Bake in a 350-degree-F oven for 4 to 5 minutes, or until lightly browned. Watch carefully because nuts burn easily.

MEATLESS ALTERNATIVE Omit the chicken. If desired, add 1½ cups cooked and cooled farro in step 3.

Gooseberry-Cherry Relish

Teamed with sweet cherries, the frisky tartness of gooseberries finds a happy medium. Serve this perky relish warm or at room temperature as a sidekick for roast lamb, venison, or pork, or with grilled tofu or baked butternut squash. It can be made ahead and refrigerated for up to 5 days.

Yields 12 servings

NUTRITIONAL INFORMATION
(per serving)

calories ... 50	sodium (mg) ... 25	vitamin A IUs ... 0%
fat calories ... 10	total carbohydrates (g) ... 10	vitamin C ... 10%
total fat (g) ... 1.5	fiber (g) ... 1	calcium ... 0%
sat fat (g) ... 0	sugars (g) ... 7	iron ... 0%
cholesterol (mg) ... 0	protein (g) ... 0	

1 tablespoon vegetable oil or canola oil

1 medium yellow onion, roughly chopped

1 cup fresh sweet cherries, pitted

¾ cup gooseberries, trimmed

⅓ cup low-sugar raspberry preserves

2 tablespoons balsamic vinegar

1 tablespoon agave syrup

2 teaspoons minced orange zest

1 teaspoon minced fresh rosemary

¼ teaspoon cayenne pepper

¼ teaspoon ground cloves

Salt

1. Heat the oil in a large, heavy-bottomed saucepan over medium-high heat. Add the onion; cook until it is softened, about 3 minutes, stirring occasionally.

2. Add the cherries, gooseberries, preserves, vinegar, syrup, zest, rosemary, cayenne, and cloves. Boil on medium-high heat until thickened, stirring occasionally, about 10 to 12 minutes. Season with salt. Serve warm or cold.

Gooseberry-Cherry Clafouti

Clafouti (also spelled "clafoutis") is a French baked custard-like dessert that is traditionally studded with fresh pitted cherries. In this version, the flan-like batter is augmented with gooseberries as well as cherries, offering an alluring spark of tartness. The final dusting of powdered sugar is optional, but it balances the flavors nicely and looks pretty.

Yields 8 servings

NUTRITIONAL INFORMATION
(per serving)

calories 110	sodium (mg) 60	vitamin A IUs 6%
fat calories 20	total carbohydrates (g)....18	vitamin C 10%
total fat (g) 2.5	fiber (g) 1	calcium 10%
sat fat (g).........................1	sugars (g) 15	iron................................4%
cholesterol (mg) 70	protein (g) 5	

Nonstick vegetable oil cooking spray

1¾ cups 1 milk

3-inch portion vanilla bean

3 eggs

⅓ cup sugar

1 tablespoon all-purpose flour

1½ teaspoons vanilla extract

1 teaspoon agave syrup

⅔ cup gooseberries, trimmed

1⅓ cups fresh sweet cherries, such as Bing, pitted

OPTIONAL GARNISH 2 tablespoons powdered sugar

1. Adjust an oven rack to the middle position. Preheat the oven to 300 degrees F. Generously coat a 9-inch pie pan with nonstick spray.

2. Put the milk in a medium saucepan. Cut the vanilla bean in half lengthwise and scrape out the seeds. Put the seeds and pod in the milk. Cook on medium heat until very hot but not boiling. Remove the pan from the heat and remove the pod.

3. In a medium-large bowl, beat the eggs and sugar until light in color. Whisk in the flour, vanilla, and syrup. Whisking constantly, add the milk in a thin stream.

4. Arrange the gooseberries and cherries in the prepared pan. Pour the milk mixture over the top. Bake until it is puffy and set, about 30 to 35 minutes. Allow the clafouti to cool for 10 to 15 minutes before cutting it into wedges and serving it lukewarm. If desired, put the powdered sugar in a sieve and shake it over the top of each wedge.

GRAPEFRUIT

Common Pink, Cocktail, Oro Blanco,
Pummelo (Pomelo), Ruby Red

There's nothing wimpy about grapefruit's flavor profile. Although the assertive tartness seems to have been somewhat tamed over the years by an increased amount of sweetness in several varieties, they still have a good degree of wake-up perkiness, and fewer seeds, too.

Grapefruits are excellent "beauty-from-within" fruits, containing a form of lecithin shown to help strengthen skin and, of course, concentrated amounts of vitamin C, needed for the body to produce and maintain healthy collagen. The antioxidants found in grapefruit are also known to prevent essential tissue damage.

NUTRITIONAL INFORMATION
(pink or red, 1 cup sections, raw with juice/white, 1 cup sections, raw with juice)

calories 97/76	sodium (mg) 0/0	vitamin A IUs 53%/2%
fat calories 3/2	total carbohydrates (g) 25/19	vitamin C 120%/128%
total fat (g) 0/0	fiber (g) 4/3	calcium 5%/3%
sat fat (g).................... 0/0	sugars (g) 16/17	iron...........................1%/1%
cholesterol (mg) 0/0	protein (g) 2/2	

CANCER PROTECTIVE POWER
Deep red grapefruit contains anthocyanin flavonoids, protecting the body against cancer and other diseases triggered by oxidative cell damage.

HEART HELPER
The vitamin A–like compound lycopene in deep-hued red-fleshed grapefruits also has demonstrated abilities to help protect against cardiovascular disease.

FAT BURNER
One grapefruit flavonoid, naringenin, aids in inhibiting the development of fat cells while helping affect lipid metabolism. A second grapefruit phytochemical, nootkatone, is believed to stimulate energy metabolism. The vitamin C and fiber in turn help regulate hunger hormones. Grapefruit also has a lot of ellagic acid, which has been noted for its effect at countering the fat-promoting inflammation process.

AVAILABLE
Cocktail: October to March

Oro Blanco: October to March

Pink (common): Year-round

Pummelo: October to March

Ruby Red: November to June

KEEP IT FRESH

Look for fragrant grapefruit that is heavy for its size, an indication that it is filled with juice. Press the skin; it should feel springy. Store it at room temperature up to 1 week in a cool, dry location (out of direct sunlight). Or refrigerate loose, up to 2 weeks.

LAST-MINUTE PREP

Wash with cold water. To eat with a spoon, cut grapefruit in half through the fruit's equator. If desired, loosen the segments from the rind with a grapefruit knife or use a grapefruit spoon to scoop out segments. To cut it into supremes (peeled segments), see page 230. Pummelos, grapefruit-like fruits that can be as large as a volleyball, have very thick rinds and less juicy flesh. Generally they are peeled and pulled into sections by hand.

QUICK COOK

Grapefruit is usually eaten raw, but it can be incorporated into warm sauces or baked goods.

try it!

IN A PERKY SORBET

Serve a tiny scoop of grapefruit sorbet accompanied with mixed berries. Prepare simple syrup by combining 1 cup water and 1 cup sugar in a medium saucepan (some like to add 4 to 6 black peppercorns) and bring it to a boil on high heat. Reduce to medium-low and simmer for 4 minutes. Cool (fish out and discard the peppercorns, if using); refrigerate. Combine 1½ cups chilled simple syrup, 1 cup fresh grapefruit juice, and ½ teaspoon minced grapefruit zest. Process in an ice-cream machine according to the manufacturer's instructions.

IN GREEN SALADS

Gently toss peeled grapefruit sections with sliced avocado, slivers of red onion, and chopped fresh mint. Use it as a garnish atop mixed green salad (or shredded cabbage) tossed with vinaigrette. If desired, sprinkle crumbled goat cheese on top.

IN SHRIMP COCKTAIL

Add peeled grapefruit sections and diced avocado to shrimp cocktail.

GRANOLA-FIED

Prepare parfaits in small stemmed glasses. Alternate layers of granola, layers of fat-free lime or orange yogurt, and peeled grapefruit sections. Serve immediately.

Broiled Halibut with Grapefruit and Orange Relish

Cara Cara oranges are such a lovely salmon-pink hue. Juicy and sweet, they are often dubbed "pink navels." Navel oranges can be substituted for the Cara Caras in this grapefruit-enriched relish, as can Valencia or blood oranges.

Yields 4 servings

NUTRITIONAL INFORMATION
(per serving)

calories 270	sodium (mg) 115	vitamin A IUs 20%
fat calories 60	total carbohydrates (g)... 23	vitamin C 120%
total fat (g) 7	fiber (g) 4	calcium 8%
sat fat (g) 1	sugars (g) 17	iron 4%
cholesterol (mg) 70	protein (g) 28	

RELISH

- 1 large grapefruit, cut into supremes (see page 230)
- 2 Cara Cara, navel, or Valencia oranges, cut into supremes (see page 230)
- ½ medium fennel bulb, trimmed, cored, cut crosswise into ¼-inch slices
- 2 green onions, trimmed, thinly sliced (including half of dark-green stalks)
- 3 tablespoons red wine vinegar
- 1½ tablespoons roughly chopped golden raisins
- 1 teaspoon honey
- Coarse salt (kosher or sea)
- Freshly ground black pepper

FISH

- Nonstick cooking spray
- Four 5-ounce halibut fillets (*see Cook's Note*)
- ¼ cup minced fresh mint
- 1½ tablespoons extra-virgin olive oil

1. To make the relish: When cutting the citrus segments, do it over a medium bowl to catch the juices. In a medium bowl, combine the segments, fennel, onions, vinegar, raisins, and honey. Season with salt and pepper. Gently toss and set aside.

2. To make the fish: Adjust an oven rack to a position about 8 inches below the broiler element. Preheat the broiler. Line a rimmed baking sheet with aluminum foil; coat the foil with nonstick cooking spray. Rub both sides of the halibut with the mint and oil. Season with salt and pepper.

3. Broil the fish until it is nicely caramelized on top, about 4 to 5 minutes. Turn the oven to 350 degrees F, shift the baking sheet to the middle rack, and bake until the fish is just barely opaque throughout, about 4 to 8 minutes more. Baking time will vary depending on the thickness of the fish. Place the fish on individual dinner plates. Top with the relish. Serve immediately.

COOK'S NOTE If desired, substitute tuna or salmon fillets for halibut.

MEATLESS ALTERNATIVE Spoon the relish over roasted root vegetables served atop cooked wild rice, brown rice, barley, or farro.

Shrimp and Grapefruit Salad

Avocado offers a bit of richness to balance grapefruit's vibrant flavor profile. This recipe makes a classic salad heartier, adding the chewiness of cooked and cooled farro, as well as minced fresh ginger. If you prefer, omit the shrimp.

Yields 6 servings

NUTRITIONAL INFORMATION
(per serving)

calories 280	sodium (mg) 340	vitamin A IUs 25%
fat calories 120	total carbohydrates (g)...29	vitamin C 70%
total fat (g) 14	fiber (g) 8	calcium 8%
sat fat (g)........................1	sugars (g) 8	iron...............................15%
cholesterol (mg) 75	protein (g) 15	

½ cup semi-pearled farro (see page 66)

VINAIGRETTE

¼ cup fresh grapefruit juice

2 teaspoons rice vinegar

1 teaspoon finely minced peeled fresh ginger

1 teaspoon honey

Salt

2 tablespoons canola oil

SALAD

6 cups baby spinach

1 ripe avocado, pitted, peeled, quartered, cut crosswise into ½-inch slices

8 ounces cooked, shelled, deveined shrimp, cut in half lengthwise

Freshly ground black pepper

1½ cups grapefruit supremes (see page 230)

½ cup slivered almonds, toasted (*see Cook's Note*)

1. Cook the farro by putting it in a small saucepan with 1½ cups water. Bring it to a boil on high heat. Reduce it to low, cover, and simmer gently for 15 to 20 minutes, or until the farro is tender but a little chewy. If any water remains, drain it well. Set aside.

2. To make the vinaigrette: In a small bowl or a measuring cup with a handle, stir together the juice, vinegar, ginger, and honey. Season with salt; stir until the salt dissolves and the honey is blended into the mixture. Whisk in the oil; set aside.

3. To make the salad: Put the spinach, avocado, shrimp, and farro in a large bowl. Toss with the vinaigrette. Taste and season with salt and pepper. Divide the mixture between six plates. Top with the grapefruit sections and almonds. Serve.

COOK'S NOTE To toast slivered almonds, place them in a single layer on a rimmed baking sheet. Bake in a 350-degree-F oven for 3 to 4 minutes, or until lightly browned. Watch carefully because nuts burn easily.

MEATLESS ALTERNATIVE If desired, scatter cubes of warm sautéed tofu (see page 54) on top of the salad instead of the shrimp.

Pink Grapefruit Compote with Yogurt Royale

Compotes, which are simple desserts that combine fruit and sugar syrup, show off the beauty of the produce. This is especially true if the compote is served in individual glass bowls. Generally, sugar syrups combine sugar and water, but here honey subs in for sugar, giving the dish a subtle floral note.

Yields 6 to 8 servings

NUTRITIONAL INFORMATION
(per serving, using 8 servings)

calories 140	sodium (mg) 10	vitamin A IUs 30%
fat calories 0	total carbohydrates (g)... 33	vitamin C 100%
total fat (g) 0	fiber (g) 2	calcium..........................4%
sat fat (g)......................0	sugars (g) 30	iron.................................2%
cholesterol (mg) 0	protein (g) 4	

COMPOTE

- ½ cup honey
- One 1-inch piece fresh ginger, thinly sliced
- 3 whole star anise
- 2 teaspoons grated grapefruit zest
- 4 large pink grapefruits, cut into supremes (see page 230)

YOGURT ROYALE

- 1 cup plain fat-free Greek-style yogurt
- 2 teaspoons honey
- 1 teaspoon minced peeled fresh ginger
- ½ teaspoon ground cinnamon

OPTIONAL GARNISH fresh mint sprigs

1. To make the compote: Combine ½ cup water with the honey, ginger, star anise, and zest in a medium saucepan on high heat, stirring until the honey melts. Bring it to a simmer and reduce the heat to medium. Gently simmer for 10 minutes. Remove from the heat; set aside at room temperature to cool for 1 hour.

2. Strain the honey mixture into a medium bowl. Add the grapefruit sections and any juice from cutting the grapefruit.

3. To make the yogurt royale: In a small bowl, stir together the yogurt, honey, ginger, and cinnamon.

4. Divide the compote between six to eight small bowls or stemmed glasses. Top each with a dollop of yogurt mixture. If desired, garnish each with a small sprig of fresh mint. Serve.

GREEN BEAN

also String Bean

These fleshy, flavorful pods are the subject of much culinary debate. Some like to briefly cook green beans to maintain a high degree of crunch and color. Others prefer a long gentle braise, rendering them limp and cushiony. Many take the middle road, blanching or steaming them until they are just barely fork tender. Then there are those who snack on them raw!

Green beans are often a warm-weather favorite with home gardeners because they are easy to grow and can be prolific producers. But in addition to being flavorful, they are a nutritional treasure chest. Vitamins, minerals, and fiber abound.

NUTRITIONAL INFORMATION
(per 1 cup raw ½-inch pieces)

calories 34	sodium (mg) 7	vitamin A IUs 15%
fat calories 1	total carbohydrates (g).....8	vitamin C 30%
total fat (g) 0	fiber (g) 4	calcium 4%
sat fat (g)........................ 0	sugars (g) 2	iron................................ 6%
cholesterol (mg) 0	protein (g) 2	

FIBER FILLER

Just 1 cup of steamed green beans adds about one-quarter of the fiber you need for the day. Fiber helps control blood sugar and improves digestive health; it is also beneficial because it creates a feeling of fullness. Green beans also contain resistant starch. It acts like fiber, giving similar benefits, but also boosts satiety by triggering certain chemical reactions in the G.I. tract.

IRON MAN

Just 1 cup of cooked green beans has nearly 1 milligram iron. That is almost as much as a 3-ounce portion of steak. Iron is important for blood, delivering oxygen to every cell of the body. Non-heme iron—the type found in plant foods—is critical to the biosynthesis of DNA.

DAMAGE CONTROL

While the iron in green beans does its work helping to deliver energy and oxygen throughout the body, phytochemical antioxidants called aglycones keep that iron from contributing to oxidative damage. Other powerful antioxidants in that group, such as quercitin and kaempferol, do their part in systemic damage control, scavenging free radicals that harm cells and their DNA.

AVAILABLE

Year-round

KEEP IT FRESH

Choose beans that snap crisply when broken and are bright green without bruises, discoloration, or soft spots. Store them dry (markets often mist the beans, and consumers bring them home and refrigerate them wet, which shortens their shelf life) and unwashed, loosely wrapped in a paper towel inside a partially closed plastic bag for 2 to 5 days. Green beans are highly perishable, so eat them as soon as possible.

LAST-MINUTE PREP

To wash beans, put them in a colander and run cold water over them; shake to remove the excess water. Snap off the ends by hand or cut them with a small knife. Leave them whole or break into 1- to 2-inch lengths, or cut on the diagonal if you prefer.

QUICK COOK

Place trimmed beans in boiling, lightly salted water; cook until they are tender-crisp, 2 to 8 minutes (time varies depending on width of beans). Drain in a colander; refresh with cold water. To steam, place the trimmed beans in a steamer basket over (but not touching) boiling water; cover and cook until they are tender-crisp, about 10 minutes for medium beans.

try it!

WITH FETA AND WALNUTS

Blanch 1 pound trimmed green beans until tender-crisp; drain well. They can be prepared ahead to this point, if desired (cool and refrigerate them, wrapped in a kitchen towel placed in a partially closed plastic bag up to 2 days). In a large saucepan, heat 1½ teaspoons extra-virgin olive oil on medium-high heat. Add the beans and season with salt and pepper. When they are hot, remove them from the heat. Add ⅓ cup toasted walnut pieces and 3 tablespoons crumbled feta cheese; toss and serve.

STEAM-SAUTÉED WITH BASIL OR TARRAGON

In a large saucepan, combine ⅓ cup water, 1 tablespoon extra-virgin olive oil, ¼ cup finely diced red onion, a pinch of salt, and 1 pound green beans (trimmed, broken into 2-inch lengths). Cover and cook on medium-high heat until the beans are starting to get tender, 6 to 9 minutes. Uncover and cook until the liquid evaporates, about 1 minute. Toss the beans with 2 teaspoons minced fresh basil or tarragon.

IN POTATO SALAD

Steam or blanch green beans that have been cut or snapped into 1-inch lengths, cooking them until tender-crisp; rinse with cold water and let them cool to room temperature. Toss with your favorite potato salad, or place the cooked green beans on a platter and top with potato salad; garnish with cherry tomatoes.

Vegetarian Lasagna

Vegetarian lasagna is such a satisfying treat. This version showcases mushrooms and green beans, but you can augment the mix by layering in a few strips of roasted red bell pepper or caramelized onion. No tomatoes or tomato sauce is used. If you wish, heat up some marinara sauce and serve it on the side as an optional topping.

Yields 6 servings

NUTRITIONAL INFORMATION
(per serving)

calories 300	sodium (mg) 430	vitamin A IUs 15%
fat calories 120	total carbohydrates (g) ... 23	vitamin C 50%
total fat (g) 14	fiber (g) 2	calcium 50%
sat fat (g) 8	sugars (g) 3	iron 10%
cholesterol (mg) 45	protein (g) 22	

4 ounces fresh green beans, trimmed, cut into 1-inch pieces

Nonstick olive oil cooking spray

2 cups part-skim ricotta cheese

⅓ cup finely chopped fresh basil

¾ cup grated Parmesan cheese

4 tablespoons finely chopped fresh Italian parsley

Coarse salt (kosher or sea)

Freshly ground black pepper

OPTIONAL pinch dried red pepper flakes

4 ounces no-boil lasagna noodles, whole wheat preferred

1 pound cremini mushrooms, thinly sliced

½ cup (loosely packed) shredded reduced-fat mozzarella cheese

1. Put a large saucepan of salted water on high heat; bring to a boil. Put the beans in the water and cook until they are tender-crisp, about 3 to 4 minutes (depending on the width of beans). Drain in a colander and refresh with cold water. Shake off the excess water and set aside.

2. Adjust an oven rack to the middle position. Preheat the oven to 350 degrees F. Generously coat an 8-inch square baking pan with cooking spray.

3. In a medium bowl, combine the ricotta, basil, ½ cup of the Parmesan, and 2 tablespoons of the parsley. Season with salt and pepper; stir to combine. If desired, stir in the pepper flakes.

4. In the prepared baking pan, put down 2 lasagna noodles. Top with about ⅔ cup cheese mixture, dropping it on in small spoonfuls to make an even layer. Top with one-third of the mushrooms and one-third of the green beans. Repeat the layering two more times. Finish with a final layer of noodles. Scatter the mozzarella and remaining ¼ cup Parmesan on top.

5. Cover with aluminum foil to tightly seal the pan on all sides. Bake for 30 minutes. Increase the oven temperature to 425 degrees F; bake for 20 minutes more. Remove the foil and bake an additional 15 minutes, or until the surface is browned. Allow the lasagna to rest out of the oven for 10 minutes before serving. Scatter it with the remaining 2 tablespoons parsley.

Couscous with Shrimp and Green Beans

This dish looks and tastes like simplified paella, the Spanish dish that showcases rice, vegetables, and seafood. Of course, couscous isn't rice; it's precooked and dried granules of dough. The green beans cook in the broth that is used to hydrate the couscous, rendering an edge of sweet-vegetal taste to the liquid.

Yields 6 servings

NUTRITIONAL INFORMATION
(per serving)

calories 150	sodium (mg) 230	vitamin A IUs 8%
fat calories 15	total carbohydrates (g)....21	vitamin C 20%
total fat (g) 1.5	fiber (g) 5	calcium.............................6%
sat fat (g)............................0	sugars (g) 2	iron..............................15%
cholesterol (mg) 70	protein (g) 14	

2 cups fat-free, low-sodium chicken or vegetable broth

4 ounces fresh green beans, trimmed, cut into ½-inch lengths

1 teaspoon curry powder

⅛ teaspoon dried red pepper flakes

10 ounces peeled and deveined medium shrimp

1 cup dry whole-wheat couscous

1 cup frozen artichoke hearts, thawed, coarsely chopped

½ cup frozen peas

⅔ cup (packed) lengthwise halved grape tomatoes

2 tablespoons minced fresh basil

Coarse salt (kosher or sea)

Freshly ground black pepper

1. Combine the broth, green beans, curry powder, and pepper flakes in a large saucepan or Dutch oven. Bring them to a boil on high heat.

2. Add the shrimp and reduce the heat to medium. Cook for 1 minute, or until the shrimp begin to turn pink.

3. Add the couscous, artichokes, and peas; stir just enough so the couscous is covered with liquid. Cover and remove from the heat. Let stand for 5 to 6 minutes, or until the liquid is absorbed. Add the tomatoes and basil. Gently toss. Taste and season with salt and pepper.

MEATLESS ALTERNATIVE Omit the shrimp. If desired, cook 2 to 3 ounces of soy-based chorizo; drain it well and crumble a little over each portion just before serving.

Curry with Green Beans, Summer Squash, and Cauliflower

Spoon this fragrant Thai-style curry over cooked brown rice or whole-wheat couscous. Yukon Gold potatoes or turnips make a lovely addition, and if you prefer, use cubed cooked chicken breast instead of tofu. The dish is only moderately spicy, so be sure to taste it when it's finished cooking. If you like, add a squeeze of hot sauce, such as Sriracha, to suit your taste.

Yields 4 servings

NUTRITIONAL INFORMATION
(per serving)

calories 130	sodium (mg) 280	vitamin A IUs 8%
fat calories 60	total carbohydrates (g)....13	vitamin C 80%
total fat (g) 7	fiber (g) 4	calcium 6%
sat fat (g) 3	sugars (g) 6	iron..............................10%
cholesterol (mg) 0	protein (g) 8	

1½ teaspoons extra-virgin olive oil

1 large yellow onion, coarsely chopped

3 ounces medium fresh green beans, trimmed, cut into ½-inch pieces

2 zucchini squash or yellow crookneck squash, trimmed, cut crosswise into ½-inch slices

1 medium garlic clove, minced

2 teaspoons red Thai curry paste

¾ cup light coconut milk

8 ounces firm tofu, cut into ¾-inch cubes

2 cups coarsely chopped cauliflower florets

About ¾ cup fat-free, low-sodium chicken or vegetable broth

Salt

OPTIONAL GARNISH chopped fresh cilantro

1. In a large saucepan or Dutch oven, heat the oil on medium-high heat. Add the onion and green beans. Cook, stirring occasionally, until the onion softens, about 3 minutes. Add the squash and garlic; cook for 1 minute.

2. In a small bowl, combine the curry paste and about 2 tablespoons of the coconut milk; stir until well combined. Add the curry paste to the vegetable mixture, along with the remaining coconut milk. Bring it to a simmer; reduce the heat to medium. Add the tofu and cauliflower. Simmer, covered, until the vegetables are tender-crisp and the tofu is heated through, about 3 minutes, reducing the heat if it's bubbling too vigorously. Add enough broth to make a thick but somewhat soupy consistency. Stir and season with salt. If desired, top each serving with a little chopped fresh cilantro.

GREEN LEAF
LETTUCE,
RED LEAF LETTUCE

Both red and green leaf lettuce have mild flavor profiles and alluring textures. They offer beguiling contrasts in rigidity; the ruffled leaves are pleasingly pliable and delicate, while the stems are crunchy-crisp and dense. Home gardeners should note that some varieties of red leaf lettuce can have a bitter edge, but most that you find in the marketplace have a delicate, bitter-free taste.

It's easy to be fooled by lettuce's ultra-low calorie count. One might assume that there is little nutrition. However, with only 4 or 5 calories per cup, red leaf and green leaf lettuces pack plenty of antioxidant vitamin A for eye function and a good amount of vitamin C, as well as iron and calcium for blood and bone health.

NUTRITIONAL INFORMATION
(per 1 cup shredded raw green leaf lettuce/per 1 cup shredded raw red leaf lettuce)

calories 5/4	sodium (mg) 10/7	vitamin A IUs 53%/42%
fat calories 0/1	total carbohydrates (g)... 1/1	vitamin C 11%/2%
total fat (g) 0/0	fiber (g) 0/0	calcium 1%/1%
sat fat (g)..................... 0/1	sugars (g) 0/0	iron.......................... 2%/2%
cholesterol (mg) 0/0	protein (g) 0/0	

GOOD SUGARS

Green and red leaf lettuces contain complex sugar molecules called polysaccharides, some of which have shown specific functional benefits to health. Inositol is an especially important member of this group, contributing to the function of insulin, the balance of calcium in nerve function, and fat and cholesterol metabolism.

GOOD MOOD FOOD

Inositol, due to its chemistry, is usually considered a member of the greater family of B vitamins. It can play a part in the metabolic pathway that balances the mood-enhancing pseudohormone serotonin.

ORGAN HELP

A type of polysaccharide in lettuce called sedoheptulose has displayed abilities to help protect the liver and kidneys from oxidative damage and abnormal fat metabolism while helping to reduce the inflammation process inherent in type 2 diabetes.

AVAILABLE

Year-round

KEEP IT FRESH

Look for lettuce that smells fresh, without soft spots or discoloration. Look closely at the tips of the leaves—the area that is generally most susceptible to deterioration. Wash before refrigerating. Separate the leaves and put them in a large tub of cold water; gently swish. Drain the leaves in a colander. Spin in a salad spinner, if available, but don't overdo it; spun too long or fast, the tender leaves get crushed, and it's good to leave a little water on the leaves or blot them partially dry with a paper towel or kitchen cloth. A little water helps to hydrate the cells to prevent wilting during storage. Wrap the lettuce loosely in a kitchen towel and place it in a partially closed plastic bag. Refrigerate it in the crisper drawer for up to 4 or 5 days.

LAST-MINUTE PREP

Gently tear clean, chilled lettuce into bite-size pieces.

try it!

IN SALAD WITH TASTY BALSAMIC DRESSING

In a small bowl, whisk together 1 teaspoon honey or agave syrup, 2 tablespoons fresh lemon juice, 1 teaspoon salt, 2 tablespoons balsamic vinegar, ¼ cup extra-virgin olive oil, and freshly ground black pepper. Stir in 3 tablespoons finely chopped red onion and 1½ tablespoons minced fresh basil. Use the dressing to lightly coat 8 handfuls of red or green leaf lettuce that have been torn into bite-size pieces. If desired, top the salads with sliced hard-cooked eggs or avocado.

WITH POTATO-GARBANZO SALAD

Simmer 12 ounces Baby Dutch Yellow potatoes or small red potatoes in a saucepan with water to cover, until just barely fork tender. Drain. When they are cool enough to handle, cut the potatoes in halves or quarters. Put the still-warm potatoes in a medium bowl; add tasty balsamic dressing as described above, but double the amount of red onion. Add one 15-ounce can garbanzo beans (drained, rinsed), 3 thinly sliced green onions (use half of dark green stalks), and 1 diced red bell pepper; toss. Taste and season with salt. Arrange 4 handfuls of bite-size pieces of red or green leaf lettuce on a platter. Top with the potato mixture.

WITH ORANGE AND CARROT SALAD

In a large bowl, whisk together 2 tablespoons fresh lemon juice, 1 tablespoon honey or agave syrup, and ¾ teaspoon ground cinnamon. Add 4 cups grated carrots and 2 tablespoons minced fresh cilantro or Italian parsley. Cut 3 peeled navel oranges into supremes, holding them over the bowl so that the juice and segments drop into the bowl (see page 230). Gently toss. Taste and adjust the seasoning. Arrange 3 to 4 large handfuls of red or green leaf lettuce that have been torn into bite-size pieces on a platter. Top with the carrot salad and serve.

Open-Faced Egg Salad Sandwiches

Each of these delectable open-faced sandwiches requires a slice of toasted rustic whole-grain bread as a foundation. What is rustic bread? It's not easy to define. Some might describe it as artisanal. It is sold whole, unsliced, usually in round or oval shapes. The bread has a crusty exterior and an interior with a chewy texture. No preservatives are used.

Yields 4 servings

NUTRITIONAL INFORMATION
(per serving)

calories 190	sodium (mg) 230	vitamin A IUs 15%
fat calories 60	total carbohydrates (g)....16	vitamin C 10%
total fat (g) 7	fiber (g) 3	calcium 8%
sat fat (g)........................ 2	sugars (g) 3	iron............................10%
cholesterol (mg) 235	protein (g) 13	

5 eggs

4 slices rustic whole-grain bread, about ⅜ inch thick

1 large garlic clove, cut in half lengthwise

2½ tablespoons plain, fat-free yogurt, plus more if needed

2 tablespoons finely chopped fresh dill

½ teaspoon minced lemon zest

Coarse salt (kosher or sea)

Freshly ground black pepper

Red leaf lettuce or green leaf lettuce

OPTIONAL GARNISH chopped fresh chives

1. Put the eggs in a small saucepan with water to cover by 1 inch. Bring it to a boil on high heat; cover and remove from the heat. Allow the eggs to sit, covered, for 12 minutes. Drain and run cold water over the eggs. When they're cool enough to handle, crack and peel them in cold water. Place them in an airtight container and refrigerate.

2. Adjust an oven rack to 6 inches below the broiler element; preheat the broiler. Put the bread on a rimmed baking sheet. Broil until the bread is toasted, about 1½ to 2 minutes; watch the progress because bread burns easily. Place each piece of toasted bread on a salad plate, toasted side up; rub the tops of the bread with a cut side of garlic.

3. In a medium bowl, stir together the yogurt, dill, and zest and season with salt and pepper. Coarsely chop the eggs and add them to the yogurt mixture; stir to combine. Taste and adjust the seasoning as needed, adding more yogurt for a creamy consistency.

4. Top each toast with a lettuce leaf or two (or more if you like). Top with egg salad. If desired, garnish with chopped chives.

Grilled Eggplant and Red Leaf Lettuce Salad

Most of the smoked paprika (*pimentón*) in the marketplace is produced in Spain. Made from ground and smoked pimiento chiles, it adds an intoxicating smoky scent to the vinaigrette used to top grilled eggplant slices and lettuce in this flavorful salad.

Yields 6 servings

NUTRITIONAL INFORMATION
(per serving)

calories 160	sodium (mg) 180	vitamin A IUs 100%
fat calories 110	total carbohydrates (g).....8	vitamin C 20%
total fat (g) 12	fiber (g) 4	calcium.......................15%
sat fat (g).......................3	sugars (g) 3	iron...............................6%
cholesterol (mg) 10	protein (g) 5	

2 small eggplants (about 1¼ pounds), unpeeled

Coarse salt (kosher or sea)

Nonstick olive oil cooking spray

1 tablespoon minced fresh Italian parsley

2 teaspoons cider vinegar

2 teaspoons balsamic vinegar

1 medium garlic clove, minced

1 teaspoon smoked paprika

Freshly ground black pepper

¼ cup extra-virgin olive oil

1 medium head red or green leaf lettuce, torn into bite-size pieces (about 8 cups)

2 Roma tomatoes, cored, diced

1 tablespoon drained capers

3 ounces grated pepper Jack cheese

1. Heat a grill to medium-high heat. Cut the eggplants crosswise into ½-inch slices; place them in a single layer on baking sheets lined with paper towels and sprinkle them with 1 teaspoon salt. Set aside for 10 minutes.

2. Pat the eggplant slices with paper towels and coat them lightly with cooking spray. Grill them on a clean grate until they are nicely browned and tender, about 4 to 5 minutes on each side. Set them aside to partially cool while preparing the dressing and salad.

3. In a small bowl or glass measuring cup with a handle, whisk together the parsley, both vinegars, garlic, and paprika and season with salt and pepper. Whisk in the oil in a thin stream. Taste and adjust the seasoning.

4. In a large bowl, toss the lettuce and tomatoes with enough dressing (about half) to lightly coat the leaves. Divide the salad between six plates. Place the eggplant on top of the greens, overlapping the slices slightly. Stir the capers into the remaining dressing and drizzle it over the eggplant. Scatter the cheese on top.

Roasted Portobello Salad

Portobello mushrooms are actually just mature cremini mushrooms. Their broad, umbrella-like caps are meaty with an underside adorned with dark gills. To prevent the dark-colored gills from discoloring a dish (such as this salad), scrape them off with a spoon; discard the gills or use them in a stock.

Yields 6 side-dish servings

NUTRITIONAL INFORMATION
(per serving)

calories 160	sodium (mg) 320	vitamin A IUs 140%
fat calories 130	total carbohydrates (g).....6	vitamin C 40%
total fat (g) 15	fiber (g) 2	calcium 6%
sat fat (g).....................2.5	sugars (g) 3	iron.............................6%
cholesterol (mg) 5	protein (g) 3	

½ medium red onion, thinly sliced

2 tablespoons seasoned rice vinegar

1 tablespoon minced fresh mint

DRESSING

2 tablespoons cider vinegar

1 tablespoon balsamic vinegar

2 teaspoons Dijon mustard

Coarse salt (kosher or sea)

Freshly ground black pepper

½ cup extra-virgin olive oil

SALAD

3 large portobello mushrooms
(*see Cook's Note*)

1½ large heads red or green leaf lettuce, torn into bite-size pieces (about 12 cups)

1 red bell pepper, cored, seeded, and cut into matchsticks

1 to 2 ounces crumbled blue cheese

1. Combine the onion, rice vinegar, and mint in a small bowl; toss and set aside to marinate.

2. Preheat the oven to 450 degrees F.

3. To make the dressing: Whisk together the cider vinegar, balsamic vinegar, and mustard in a small bowl or glass measuring cup with a handle, and season with salt and pepper. Whisk in the oil in thin stream. Taste and adjust the seasoning if needed.

4. To make the salad: Put the mushrooms on a rimmed baking sheet. Using a pastry brush, brush the mushrooms on both sides with dressing. Turn them stem-side up and roast until tender, about 15 minutes, brushing with dressing at 5-minute intervals, reserving the leftover dressing. Set them aside to cool slightly.

5. Drain the onions, reserving the vinegar. Put the onions in a large bowl. Add the lettuce, bell pepper, and reserved dressing; toss. Taste and, if needed, season with the reserved rice vinegar, salt, and/or pepper. Divide the salad between six plates. Cut the mushrooms into ½-inch slices. Fan them on top of the salads. Top with the cheese.

COOK'S NOTE Snap or cut off the stems and wipe the mushroom caps with a moist paper towel.

GREEN ONION

also Scallion, Spring Onion

Two complementary but different tastes and textures make the green onion a culinary powerhouse. The petite white bulb offers a flavor and aroma that are milder than larger yellow or brown onions. A subtle edge of sweetness makes this portion of the green onion a suitable substitute for shallots. The hollow, bright-green stalks have a more vegetal character, with a decisive scent that makes them appropriate to stand in for chives.

Green onions are versatile and can enhance a wide variety of dishes, but they also offer many health benefits.

NUTRITIONAL INFORMATION
(per 1/4 cup raw, chopped)

calories 10	sodium (mg) 10	vitamin A IUs 2%
fat calories 0	total carbohydrates (g)..... 2	vitamin C 8%
total fat (g) 0	fiber (g) 1	calcium 2%
sat fat (g).........................0	sugars (g) 1	iron............................... 0%
cholesterol (mg) 0	protein (g) 0	

IRON BOOSTER
The sulfur compounds in onions are able to enhance the body's ability to absorb iron in grain foods, in some cases doubling the amount absorbed without onions in the mix. Iron is a necessary element for helping the blood cells carry and release oxygen throughout the body.

ZINC ON TAP
Onions also help boost the absorption of zinc. The metal is indispensable to hundreds of metabolic functions, including those related to taste, fertility, and immunity.

A-OK
A single stalk of green onion has 10 percent of your daily vitamin A needs and 25 percent of vitamin K. Vitamin A is important for eye health, skin health, and immunity as well as the formation of red blood cells. Vitamin K is a major component in bone growth and blood vessel growth in addition to its best-known function of facilitating blood coagulation.

AVAILABLE
Year-round

KEEP IT FRESH
Look for bright green stalks without any hint of sliminess, soft spots, or discoloration. The bulbs should be firm and smell fresh. Refrigerate them, dry and unwashed, loosely packed in a plastic bag in the crisper drawer for up to 6 days.

LAST-MINUTE PREP

Wash with cold water. Trim off and discard the roots. Many recipes call for using both the light-colored bulb and dark green stalks, while others may specify just one or the other.

QUICK COOK

Grilling brings out the sweetness in green onions. Toss them with enough extra-virgin olive oil to lightly coat; season with coarse salt. Heat a grill or grill pan to medium-high heat. Grill (placing them perpendicular to the grates) until they are softened and lightly marked, about 1½ to 2 minutes on each side. Serve as is, or squeeze a little fresh lime juice on top.

try it!

WITH CROOKNECK SQUASH AND TORTELLINI

Cook an 8-ounce package of refrigerated ricotta tortellini or tofu tortellini according to the package directions; drain. In a medium skillet, heat 1 tablespoon extra-virgin olive oil on medium-high heat; add 2 yellow crookneck squash (sliced), 1 garlic clove (minced), and 2 green onions (sliced, including half of dark green stalks). Lower the heat to medium and cook, stirring occasionally, until the squash is tender-crisp. Add the drained tortellini and gently toss. Season with freshly ground black pepper.

IN LENTIL SALAD

In a bowl, combine 2 cups cooked (cooled) lentils, 5 Roma tomatoes (cored, diced), 4 ounces feta cheese (crumbled), and 3 green onions (sliced, including half of dark green stalks). In a small bowl, combine 2 tablespoons red wine vinegar, 1 teaspoon Dijon mustard, ½ teaspoon garlic salt, and ⅓ cup extra-virgin olive oil; whisk to combine and add to the lentil mixture. Toss.

IN RICOTTA-CHILE BROWN RICE

Bring 4 cups fat-free, low-sodium chicken or vegetable broth to a boil in a large saucepan on high heat. Add 1¾ cups dry long-grain brown rice; cover and reduce the heat to medium-low and simmer for 35 minutes (or according to the package directions), until the broth is absorbed and the rice is tender. Stir in one 4-ounce can chopped mild green chiles, ⅔ cup part-skim ricotta, and ¼ cup sliced green onions. Cook on medium heat, stirring, just until heated through.

Cream of Mushroom Soup with Green Onions

The dark brown caps of cremini mushrooms add a delightful earthiness to this puréed soup. Green onions contribute their subtle sweetness and aroma on two fronts: The white and light green portions cook with the mushrooms, and the dark stalks are used as a colorful garnish. If you prefer a lighter-hued soup, substitute common white (button) mushrooms for cremini, or use a combination of white and cremini mushrooms.

Yields 6 servings

NUTRITIONAL INFORMATION
(per serving)

calories 60	sodium (mg) 560	vitamin A IUs 8%
fat calories 0	total carbohydrates (g) 11	vitamin C 6%
total fat (g) 0	fiber (g) 1	calcium 15%
sat fat (g) 0	sugars (g) 8	iron 4%
cholesterol (mg) 0	protein (g) 5	

6 to 8 green onions

Nonstick olive oil cooking spray

14 ounces sliced cremini mushrooms (about 3 cups)

2 medium garlic cloves, minced

Coarse salt (kosher or sea)

Freshly ground black pepper

2 cups fat-free, low-sodium chicken or vegetable broth

One 12-ounce can fat-free evaporated milk

1. Cut the onions into ¼-inch slices. Make two piles: one with the white and light green slices, the other with the dark green stalks. Use enough onions to make about ½ cup of white and light green slices.

2. Coat a large saucepan or Dutch oven with the cooking spray and put it on medium-high heat. Add the white and light green slices of the onions, the mushrooms, and garlic. Cook until the mushrooms are tender-crisp and starting to release liquid, about 5 minutes, stirring occasionally. Season with salt and pepper.

3. Add the broth and milk. Cover and bring to a boil; reduce the heat to medium-low and gently simmer until the mushrooms are tender, about 10 minutes. Remove from the heat.

4. Working in three batches, purée the soup in a blender (use caution and hold down the lid with a pot holder), or use a food processor. Return the soup to medium-low heat and cook, stirring frequently until it is reheated, about 2 minutes. Ladle the soup into bowls and grind a little pepper on each serving. Top with slices of dark green onion stalks.

Pita Sandwiches with Indian Spices and Endive Salad

Cucumbers make such a welcome crunchy addition to sandwiches. Hothouse (also called English) cucumbers have thin skin and few, if any, seeds, so they don't require peeling or seeding. They are the long, slender variety, usually about 12 to 15 inches long, that are commonly sealed in a clear plastic wrap.

Yields 8 half or 4 whole servings

NUTRITIONAL INFORMATION
(per half-pita serving)

calories 300	sodium (mg) 95	vitamin A IUs 6%
fat calories 120	total carbohydrates (g)... 32	vitamin C 10%
total fat (g) 13	fiber (g) 8	calcium 10%
sat fat (g)......................2	sugars (g) 7	iron...............................15%
cholesterol (mg) 60	protein (g) 16	

Nonstick vegetable oil cooking spray

- 2 teaspoons garam masala (*see Cook's Note*)
- 1 teaspoon coarse salt (kosher or sea)
- 1 pound boneless, skinless chicken breasts
- ¾ cup plain fat-free Greek-style yogurt
- ⅔ cup roughly chopped unpeeled hothouse cucumber
- 1½ tablespoons chopped fresh mint
- 2 teaspoons fresh lemon juice
- 4 heads Belgian endive, trimmed, halved lengthwise, cut into ½-inch slices
- 4 green onions, thinly sliced (including half of dark green stalks)
- ⅓ cup halved grape tomatoes

Freshly ground black pepper

Four 6-inch whole-wheat pitas, warmed

1. Adjust an oven rack to the upper third of the oven. Preheat the broiler. Line a broiler pan or a sturdy rimmed baking sheet with aluminum foil. Coat it with nonstick cooking spray. In a small bowl, toss 1½ teaspoons of the garam masala and the salt together; sprinkle the chicken on both sides with the mixture. Place the chicken on the foil. Broil until it is opaque in the thickest part, turning halfway through cooking, about 7 to 8 minutes per side. Set it aside to cool for 5 to 10 minutes.

2. In a large bowl, combine the yogurt, cucumber, mint, lemon juice, and ½ teaspoon remaining garam masala; stir to combine. Add the endive, green onions, and tomatoes; season with salt and pepper and toss.

3. Cut the chicken crosswise into ¼-inch slices. Cut the pitas in half across the middle and open the pockets. Fill them with chicken slices and salad.

COOK'S NOTE Garam masala is an Indian spice blend that is sold in Indian markets and many supermarkets. The dry, ground concoction often contains pepper, cloves, mace, cumin, cinnamon, cardamom, nutmeg, star anise, and coriander seeds.

MEATLESS ALTERNATIVE Omit the chicken. Substitute 1 pound extra-firm tofu. Drain it and pat it dry with paper towels. Cut it into 1-inch cubes and season with the garam masala–salt mixture. Stir-fry as for step 2 of the Broccoli-Tofu Stir-Fry (page 54).

Garbanzo Patties with Green Onion Tzatziki Sauce

Eggs, bread crumbs, and partially mashed garbanzo beans are the backbone of these vegetarian patties. They are spiked with harissa, the North African chile paste that adds spicy heat and hints of smokiness. Look for it in Middle Eastern markets, natural food stores, and some supermarkets with large imported specialty food sections.

Yields 6 servings

NUTRITIONAL INFORMATION
(per serving)

calories 300	sodium (mg) 95	vitamin A IUs 6%
fat calories 120	total carbohydrates (g)... 32	vitamin C 10%
total fat (g) 13	fiber (g) 8	calcium 10%
sat fat (g) 2	sugars (g) 7	iron.............................15%
cholesterol (mg) 60	protein (g) 16	

½ hothouse cucumber, unpeeled, grated

Coarse salt (kosher or sea)

PATTIES

Two 1-inch slices rustic whole-wheat bread, torn into bite-size pieces

2 eggs

4 tablespoon extra-virgin olive oil

1 teaspoon garam masala (*see Cook's Note*, page 175)

½ teaspoon harissa

Two 16-ounce cans garbanzo beans, drained, rinsed

2 green onions, minced (including half of dark green stalks)

⅓ cup plain fat-free Greek-style yogurt

TZATZIKI

1 cup plain fat-free Greek-style yogurt

2 green onions, minced (including half of dark green stalks)

1 tablespoon fresh lemon juice

1 teaspoon chopped fresh mint

1 teaspoon chopped fresh cilantro

1 teaspoon minced garlic

1 teaspoon harissa

GARNISH thinly sliced dark green stalks of 1 or 2 green onions; coarse salt such as fleur de sel; freshly ground black pepper; lime wedges

OPTIONAL GARNISH 12 pita chips

1. Preheat the oven to 350 degrees F. Put the cucumber in a colander; sprinkle it with a little salt and set aside to drain.

2. To make the patties: Pulse the bread in a food processor until coarse crumbs form. Spread them on a rimmed baking sheet. Toast in the oven until they are dry and golden brown, about 10 minutes, checking after 5 minutes and tossing the crumbs to help them evenly brown. You should have about ½ to ⅔ cup crumbs.

3. In a medium bowl, whisk the eggs with 2 tablespoons of the oil, the garam masala, and harissa. In a large bowl, coarsely mash the garbanzos until half of the mixture is smooth and the other half is a little chunky. Stir in the bread crumbs, egg mixture, onions, and yogurt. Form the mixture into six patties.

4. To make the tzatziki: Shake the colander to remove water from the grated cucumber. In a bowl, combine the cucumber with the yogurt, onions, lemon juice, mint, cilantro, garlic, and harissa. Gently toss and set aside.

5. Heat 1 tablespoon of the remaining oil in a large nonstick skillet on medium-high heat. Add half of the patties and cook until they are golden brown on both sides and heated through. Place them on a paper towel–lined plate and cover with aluminum foil. Add the last 1 tablespoon of the oil and cook the remaining patties.

6. Garnish each patty with a good dollop of tzatziki sauce. Top with some thinly sliced green onions and a pinch of salt and pepper. Place a lime wedge next to each patty. If desired, accompany each serving with 1 or 2 pita chips.

GUAVA

True guavas have edible, knobby green skin that often turns yellow when they are thoroughly ripe. Round or sometimes pear shaped and 2 to 4 inches in diameter, guavas are generally off-white inside but can be pink or yellow. Domestic varieties generally have a firmer, crisper texture. Redolent of exotic floral notes, the mildly sweet-tart flesh is dotted with seeds that vary in size and rigidity. Although they can be eaten, they are strained out when the fruit is mashed for use in sauces, jams, and pastes.

Don't confuse true guava with feijoa, that semi-sweet ovoid fruit with inedible rind that is often labeled "pineapple guava."

Guavas have one of the highest concentrations of vitamin C of any fruit or vegetable—four times that of oranges. Vitamin C helps counter inflammation, plus it lowers the risks of heart disease, strokes, cataracts, and certain types of cancer. Another job this common vitamin manages is to aid the body in absorbing important minerals, such as iron and zinc.

NUTRITIONAL INFORMATION
(per 1 cup raw)

calories 112	sodium (mg) 3	vitamin A IUs 21%
fat calories 13	total carbohydrates (g)...24	vitamin C 628%
total fat (g) 2	fiber (g) 9	calcium 3%
sat fat (g).........................0	sugars (g) 15	iron..............................2%
cholesterol (mg) 0	protein (g) 4	

FILLING FIBER
Guavas are fiber rich, offering a whopping 9 grams a cup. The same amount of fruit contains 4 grams of protein. Both of these nutrients help increase satiety and encourage the body to burn calories longer to balance blood sugar and reduce symptoms of diabetes.

JOINT JUICER
Some research studies indicate that people with arthritis, high blood pressure, or Alzheimer's disease can benefit greatly from a vitamin C–rich diet—so much so that the National Academy of Sciences recommends increasing the daily vitamin C requirement from 60 milligrams to 75 to 90 milligrams per day.

AVAILABLE
Domestic (about the size of a ping-pong ball): October to June
Imported (about the size of a raquet ball): Year-round

KEEP IT FRESH
Select firm, unblemished fruit. It may take up to 2 weeks for the fruit to ripen at room temperature (out of direct sunlight). Refrigerate unwashed ripe fruit, loose in the crisper drawer, up to 1 week.

LAST-MINUTE PREP
Wash guavas thoroughly with cold water. Trim off the stem and blossom ends.

QUICK COOK
Guavas are eaten skin-on, raw or cooked. To cook, sauté or broil them. For a sweet sauce, gently simmer guavas until tender in a sugar syrup or a combination of equal parts agave syrup or honey and water or sherry; push through a strainer and discard the seeds.

try it!

IN SMOOTHIES

In a blender, combine 1 ripe guava (ends trimmed and discarded, quartered), 6 hulled strawberries, 1 tablespoon dark honey, 1 cup fat-free plain yogurt, 1 cup 2% milk, and 6 ice cubes. Whirl until icy smooth. Pour it into 2 large glasses.

AS A GRILLED GARNISH

Slice off the stem and blossom ends of several ripe guavas. Cut them crosswise into ¼-inch unpeeled rounds. Place them on a rimmed baking sheet in a single layer and brush with extra-virgin olive oil. Roast in a 375-degree-F oven until tender-crisp. Drizzle them with honey and sprinkle with coarse salt. Broil about 8 inches below the broiler element until they are nicely browned on the edges, about 3 minutes. Transfer them to a plate; let cool to room temperature. Use as a garnish for a cheese course or atop green salads or grilled chicken.

MEXICAN-STYLE

Trim the ends off ripe guavas, slice, and place them on a plate; squeeze fresh lime juice on top. Sprinkle with Pico de Gallo seasoning mix to taste. Buy the spice mixture at Latin American markets or make your own blend by stirring together 1 teaspoon kosher salt, 2 teaspoons chili powder, 2 teaspoons paprika, and 3 to 4 teaspoons cayenne pepper.

Warm Goat Cheese Appetizers with Guava Salsa

The crisp perkiness of guava-spiked salsa teams beautifully with creamy-warm goat cheese coated with toasty nuts and bread crumbs. One of the easiest ways to cut a log of chilled goat cheese into slices is to use unflavored dental floss. Stretch the floss tightly between two hands and pull it down through the cheese. This method avoids the problem of cheese sticking to a knife blade.

Yields 10 to 12 servings

NUTRITIONAL INFORMATION
(per serving)

calories 90	sodium (mg) 75	vitamin A IUs 15%
fat calories 40	total carbohydrates (g).....11	vitamin C 60%
total fat (g) 4	fiber (g) 2	calcium..........................4%
sat fat (g)......................1.5	sugars (g) 7	iron.................................4%
cholesterol (mg) 5	protein (g) 3	

SALSA

- 1 large ripe guava, finely diced, with skin (*see Cook's Notes*)
- 1 mango, peeled, pitted, finely diced
- 4 medium strawberries, hulled, finely diced
- ¾ cup finely diced peeled and cored pineapple
- 1½ tablespoons minced fresh cilantro
- 1 tablespoon fresh lime juice

Pinch dried red pepper flakes

Pinch salt

WARM BAKED GOAT CHEESE

- ½ cup fresh sourdough or rustic whole-wheat bread crumbs (*see Cook's Notes*)
- ¼ cup finely chopped pecans

Nonstick olive oil cooking spray

- Six ¾-inch slices chilled log-style goat cheese

GARNISH microgreens

FOR SERVING crackers, crostini, or toasted lavash

1. Preheat the oven to 375 degrees F.

2. To make the salsa: In a medium bowl, combine the guava, mango, straw-berries, pineapple, cilantro, lime juice, pepper flakes, and salt. Set aside.

3. To make the baked cheese: Stir together the bread crumbs and nuts on a rimmed baking sheet. Bake until they are golden brown and crisp, 5 to 8 minutes, stirring twice during baking.

4. Spray the cheese slices with olive oil on each side and dredge them in the bread crumb mixture on all sides. Spray the baking sheet with oil. Place the coated cheese on the sheet and bake until warmed through and soft when the center is pressed, about 6 to 7 minutes.

5. Spread the salsa on a serving platter. Use a thin metal spatula to remove the cheese rounds from the baking sheet and place them atop the salsa. Sprinkle the microgreens on top. Accompany with crackers, crostini, or toasted lavash.

COOK'S NOTES A large guava is about 2¼ inches in diameter. If using smaller guavas, use 2 or 3.

Use a food processor fitted with the metal blade to produce bread crumbs. Use the pulsing technique, processing until the bread crumbs are still coarse, not finely ground.

Apple and Raisin–Stuffed Pork Tenderloin with Guava Sauce

True guavas (as opposed to feijoas, which are often labeled "pineapple guavas" but aren't really "true" guavas) combine with apples and raisins to make a silky puréed sauce to accompany braised, stuffed pork tenderloin. Adding an appealing aroma and texture to the sauce, the guavas also bring a nice spark of acidity to the raisin-sweetened purée.

Yields about 4 servings

NUTRITIONAL INFORMATION
(per serving, with ½ cup sauce)

calories ... 390	sodium (mg) ... 200	vitamin A IUs ... 15%
fat calories ... 110	total carbohydrates (g) ... 32	vitamin C ... 400%
total fat (g) ... 12	fiber (g) ... 7	calcium ... 4%
sat fat (g) ... 3	sugars (g) ... 22	iron ... 15%
cholesterol (mg) ... 115	protein (g) ... 41	

1½ pounds pork tenderloin

1 green apple, such as Granny Smith, finely diced

⅓ cup raisins

Salt

Freshly ground black pepper

1 tablespoon extra-virgin olive oil

1 cup fat-free, low-sodium beef broth

½ teaspoon dried basil or 1½ teaspoons minced fresh basil

GUAVA SAUCE

1 tablespoon extra-virgin olive oil

1 sweet onion, such as Maui, thinly sliced

2½ cups finely diced ripe guava (including skin, seeds, and flesh)

1. Preheat the oven to 350 degrees F.

2. Butterfly the tenderloin lengthwise, cutting only about three-fourths of the way through.

3. In a small bowl, mix together the apple and raisins and fill the tenderloin. Do not overfill; any extra filling will be used in the sauce. Using cotton string, tie the tenderloin closed at 1-inch intervals; season with salt and pepper.

4. Heat the oil in an ovenproof deep skillet on medium-high heat. Brown the meat on all sides. Add the broth and sprinkle with basil. Cover with foil and roast for 45 minutes to 1 hour, or until an internal temperature of 160 degrees F.

5. During the last 20 minutes of cooking, start making the sauce: In a saucepan, heat the oil on medium-high heat; add the onion and cook until brown, stirring occasionally, about 10 minutes. Add 2 cups hot water, the guava, and any reserved filling and bring to a boil on high heat. Reduce the heat to medium-low and simmer for 20 minutes, or until the apple is very tender, stirring occasionally. Remove from the heat and carefully purée the sauce in batches in a blender (hold down lid with a pot holder). Strain the sauce; discard the seeds. Season with salt.

6. Cut the meat into 1-inch slices (a serrated knife works well) and remove the strings. Serve it with the sauce spooned over the top.

MEATLESS ALTERNATIVE Serve the sauce over grilled tofu atop wild rice or brown rice. When cooking the onion, add 1 teaspoon maple syrup, 2 tablespoons raisins, and ½ Granny Smith apple (peeled, cored, and finely chopped). Proceed with the remaining sauce directions.

KALE

Common Curly, Tuscan

Don't let kale's appearance deceive you. Many assume that common curly kale's thick, deep-green leaf has bold bitterness or tough texture. Neither is true. These ruffled greens are mild and delicious, their leathery appearance easily softened with quick cooking. Served raw, cut into narrow pieces, and allowed to soften a few minutes with a little vinaigrette, kale attains a more lettuce-like consistency.

Common, frilly edged green kale is the variety that is easiest to find in the marketplace. Its leaves are tougher than the almost-black, deeper green puckered leaves of Tuscan kale (*cavolo nero* in Italian), that is sometimes called "dinosaur kale."

NUTRITIONAL INFORMATION
(per 1 cup raw, chopped)

calories 33	sodium (mg) 29	vitamin A IUs 206%
fat calories 4	total carbohydrates (g)..... 7	vitamin C 134%
total fat (g) 0	fiber (g) 1	calcium 9%
sat fat (g).........................0	sugars (g) 0	iron...............................6%
cholesterol (mg) 0	protein (g) 2	

There's a good explanation for kale's inclusion on every "vegetable superstar" list. Leafy greens of the genus *Brassica* (which includes mustard greens as well as broccoli and its cousins, rapini and cauliflower) are intensely concentrated sources of vitamins A and C, a good source of B and K, plus lots of important minerals.

HEARTS AND BABIES
The B vitamin in which kale is richest is folate, long lauded for its role in reducing the risk of neural tube birth defects in developing fetuses. And folate also helps the heart by regulating a chemical compound in the blood called homocysteine, implicated in cardiovascular disease.

BLOOD SUGAR BALANCER
Kale also is a good source of vitamin B_6. It is critical to scores of metabolic reactions, including the release of glucose from its storage form of glycogen and helping the body convert protein fractions into glucose. Better glucose balance, combined with the high fiber content of kale, means calories burn better and longer to reduce the risk of diabetic symptoms.

AVAILABLE
Year-round

KEEP IT FRESH
Look for kale with a fresh scent and crisp leaves, without wilting or discoloration. Smaller leaves with stems no wider than ¼ inch have the best texture. Rinse them in a tub of cold water, gently swishing the leaves around to remove any dirt or grit; repeat if necessary until the water is clear. Shake them to remove excess water. Wrap the leaves in a clean kitchen towel or paper towels and place them in a partially closed plastic bag. Refrigerate in the crisper drawer up to 3 days.

LAST-MINUTE PREP

Most recipes just call for kale's leafy greens; the thick stalks (ribs) are usually removed before use. The stalks can be discarded or composted or reserved for another use; they can be coarsely chopped and added to soups or stews. To remove the stalks, cut around them with a knife or use your hand by cupping the fingers and thumb around the stem below the leaf; holding the stem with the opposite hand, move the cupped hand toward the leaf's tip, scraping the leaf from the stem in the process. To chop or cut the leaves into ribbons, stack several together. Make a manageable package by folding the leaves in half in one direction, then in half in the other direction. Coarsely chop or cut them into ¼-inch crosswise slices.

QUICK COOK FOR COMMON CURLY KALE

In a large pan or Dutch oven, bring about 2 quarts water to a boil on high heat. Add 1 teaspoon salt and 2 pounds stemmed, coarsely chopped kale. Cover and cook until the leaves are tender, about 5 to 6 minutes. Drain them in a colander; refresh with cold water. Press out the excess water with the back of a spoon, or when the leaves are cool enough to handle, squeeze out the excess water in handfuls. Season with salt and pepper. Serve accompanied with lemon wedges.

QUICK COOK FOR TUSCAN KALE

Cut several handfuls of (clean, trimmed) leaves into ½-inch crosswise slices. In a deep skillet or large saucepan, bring ½ cup vegetable broth, chicken broth, or water to a boil on medium-high heat. Add the kale and cover; cook until tender, about 3 to 4 minutes. Season the kale with fresh lemon juice or red wine vinegar, plus salt and pepper. If desired, add a smidgen of extra-virgin olive oil.

WITH ROASTED GARLIC DRESSING

Preheat the oven to 450 degrees F. Using a sharp knife, cut off one-third of an unpeeled large head of garlic at the pointed end. Enclose the remaining garlic in aluminum foil, cut-side up; open it slightly and drizzle with 1 tablespoon olive oil (or to reduce fat, use 1 tablespoon water). Roast the garlic for about 30 minutes, or until the cloves are soft. When cool enough to handle, invert and squeeze the cloves from the papery sheaths into a blender. Add 2½ tablespoons extra-virgin olive oil, 2 tablespoons balsamic vinegar, 1 tablespoon fresh lemon juice, and season with salt and pepper. Whirl until the dressing is smooth. Toss with 2 pounds of trimmed, cooked kale.

IN BEAN SOUP

Five minutes before the end of cooking, add a generous handful of coarsely chopped kale to bean soup.

ATOP BAKED SWEET POTATOES

In a skillet, heat 2 teaspoons extra-virgin olive oil on medium-high heat. Add 1 medium onion (chopped) and 1 large garlic clove (minced); cook until softened. Stir in a pinch of dried red pepper flakes and 2 cups cooked, chopped kale (see Quick Cook for both varieties); cook until heated through. Taste and adjust the seasoning. Cut lengthwise slits in 3 or 4 baked sweet potatoes (leaving the bottoms intact). Spoon the kale mixture on top. If desired, top with a little grated Parmesan cheese.

Kale and Cannellini Beans with Crumbled Sausage

Cannellini beans, which are large white kidney beans, have a lovely starchy-sweet taste. Many supermarkets sell canned cannellini, but if you prefer, substitute canned great Northern beans. This hearty concoction pairs the flavorful beans with curly edge kale and Italian sausage made with turkey. Use the sweet variety for the mildest taste, or add spicy attitude with hot sausage.

Yields 4 main-course servings

NUTRITIONAL INFORMATION
(per serving)

calories 320	sodium (mg) 780	vitamin A IUs 610%
fat calories 120	total carbohydrates (g) ... 35	vitamin C 400%
total fat (g) 13	fiber (g) 8	calcium 30%
sat fat (g) 1	sugars (g) 1	iron 30%
cholesterol (mg) 35	protein (g) 21	

8 ounces Italian turkey sausage, bulk or casings removed

1½ tablespoons extra-virgin olive oil

1¾ pounds curly kale (about 2 large bunches), washed, stemmed, coarsely chopped

4 large garlic cloves, thinly sliced

Salt

Freshly ground black pepper

One 15-ounce can cannellini beans, undrained

2 tablespoons red wine vinegar

1. Put the sausage in a small skillet on medium-high heat. Break it up with a spatula, heating until the sausage is thoroughly cooked and no pink color remains, about 4 to 5 minutes. Drain it on a paper towel and set aside.

2. Heat the oil in a large, deep skillet on medium-high heat. Add the kale, garlic and ½ cup water; season with salt and pepper. When the liquid comes to a boil, cover and cook until the kale is tender, about 10 minutes, tossing the mixture two or three times during cooking.

3. Stir in the beans and vinegar; cook until the beans are hot, about 2 minutes. Taste and adjust the seasoning if needed. Serve the kale in shallow bowls topped with the crumbled sausage.

MEATLESS ALTERNATIVE Omit the sausage. For a spicier version, add a good pinch of dried red pepper flakes along with the beans. If desired, top each serving with chopped fresh Italian parsley or fresh basil.

Kale Salad with Dates and Almonds

This dish could turn kale doubters into true-blue kale fans. Dates, dried cranberries, and a small amount of maple syrup bring sweetness to the salad, while toasted almonds add welcome crunch and richness. Be sure to allow the salad to sit at room temperature before serving: 10 minutes if made with Tuscan kale, 30 minutes if made with curly kale.

Yields 6 side-dish servings

NUTRITIONAL INFORMATION
(per serving)

calories 200	sodium (mg) 230	vitamin A IUs 210%
fat calories 120	total carbohydrates (g)....19	vitamin C 140%
total fat (g) 14	fiber (g) 3	calcium 10%
sat fat (g).....................1.5	sugars (g) 9	iron..............................8%
cholesterol (mg) 0	protein (g) 4	

VINAIGRETTE

- 3 tablespoons fresh lemon juice
- 1 tablespoon maple syrup

Coarse salt (kosher or sea)

Freshly ground black pepper

- 4 tablespoons extra-virgin olive oil
- 2 tablespoons diced dates
- 1 medium garlic clove, minced

Dried red pepper flakes

- 6 loosely packed cups washed, patted dry, stemmed, ¼-inch crosswise slices Tuscan kale (*cavolo nero*) or curly kale

GARNISH ½ cup toasted slivered almonds (*see Cook's Note*); ⅓ cup dried cranberries

1. To make the vinaigrette: In a small bowl, whisk together the lemon juice and syrup; season with salt and pepper. Add the oil in a thin stream, whisking constantly. Stir in the dates, garlic, and a generous pinch (or more) of pepper flakes. Set aside.

2. Put the kale in a medium-large bowl. Stir the vinaigrette and pour it on the kale; toss well. If using Tuscan kale, allow it to sit at room temperature for 10 minutes before serving. If using curly kale, allow it to sit at room temperature for 30 minutes before serving.

3. Taste and adjust the seasoning as needed. Divide the salad between 6 plates. Top with the almonds and cranberries. Serve.

COOK'S NOTE To toast slivered almonds, place them in a single layer on a rimmed baking sheet. Bake in a 350-degree-F oven for 3 to 4 minutes, or until lightly browned. Watch carefully because nuts burn easily. Let them cool before use.

Breakfast Toasts with Kale and Sunny-Side Up Eggs

Kale-topped toasts adorned with sunny-side up eggs make a nutritious breakfast treat, but they also could be the centerpiece of a tasty lunch or supper. If you prefer firmer yolks, turn the eggs to cook them on both sides, or substitute moist scrambled eggs or scrambled egg whites.

Yields 4 servings

NUTRITIONAL INFORMATION
(per serving)

calories 300	sodium (mg) 700	vitamin A IIUs............310%
fat calories 120	total carbohydrates (g)... 27	vitamin C 210%
total fat (g) 14	fiber (g) 5	calcium 30%
sat fat (g)........................4	sugars (g) 4	iron...........................20%
cholesterol (mg) 190	protein (g) 17	

Four ⅜-inch slices rustic whole-wheat bread

1½ tablespoons extra-virgin olive oil

5 tablespoons grated Parmesan cheese

6 loosely packed cups washed, patted dry, stemmed, ¼-inch crosswise slices Tuscan kale (*cavolo nero*) or curly kale

1 large garlic clove, minced

1½ tablespoons fresh lemon juice

Nonstick vegetable oil cooking spray

4 eggs

Seasoned salt

1. Adjust an oven rack to 8 inches below the broiler element. Preheat the broiler. Put the bread in a single layer on a rimmed baking sheet. Broil until it is just lightly browned, about 30 seconds. Turn the bread over and lightly brush it with about ½ tablespoon of the oil. Sprinkle each toast with 1 tablespoon of the cheese. Return them to the broiler. Keep a close eye on the toast; broil until it is lightly browned on the second side, about 40 to 50 seconds.

2. Line a large plate with paper towels. Heat the remaining 1 tablespoon oil in a large, deep skillet on medium-high heat. Add the kale, garlic, and ¼ cup water; season with salt and pepper. When the liquid comes to a boil, cover and cook until the kale is tender, about 6 to 8 minutes, tossing the mixture two or three times during cooking (curly kale will take longer to cook than Tuscan kale). Remove the lid and cook until most of the liquid evaporates, about 1 minute. Add the lemon juice and toss. Place the kale on the paper towel–lined plate.

3. Generously coat a medium nonstick skillet with cooking spray. Place it on medium-high heat. When it is hot, add the eggs one at a time, spacing them apart. Reduce the heat to low. Cook until the whites are set, about 2 minutes.

4. Place the toasts on four plates. Divide the kale between the toasts. Using a spatula, remove each egg from the skillet and place it on top of a layer of kale. Sprinkle the eggs with seasoned salt and the remaining cheese. Serve immediately.

KIWI

also Chinese Gooseberry, Kiwifruit

Don't let the itchy exterior fuzz deceive you. Inside kiwi's brown skin is a juicy, sweet-tart treat. The flesh is most often a bright lime green, but there are varieties that are gold. No matter the hue, the delicious flesh is dotted with tiny edible seeds that line up around a soft whitish core.

For a funny little furry fruit, the kiwi is a giant in nutrition, with vitamins, minerals, and phyto-chemicals in abundance.

NUTRITIONAL INFORMATION
(per 1 cup raw, chopped)

calories 108	sodium (mg) 5	vitamin A IUs 3%
fat calories 8	total carbohydrates (g)... 26	vitamin C 273%
total fat (g) 1	fiber (g) 5	calcium 6%
sat fat (g).........................0	sugars (g) 16	iron.............................. 3%
cholesterol (mg) 0	protein (g) 2	

ACES HIGH
Kiwis are near the top of the food chain when it comes to antioxidant vitamins. They contain abundant vitamin C, plus a good amount of vitamin E and even vitamin A. While all three help protect your DNA from damage by pollution and toxins, the vitamin C is concentrated enough to contribute twice the daily value to your diet as it goes toward building the collagen that supports your skin. The vitamin E is part of the structure of every cell in your body, keeping the immune system on track and contributing to the efficiency of nerve functions. And vitamin A helps prevent cataracts and keeps the retina functioning.

GOOD FUNCTION
Scientists in Taiwan recently discovered that kiwifruit can significantly improve the function of the lower digestive system, especially in people with disorders of that organ. A well-functioning lower G.I. means better health and balance for the entire immune system, plus enhanced weight and blood sugar management.

OMEGAS ALL AROUND
Kiwi is a surprising source of omega-3 oils, with 32 milligrams in a single fruit. Omega-3s have been connected to multiple health benefits, protecting against cancer; boosting heart, nerve, and brain function; and possibly lowering risks of cognitive deficit, symptoms of asthma, and depression.

AVAILABLE
Year-round

KEEP IT FRESH

The skin should be unblemished, without nicks or cracks. The fruit should give to gentle pressure but shouldn't be too soft or mushy. Size doesn't affect taste. The fruit should smell fragrant, but if it needs ripening, leave it at room temperature out of direct sunlight for 2 to 3 days. Ripening time can be shortened by placing kiwi in a loosely sealed paper bag with an apple, banana, or pear at room temperature out of direct sunlight. Refrigerate ripe kiwi (unwashed, dry, unpeeled) in the crisper drawer for up to 3 to 4 days.

LAST-MINUTE PREP

Wash with cold water. The skin, especially with smaller "baby" kiwi, is paper-thin and can be eaten. Or when the skin is fuzzy or thick, peel it with a paring knife, cutting just deep enough to remove the exterior. If kiwi is fairly large and you want to eat it out of hand, cut off one end and scoop out the flesh with a small spoon.

QUICK COOK

Kiwi is most often eaten raw. When adding it to a mixture such as fruit salad, or using it as a topping such as a fruit tart, add it at the last minute. It tends to break down the other fruits, making them a little mushy.

try it!

IN MINI TARTS

Buy or make tiny graham cracker tartlet shells. Just before serving, fill the cooled shells half full with plain Greek-style yogurt lightly sweetened with honey. Top each with a slice of peeled kiwi and 2 or 3 fresh blueberries.

IN NUT-BREAD TEA SANDWICHES

Cut moist, dense date-nut quick bread into ¼-inch slices (if the bread is crumbly, it won't work for this recipe). Spread half the slices with a layer of whipped cream cheese and top with a single layer of peeled kiwi slices. Top each adorned bread slice with a second slice of bread and press gently to slightly compact. Cut them crosswise into ¾-inch strips and serve.

IN SALAD WITH POMEGRANATE AND ORANGES

Combine 1½ tablespoons white wine vinegar and ¼ cup extra-virgin olive oil in a small bowl. Season with salt and pepper and ⅛ teaspoon dried red pepper flakes; stir to combine. Put 6 cups mixed baby greens in a salad bowl and toss with just enough dressing to barely coat the leaves. Divide the salad between six salad plates. Peel and slice 3 kiwis. Peel 2 navel oranges (or seeded Valencia oranges) and cut them into slices. Alternate kiwi and orange slices atop the salads. Drizzle with the remaining dressing. Scatter ¾ cup pomegranate seeds on top and serve.

Tilapia with Kiwi-Papaya Salsa

Known for its mild flavor and white flesh, tilapia is an extremely versatile fish. Here it is lightly coated with a beer batter that is spiked with cayenne and cumin, then sautéed in a bit of oil. The fruit-based salsa steals the show, offering a sweet-spicy-tart balance to the dish.

Yields 4 servings

NUTRITIONAL INFORMATION
(per serving)

calories 250	sodium (mg) 165	vitamin A IUs 8%
fat calories 60	total carbohydrates (g)...20	vitamin C 110%
total fat (g) 7	fiber (g) 3	calcium 4%
sat fat (g) 1	sugars (g) 8	iron................................ 8%
cholesterol (mg) 55	protein (g) 25	

SALSA

- 1 cup peeled, diced kiwi
- 1 cup peeled, seeded, diced papaya
- ¼ cup finely diced red onion
- ½ seeded, minced jalapeño
  (*see Cook's Note*)
- 1½ tablespoons fresh lime juice
- 1 tablespoon chopped fresh cilantro
- 1 teaspoon minced peeled fresh ginger
- Coarse salt (kosher or sea)

FISH

- 3 tablespoons whole-wheat flour
- 2 tablespoons all-purpose flour
- ½ teaspoon ground cumin
- ½ teaspoon seasoned salt
- ¼ teaspoon cayenne
- ½ cup beer (lager)
- 4 teaspoons canola oil
- 1 pound tilapia fillets, each cut in half crosswise

1. To make the salsa: Prepare this just before cooking the fish so that the fruit maintains the desired texture. Combine the kiwi, papaya, onion, jalapeño, lime juice, cilantro, and ginger in a nonreactive bowl, such as glass or ceramic. Season with salt. Gently toss and set aside.

2. To make the fish: In a medium bowl, combine both flours, the cumin, seasoned salt, and cayenne. Stir to combine. Whisk in the beer. Heat 2 teaspoons of the oil in a large nonstick skillet on medium-high heat. Coat half the fillets with batter, allowing the excess to run back into the bowl. Add the fillets in a single layer to the skillet. Cook until they are golden and just barely cooked through, about 3 minutes on each side. Repeat with the remaining oil and fillets.

3. Taste the salsa and adjust the seasoning if needed. Spoon the salsa over the fish.

COOK'S NOTE Use caution when working with fresh chiles. Upon completion, wash your hands and work area thoroughly. Do *not* touch your eyes or face.

MEATLESS ALTERNATIVE Serve this salsa over grilled tofu (see page 112).

Skinny Cheesecake Parfaits

This thick, cream cheese pudding-like mixture contrasts beautifully with the refreshing mixture of kiwis and strawberries. Feel free to tinker with the fruit formula. Tangerine sections are a beautiful counterpoint to the kiwi slices, as are raspberries, blueberries, or blackberries.

Yields 8 small servings

NUTRITIONAL INFORMATION
(per 8 servings)

calories 80	sodium (mg) 100	vitamin A IUs 0%
fat calories 0	total carbohydrates (g).... 17	vitamin C 80%
total fat (g) 0	fiber (g) 1	calcium 8%
sat fat (g)........................0	sugars (g) 14	iron............................0%
cholesterol (mg) 0	protein (g) 4	

4 ounces fat-free cream cheese

4 ounces vanilla fat-free Greek-style yogurt

¼ cup agave syrup, plus more if needed

½ teaspoon vanilla extract

4 kiwis, peeled, halved lengthwise, cut crosswise into ⅜-inch slices

10 ripe strawberries, sliced lengthwise

1. In a food processor bowl, combine the cream cheese, yogurt, syrup, and vanilla. Whirl until smooth and well combined.

2. Just before serving, in a medium bowl, gently toss together the kiwi and strawberries using a rubber spatula. Taste. If the berries aren't very sweet, add a drizzle of agave syrup and gently toss again.

3. Divide the cheese mixture between eight small stemmed bowls or wine glasses. Top with the fruit and serve.

COOK'S NOTES It is best to assemble these desserts no more than 10 minutes before serving, but the cheese mixture can be mixed in advance, placed in serving dishes, and covered airtight in the refrigerator.

If desired, garnish each serving with a small sprig of fresh mint or a fresh, pesticide-free lavender blossom.

Breakfast Bowls with Toasted Quinoa, Kiwi, and Strawberries

This recipe makes more of the crunchy quinoa topping than is used in the dish. The mixture can be thoroughly cooled and stored airtight up to 1 week at room temperature. Use it atop rice, baked apples, or sliced stone fruit.

Yields 6 servings

NUTRITIONAL INFORMATION
(per serving)

calories 290	sodium (mg) 60	vitamin A IUs 2%
fat calories 70	total carbohydrates (g)... 39	vitamin C 60%
total fat (g) 8	fiber (g) 3	calcium 15%
sat fat (g)..................... 2.5	sugars (g) 13	iron............................. 15%
cholesterol (mg) 10	protein (g) 18	

1¼ cups white quinoa

1 tablespoon plus 1 teaspoon agave syrup

1 tablespoon vegetable or canola oil

1 cup sliced ripe strawberries

2 kiwis, peeled, halved lengthwise, cut into crosswise slices

4 cups plain or vanilla 2 Greek-style yogurt

1. Preheat the oven to 375 degrees F. Rinse the quinoa in a fine strainer under cold running water for about 45 seconds; shake the strainer to remove as much water as possible.

2. Put the well-drained quinoa on a rimmed baking sheet. Pour 1 tablespoon of the syrup and the oil on top; mix with a rubber spatula or clean hands to combine. Spread the quinoa into a single layer as much as possible. Bake until it is crisp, stirring occasionally, about 10 to 11 minutes. Remove the baking sheet to a cooling rack to cool thoroughly.

3. In a medium bowl, toss the strawberries and kiwis with the remaining 1 teaspoon syrup.

4. Divide the yogurt between six bowls. Top each with some fruit mixture and about 2 tablespoons of the crunchy quinoa. Serve.

KUMQUAT

Tastewise, kumquats are like inside-out oranges. The peel is sweet, while the interior is tart. When eaten together, skin and all, the two flavors balance in an appealing way, making a sweet-sour marmalade-style taste.

If you are a first timer at eating a whole kumquat, give it a chance. With the initial chew, it will taste a little bitter, but keep chewing. Give the flavors a chance to develop in your mouth. Most likely you will be hooked by the sweet-tart flavor and citrus fragrance.

Small seeds generally dot the interior and are soft and edible. If large seeds are present, they should be removed and discarded. Cut the fruit in half lengthwise or into slices. If there are any large seeds, use the point of a paring knife to pluck them out.

The kumquat's edible skin is a source of concentrated sesquiterpenes, a class of natural chemicals that have demonstrated pronounced therapeutic actions as antioxidants throughout the body.

NUTRITIONAL INFORMATION
(per 1 cup raw, sliced kumquats)

calories 140	sodium (mg) 20	vitamin A IUs 12%
fat calories 14	total carbohydrates (g).... 31	vitamin C 146%
total fat (g) 2	fiber (g) 12	calcium 12%
sat fat (g).......................... 0	sugars (g) 4	iron............................... 12%
cholesterol (mg) 0	protein (g) 0	

INFLAMMATION FIGHTER
Kumquats are sources of dozens of phytochemicals, which together include antioxidant, anti-bacterial, antimicrobial, and anti-inflammatory abilities. Inflammation often is the cause of joint pain and results from disorders such as obesity and impaired vascular dysfunction.

PAIN RELIEVER
Studies indicate that compounds in kumquat peel can act as an analgesic, fighting pain both orally and psychologically as a component of aromatherapy.

OXYGEN PUMP
The sesquiterpenes in kumquats have a unique function. They mimic hemoglobin by carrying oxygen molecules in the blood. This allows them to help arrest cancer cells directly by preventing DNA damage through effectively "smothering" with oxygen the cancer development process in cells.

AVAILABLE
November to July

KEEP IT FRESH

Buy kumquats that are plump and firm, without shriveling. The fruit should feel heavy for its size. Refrigerate kumquats, unwashed and dry in a plastic bag in the crisper drawer, up to 1 week.

LAST-MINUTE PREP

Wash kumquats in cold water before use. Pat them dry. Cut them in half lengthwise or slice, removing any large seeds with the point of a paring knife.

QUICK COOK

Kumquats can be eaten raw or cooked. When cooked, they are most often sliced and gently simmered in a simple sugar syrup made with equal parts sugar and water. They can also be cooked in syrup made with half water and half agave syrup, or half water and half honey.

try it!

IN FRUIT SALADS

Thinly slice and add a small amount of kumquats to fruit salad to balance sweet fruit such as ripe strawberries, pears, or grapes.

GLAZED

A glazed kumquat and dried cranberry jumble is an irresistible topping. It can be scattered over anything from pancakes to cottage cheese, green salads to angel food cake. In a small, heavy-bottomed skillet or saucepan, combine 6 kumquats (cut crosswise into ¼-inch slices, large seeds removed), 1 tablespoon dried cranberries, ⅔ cup water, and 1½ tablespoons sugar or agave syrup. Bring them to a boil on high heat. Reduce the heat to medium to maintain vigorous bubbling around the edge of the pan. Cook for 10 to 12 minutes, or until almost no liquid remains. Remove from the heat, stir, and transfer to a rimmed plate to cool.

IN ICED TEA TO ADD DAZZLE

Use sliced kumquats as a colorful garnish for iced tea.

Beet Salad with Kumquat-Almond Relish

The earthiness of roasted beets teams beautifully with any kind of citrus, especially oranges, tangerines, or kumquats. In this salad, a relish serves as the dressing. It is made by combining finely chopped raw kumquats with toasted almonds, a smidgen of cayenne pepper, and extra-virgin olive oil. The dressed beets sit atop mixed baby greens and are crowned with a small portion of crumbled blue cheese.

Yields 8 first-course servings

NUTRITIONAL INFORMATION
(per serving, without cheese)

calories 150	sodium (mg) 300	vitamin A IUs 40%
fat calories 80	total carbohydrates (g)....15	vitamin C 25%
total fat (g) 9	fiber (g) 5	calcium.........................4%
sat fat (g)........................1	sugars (g) 9	iron...............................8%
cholesterol (mg) 0	protein (g) 3	

2 **pounds beets, each with 1-inch stem attached**

2 **tablespoons sherry vinegar or champagne vinegar**

Coarse salt (kosher or sea)

4 **tablespoons extra-virgin olive oil**

3 **tablespoons finely chopped shallot**

2½ **tablespoons finely chopped chives**

1 **medium garlic clove, peeled**

⅓ **cup slivered almonds, toasted** (*see Cook's Note*)

Pinch cayenne pepper

⅓ **cup finely chopped, seeded kumquats**

7 **cups mixed baby greens**

OPTIONAL GARNISH 8 teaspoons crumbled blue cheese

1. Preheat the oven to 400 degrees F. Wash the beets thoroughly in cold water. Wrap the wet beets 3 or 4 to a packet in heavy-duty aluminum foil. Place the packets in a single layer on a rimmed baking sheet. Roast until they are fork tender, 30 to 60 minutes, depending on their size. When cool enough to handle, slip off the peels and cut off the stems. Cut the beets into ½-inch chunks.

2. In a medium bowl, combine the vinegar and ¾ teaspoon salt; whisk to dissolve the salt. Whisk in 3 tablespoons of the oil. Stir in the shallots and chives. Add the beets and gently toss to combine.

3. In a food processor fitted with the metal blade, with the motor running, drop the garlic through the feed tube and process until it is minced. Add the almonds, a pinch of salt, and the cayenne. Pulse just enough to finely chop the almonds. Stir in the remaining 1 tablespoon oil and the kumquats. Add the relish to the beets and gently toss. Taste and adjust the seasoning as needed.

4. Divide the greens between eight salad plates. Top with the beet salad. If desired, top each salad with 1 teaspoon blue cheese.

COOK'S NOTE To toast slivered almonds, place them in a single layer on a rimmed baking sheet. Bake in a 350-degree-F oven for 3 to 4 minutes, or until lightly browned. Watch carefully because nuts burn easily. Cool the nuts before using them in this recipe.

Roasted Broccoli and Kumquats

Kumquats take on an inviting caramelization when roasted, giving them a little added sweetness without depleting their signature spark. Roasting them alongside broccoli florets brings out the sweeter side of the vegetable as well. A pinch of dried red pepper flakes brings an alluring balance, adding a spicy heat to the dish.

Yields 6 to 8 side-dish servings

NUTRITIONAL INFORMATION
(per serving)

calories 90	sodium (mg) 170	vitamin A IUs 50%
fat calories 60	total carbohydrates (g).....7	vitamin C 140%
total fat (g) 6	fiber (g) 4	calcium 6%
sat fat (g)........................1	sugars (g) 1	iron.................................6%
cholesterol (mg) 0	protein (g) 3	

1½ **pounds broccoli florets (about 8 cups)**

6 **kumquats, thinly sliced, large seeds removed**

⅛ **teaspoon dried red pepper flakes**

3½ **tablespoons extra-virgin olive oil**

3 **medium garlic cloves, finely chopped**

Salt

Freshly ground black pepper

1. Preheat the oven to 425 degrees F. In a large bowl, toss together the broccoli, kumquats, and pepper flakes. Drizzle on 3 tablespoons of the oil and toss to coat. Spread the mixture out on a rimming baking sheet, leaving a little space between the broccoli and kumquats. Roast for 15 minutes.

2. In the same bowl, toss the garlic and remaining ½ tablespoon oil. Add it to the broccoli on the baking sheet; gently toss. Roast an additional 10 to 12 minutes, until the broccoli is nicely browned. Season with salt and pepper.

Bulgur Wheat Salad with Kumquats, Cranberries, and Nuts in Lettuce Cups

Bulgur (wheat kernels that have been steamed, dried, and crushed) has a slightly chewy texture when rehydrated. It is sold in many supermarkets, Middle Eastern markets, and natural foods stores. Often it is labeled according to its size; fine is number 1, medium is number 2, coarse is number 3, and extra-coarse is number 4. The coarse-ground number 3 bulgur is best for this delicious concoction.

Yields 8 servings

NUTRITIONAL INFORMATION
(per serving)

calories 80	sodium (mg) 150	vitamin A IUs 15%
fat calories 60	total carbohydrates (g).....6	vitamin C 25%
total fat (g) 7	fiber (g) 2	calcium.......................2%
sat fat (g)........................1	sugars (g) 3	iron.............................4%
cholesterol (mg) 0	protein (g) 2	

Salt

1 cup coarsely ground bulgur (number 3 grind preferred)

6 kumquats, quartered lengthwise, large seeds removed

1 tablespoon dried cranberries

½ cup packed fresh Italian parsley

3 tablespoons fresh lemon juice, plus more if needed

2½ tablespoons extra-virgin olive oil

2 tablespoons plain fat-free Greek-style yogurt

OPTIONAL ¼ teaspoon harissa or hot sauce, such as Sriracha

⅓ cup diced red onion

¼ cup dry-roasted mixed nuts, roughly chopped (*see Cook's Note*)

8 butter or Bibb lettuce leaves

1. Bring 2 cups water and ½ teaspoon salt to a boil in a medium saucepan on high heat. Add the bulgur and stir to combine. Cover and reduce the heat to low. Simmer 10 to 15 minutes, or until the bulgur is tender. Drain it if all the water is not absorbed. Transfer the bulgur to a bowl; fluff it with a fork. Add the kumquats and cranberries; toss and let cool.

2. In a food processor or blender, combine the parsley, juice, oil, yogurt, and harissa, if using. Whirl until smooth. Stir in the onion.

3. Spoon the dressing over the bulgur mixture. Add the nuts and toss. Taste and add salt and/or more lemon juice if needed. Spoon the mixture into the lettuce leaf "cups" and serve.

COOK'S NOTE If you use salted mixed nuts, you probably won't need to add any salt to the mixture.

Curried Kumquat Sauce

A good dose of curry powder gives this sweet-sour sauce the scent and taste of a wide variety of warm spices. Although formulas vary, most curry powders contain coriander, turmeric, cumin, fenugreek, and red pepper. Many also contain ginger, fennel seed, cinnamon, cloves, mustard seed, green cardamom, black cardamom, nutmeg, and black pepper. Try the sauce spooned over grilled tofu or fish.

Yields about 3 cups

NUTRITIONAL INFORMATION
(per 1/4 cup serving)

calories 70	sodium (mg) 45	vitamin A IUs 2%
fat calories 20	total carbohydrates (g) 11	vitamin C 20%
total fat (g) 2	fiber (g) 2	calcium 4%
sat fat (g) 0	sugars (g) 8	iron 1%
cholesterol (mg) 0	protein (g) 1	

1½ tablespoons extra-virgin olive oil

1 medium red onion, roughly chopped

¼ cup sherry vinegar

¼ cup (packed) dark brown sugar

1 tablespoon granulated sugar or maple syrup

2½ tablespoons dry white wine

3½ cups fat-free low-sodium vegetable or chicken broth

1¾ cups kumquats, about 18, quartered lengthwise, large seeds removed

1 tablespoon curry powder, mild or hot

1 star anise

1 tablespoon minced fresh thyme

Salt

1. Heat the oil in a large, deep skillet on medium-high heat. Add the onion and cook until it is softened, stirring occasionally, about 5 minutes. Reduce the heat to medium-low and cook until it is lightly browned, about 5 minutes. Add the vinegar, both sugars, and the wine; stir to combine and cook until the pan is almost dry.

2. Stir in the broth, kumquats, curry powder, and star anise. Bring to a boil on high heat; reduce the heat to medium-low and simmer vigorously until the mixture is reduced by two-thirds, about 45 minutes. Remove and discard the star anise. Stir in the thyme. Season with salt. Let the sauce cool or serve warm over grilled fish or tofu.

MÂCHE
also Lamb's Lettuce, Field Lettuce, Corn Salad

Mâche's spoon-shaped leaves grow in a cluster in small loose heads. Bright green and tender, the delicate leaves have pronounced sweetness and a subtle nuttiness. Sometimes mâche is labeled "lamb's lettuce," a name acquired due to the leaf's resemblance to the shape of a lamb's tongue.

While all fruits and veggies are good sources of dietary potassium, mâche is one of the best sources in its class, with about double the amount of this crucial mineral compared to other lettuces. Just a 3-ounce portion has almost 25 percent of the daily requirement.

NUTRITIONAL INFORMATION
(per 1 packed cup raw)

calories 12.5	sodium (mg) 10	vitamin A IUs 50%
fat calories 0	total carbohydrates (g)... 1.5	vitamin C 20%
total fat (g) 0	fiber (g) 1	calcium 5%
sat fat (g) 0	sugars (g) 0	iron 10%
cholesterol (mg) 0	protein (g) 1.5	

NITROGEN NEUTRALIZER

Although it's a key component in protein, nitrogen can be toxic. Our body uses the mineral manganese to help the body metabolize nitrogen. That's where mâche comes in: It is one of the better vegetable sources of manganese.

OMEGA SURPRISE

Mâche is a uniquely good source of vegetarian omega-3 fatty acids. It's been estimated that around half of the fat-acid content in mâche is of the omega-3 class, with more than 300 milligrams in 4 ounces. Omega-3s help to promote cognitive function and heart health, keep arteries clear, and protect against cancer and birth defects while relieving symptoms of diabetes, arthritis, and even depression.

AVAILABLE

Year-round

KEEP IT FRESH

Mâche leaves are tender and delicate; they can be a little limp but still be fresh. They should be free of discoloration and have a fresh scent. Refrigerate it unwashed, loose in an unsealed plastic bag, up to 3 days (but because it is highly perishable, use as soon as possible).

LAST-MINUTE PREP

Wash the leaves in a tub of cold water. Drain well in a colander. If using raw, gently pat them dry with a clean kitchen cloth or paper towels. Mâche is somewhat fragile, so treat it with a light touch.

QUICK COOK

Mâche is most often eaten raw. If served as a hot vegetable, the best method to cook it is steaming just until it is barely tender. It is also delicious in soup, generally added in the last few minutes of cooking.

try it!

WITH A WATERMELON-TOMATO SALAD

Toss together 2 cups watermelon cubes, 1 cup ripe yellow tomato chunks, 1 cup fresh mozzarella cubes, and 2 tablespoons chopped fresh mint. Make a vinaigrette by mixing 1½ tablespoons red wine vinegar with 5 tablespoons extra-virgin olive oil; season with salt and red pepper flakes. Gently toss the salad with the vinaigrette. Taste and season as needed. Serve the salad over beds of mâche.

IN TACOS OR SANDWICHES

Instead of traditional shredded cabbage or standard lettuce in tacos or sandwiches, use mâche.

WITH A CLASSIC FRUIT AND CHEESE COMBO

Gently toss 6 cups mâche with 2 apples (cored, thinly sliced unpeeled Fuji, Ambrosia, or Gala), 1 tablespoon fresh lemon juice, and ½ cup toasted walnut pieces. In a separate bowl, make the dressing: Whisk ⅓ cup extra-virgin olive oil with 2 tablespoons balsamic vinegar, season with salt and pepper, then stir in 3 ounces crumbled blue cheese. Add the dressing to the salad; toss and taste. Adjust the seasoning.

Mâche and Beet Salad Platter

A stunning addition to a buffet table, this colorful salad is arranged in three portions on an elongated platter. A tangle of mâche salad sits in the middle, with red beets on one side and yellow on the other. The beets can be cooked and tossed with vinaigrette several hours in advance, making it a very practical dish for entertaining.

Yields 10 servings

NUTRITIONAL INFORMATION
(per serving)

calories 170	sodium (mg) 125	vitamin A IUs 20%
fat calories 100	total carbohydrates (g).... 17	vitamin C 20%
total fat (g) 11	fiber (g) 5	calcium 2%
sat fat (g) 1.5	sugars (g) 11	iron 8%
cholesterol (mg) 0	protein (g) 3	

8 medium red beets, with 1-inch stem attached

8 medium golden beets, with 1-inch stem attached

1 large lemon, zested and juiced (*see Cook's Note*)

1 lime, zested and juiced

1½ tablespoons honey

1 teaspoon Dijon mustard

Salt

Freshly ground black pepper

½ cup extra-virgin olive oil

5 cups mâche

1. Preheat the oven to 400 degrees F. Wash the beets thoroughly in cold water. Wrap the wet beets 3 or 4 to a packet in heavy-duty aluminum foil. Place the packets in a single layer on a rimmed baking sheet. Roast until they are fork tender, 30 to 60 minutes, depending on their size. When cool enough to handle, slip off the peels and cut off the stems. Cut the beets into ½-inch chunks. Place each color of beets in a separate bowl.

2. In a bowl or measuring cup with a handle, whisk together the juices, zests, honey, and mustard, and season with salt and pepper. Add the oil in a thin stream, whisking constantly. Pour one-third of the vinaigrette over each color of beets and gently toss.

3. Place the mâche in a bowl. Toss it with the remaining vinaigrette.

4. Taste the beets and adjust the seasoning if needed. On a rectangular or oval platter, arrange the red beets at one end and the yellow beets at the opposite end. Place the mâche in the center. Serve.

COOK'S NOTE Always remove zest from citrus before juicing.

Cream of Mâche Soup

Mâche's sweet side is showcased in this creamy, puréed soup. The amount of evaporated nonfat milk needed to make a rich, spoonable purée varies, so add it ¼ cup at a time until the desired consistency is reached.

Yields 6 servings

NUTRITIONAL INFORMATION
(per serving)

calories 110	sodium (mg) 160	vitamin A IUs 35%
fat calories 5	total carbohydrates (g).... 21	vitamin C 40%
total fat (g) 0	fiber (g) 3	calcium 15%
sat fat (g) 0	sugars (g) 9	iron............................. 4%
cholesterol (mg) 0	protein (g) 5	

4 cups fat-free low-sodium vegetable or chicken broth

1½ (packed) cups mâche

1 large onion, coarsely chopped

1 cup coarsely chopped celery

1 cup coarsely chopped peeled carrots

1 small green pepper, cored, seeded, coarsely chopped

½ cup coarsely chopped fresh parsley

1 bouquet garni (see Cook's Note)

⅓ cup dry long-grain brown rice

About 1 cup evaporated nonfat milk

Coarse salt (kosher or sea)

Freshly ground black pepper

OPTIONAL GARNISH plain fat-free Greek-style yogurt

1. In a 6-quart pan or Dutch oven, combine the broth, mâche, onion, celery, carrots, green pepper, parsley, and *bouquet garni*. Stir in the rice and bring the mixture to a boil on high heat. Reduce the heat to medium and cook, partially covered, for 35 minutes or until the vegetables are very soft. Remove the *bouquet garni* and discard it.

2. Working in three or four batches, process the soup in a food processor fitted with the metal blade or a blender (hold down the lid with a pot holder). Return the purée to the saucepan. Add enough milk to make a creamy consistency. Reheat the soup on medium heat until hot. Taste and season with salt and/or pepper.

3. Ladle the soup into bowls and serve. If desired, top each serving with a small spoonful of yogurt.

COOK'S NOTE To make a *bouquet garni*, enclose 1 bay leaf, 1 peeled garlic clove, 2 whole cloves, and 1 or 2 sprigs of fresh thyme (or 1 teaspoon dried) in a double layer of cheesecloth; tie the ends together to secure the bundle, or tie them with cotton string.

Stuffed Chicken Breasts with Herbed Cheese and Mâche

Reduced-fat "light" versions of store-bought spreadable cheeses are made using nonfat milk. Brands such as Alouette offer these spreadables amped with garlic and herbs. They add both flavor and creaminess to fillings. Toasted pecans augment the cheese in this filling for pockets cut into boneless, skinless chicken breasts. Once cooked, the chicken is sliced and fanned over a tasty mâche salad.

Yields 4 servings

NUTRITIONAL INFORMATION
(per serving)

calories 280	sodium (mg) 230	vitamin A IUs 60%
fat calories 120	total carbohydrates (g).....6	vitamin C 25%
total fat (g) 14	fiber (g) 3	calcium.........................4%
sat fat (g)..........................2	sugars (g) 2	iron.............................10%
cholesterol (mg) 80	protein (g) 33	

- 3 tablespoons coarsely chopped pecans, toasted (*see Cook's Note*)
- ⅓ cup light garlic-herb spreadable cheese
- Four 5- to 6-ounce boneless, skinless chicken breasts
- Coarse salt (kosher or sea)
- Freshly ground black pepper
- 2 tablespoons extra-virgin olive oil
- 5 cups mâche
- ½ red bell pepper, cored, seeded, diced
- 2 teaspoons fresh lemon juice

1. Adjust an oven rack to the middle position. Preheat the oven to 350 degrees F. In a small bowl, stir together the nuts and cheese.

2. Using a small sharp knife, cut a horizontal pocket in each chicken breast. Leave three sides intact and try not to pierce the top or bottom (if you do, it still will work—it just won't look as good). Fill each pocket with the cheese mixture and close with a wooden toothpick. Season with salt and pepper.

3. Heat 1 tablespoon of the oil in a large ovenproof skillet. Add the chicken breasts top-side down. Cook until they are nicely browned, about 5 minutes. Turn over the chicken. Place the pan in the oven; cook 10 to 12 minutes, or until no pink color remains in the meat (cooking times will vary depending on the size). Set aside for 5 minutes.

4. Meanwhile, in a large bowl, toss the mâche and bell pepper with the remaining 1 tablespoon oil. Sprinkle it with the lemon juice. Toss. Season with salt and pepper; toss.

5. Divide the mâche between four plates. Cut each chicken breast into ¾-inch slices. Fan the slices atop the mâche mixture. Serve.

COOK'S NOTE To toast coarsely chopped pecans, place them in a single layer on a rimmed baking sheet. Bake in a 350-degree-F oven for about 3 minutes, or until lightly browned. Watch carefully because nuts burn easily. Let cool.

MEATLESS ALTERNATIVE Toss the mâche mixture with chunks of room temperature roasted root vegetables. Mix crumbled goat cheese with minced sun-dried tomatoes and minced basil. Scatter the cheese mixture over the vegetables. Garnish with toasted walnut or pecan halves.

MUSTARD
GREEN

The tender greens of the mustard plant have a bold flavor profile. They have straightforward peppery appeal with a radish-like edge, an attribute that makes them especially gratifying when teamed with something rich. Assertive cheese or rich dishes such as braised short ribs make perfect partners for these spicy greens.

Mustard greens, a relative of broccoli and horseradish, have long been associated with health, including protection against cancer and other diseases.

NUTRITIONAL INFORMATION
(per 1 cup chopped raw)

Calories 15	sodium (mg) 14	vitamin A IUs 118%
fat calories 1	total carbohydrates (g).....3	vitamin C 65%
total fat (g) 0	fiber (g) 2	calcium 6%
sat fat (g)..........................0	sugars (g) 1	iron................................5%
cholesterol (mg) 0	protein (g) 2	

NUTRITION BANK
A full 1 cup of raw mustard greens has only 15 calories yet 2 grams each of protein and fiber, plus two-thirds of your daily vitamin C needs, a day's worth of vitamin A, and more than three times the recommended intake of vitamin K.

LOWER CHOLESTEROL
The fiber content and phenolic components in the leaves and stems of mustard greens help prevent the uptake of cholesterol, acting as a natural cholesterol-lowering agent. Mustard greens and its cousins kale, broccoli, and collard greens can help reduce the risk of atherosclerosis and other cardiovascular diseases.

LIVER LOVER
Other phytochemical compounds in mustard greens have been shown in animal studies to act against impurities taken up by the liver, helping to detoxify it and protect it.

AVAILABLE
Year-round

KEEP IT FRESH
Look for leaves that smell fresh and are free of wilting or discoloration. Refrigerate them unwashed and dry, in a partially closed plastic bag, for up to 3 days, but use as soon as possible because they are highly perishable. Discard any yellowed leaves.

LAST-MINUTE PREP

Place the leaves in a large tub of cold water and swish them; repeat if necessary until the water is clean. Drain in a colander. If the stems are tough, remove by cutting around them with a small, sharp knife. The stems can be used in soups, or composted or discarded. If the leaves are to be used raw in salad, pat them dry with paper towels or a clean kitchen cloth.

QUICK COOK

Mustard greens can be eaten raw; cut clean, trimmed leaves into bite-size pieces and toss them into salads along with milder greens such as baby spinach. Or cut several handfuls of (clean, trimmed) leaves into ½-inch crosswise slices. In a deep skillet or large saucepan, bring ½ cup fat-free low-sodium vegetable or chicken broth or water to a boil on medium-high heat. Add the greens and cover; cook about 3 to 4 minutes. Season with fresh lemon juice or red wine vinegar, salt and pepper, and a drizzle of extra-virgin olive oil.

try it!

IN NOODLE SOUP WITH ATTITUDE

Add a handful of coarsely chopped mustard greens to noodle soup in the last 3 to 4 minutes of cooking.

IN POTATO SALAD

Dress chunks of still-warm fork-tender potatoes with a simple oil and vinegar dressing. Add coarsely chopped mustard greens as desired. Place each serving atop a slice of ripe heirloom tomato.

A LITTLE ATOP RISOTTO

For a garnish, sprinkle about 1 tablespoon finely chopped mustard greens atop individual servings of risotto. If desired, crumble on some goat cheese, too.

Orecchiette with Mustard Greens, Basil, and Pecorino Cheese

Orecchiette translates from Italian as "little ears." Their small, cupped shapes turn them into reservoirs to scoop up and hold tasty ingredients. In this pasta dish, those little cups capture bits and pieces of pungent mustard greens, tangy cheese, garlic, and herbs, along with pine nuts and a smidgen of dried red pepper flakes. To save time and energy, you can use only one pot of double-duty boiling water—first to cook the greens, then to cook the pasta.

Yields 6 first-course or side-dish servings

NUTRITIONAL INFORMATION
(per serving)

calories 370	sodium (mg) 320	vitamin A IUs 160%
fat calories 80	total carbohydrates (g)...58	vitamin C 60%
total fat (g) 8	fiber (g) 4	calcium 10%
sat fat (g)........................1	sugars (g) 3	iron............................10%
cholesterol (mg) 0	protein (g) 13	

2 pounds mustard greens, thick ribs removed, leaves washed and cut crosswise into 1-inch strips (still damp), 10 to 11 cups

1 pound dry whole-grain orecchiette or gemelli pasta

2 tablespoons extra-virgin olive oil

3 large garlic cloves, minced

¼ to ½ teaspoon dried red pepper flakes

1 tablespoon chopped fresh basil

3 tablespoons toasted pine nuts (*see Cook's Note*)

Coarse salt (kosher or sea)

Freshly ground black pepper

GARNISH ⅓ cup grated Pecorino Romano cheese

1. Put a large pot of salted water on high heat and bring it to a boil. Add the greens and cook until they are tender, about 5 minutes. Remove the greens with a slotted spoon and put them in a colander, refresh with cold water, and drain.

2. Add the pasta to the boiling water and cook until it is al dente (following the package directions). Drain the pasta, reserving 1 cup of the cooking water. Working one handful at a time, squeeze the greens to remove excess water.

3. Heat the oil in a large, deep skillet on medium-high heat. Add the garlic and pepper flakes; cook until the garlic is starting to soften, about 30 seconds. Add the greens and cook, separating the leaves with a spatula. Add the basil and pine nuts; toss. Add the pasta; toss. Add enough of the reserved pasta water to make a creamy sauce. Season with salt and pepper.

4. Spoon the pasta into individual small bowls. Top with the cheese.

COOK'S NOTE To toast pine nuts, place them in a small skillet on medium-high heat. Shake the skillet to redistribute the nuts so they won't overbrown on one side. Cook until lightly browned. Watch carefully because nuts burn easily.

Salad with Mustard Greens and Baby Spinach

The sweetness in baby spinach and a dressing made with maple syrup help balance the pungent spiciness of mustard greens. If you like, place each serving on top of a toasted slice of rustic whole-wheat bread.

Yields 8 servings

NUTRITIONAL INFORMATION
(per serving)

calories 120	sodium (mg) 230	vitamin A IUs 40%
fat calories 90	total carbohydrates (g).....6	vitamin C 15%
total fat (g) 11	fiber (g) 1	calcium 8%
sat fat (g)........................2	sugars (g) 3	iron...............................4%
cholesterol (mg) 5	protein (g) 3	

DRESSING

- 3 tablespoons seasoned rice vinegar
- ⅛ teaspoon salt
- 2 tablespoons maple syrup
- 2 teaspoons Dijon mustard
- ⅓ cup extra-virgin olive oil
- 1 large garlic clove, minced
- 1 tablespoon finely sliced fresh chives

SALAD

- 1 pound mustard greens, thick ribs removed, leaves washed, patted dry, torn into bite-size pieces, about 4 cups
- 4 cups baby spinach leaves, washed, patted dry

OPTIONAL ¼ cup dried cranberries

Freshly ground pepper to taste

- ⅓ cup shaved Parmesan cheese

1. To make the dressing: In a small bowl or glass measuring cup with a handle, stir together the vinegar and salt until the salt dissolves. Add the syrup and mustard; whisk to combine. Drizzle in the oil while whisking. Stir in the garlic and chives.

2. To make the salad: Put the mustard greens and spinach in a large bowl. Add the cranberries, if using. Stir the dressing and pour it over the greens. Toss to coat. Season with pepper. Taste and adjust the seasoning.

3. Divide the salad between eight small bowls or salad plates. Top with the Parmesan and serve.

Southeast Asian Chicken Soup with Mustard Greens

Thai yellow curry paste gives this soup its signature wealth of flavors and aromas. The paste's warm spices, such as cinnamon, cloves, and nutmeg, along with lemongrass, garlic, and chiles, give the soup its sour-sweet profile. And mustard greens add a just-right note of peppery hot verve.

Yields 6 servings

NUTRITIONAL INFORMATION
(per serving)

calories 290	sodium (mg) 490	vitamin A IUs 30%
fat calories 170	total carbohydrates (g)....13	vitamin C 20%
total fat (g) 19	fiber (g) 2	calcium.........................4%
sat fat (g).......................14	sugars (g) 1	iron............................20%
cholesterol (mg) 65	protein (g) 19	

5 cups fat-free low-sodium chicken or vegetable broth

One 15-ounce can unsweetened coconut milk or "light" coconut milk

2½ teaspoons Thai yellow curry paste

1 pound bone-in chicken thighs, skin removed

3 Roma tomatoes, diced

8 ounces mustard greens, thick ribs removed, leaves washed, patted dry, torn into bite-size pieces, about 2 cups

1 cup cooked brown or black rice

3 tablespoons fresh lime juice

¼ cup chopped fresh cilantro

3 green onions, thinly sliced (including dark green stalks)

Coarse salt (kosher or sea)

OPTIONAL GARNISH fish sauce, Asian-style hot sauce (such as Sriracha), torn fresh mint, bean sprouts, lime wedges

1. In a 4- to 6-quart pot or Dutch oven, stir together the broth, coconut milk, and curry paste. Bring them to a simmer on medium heat. Add the chicken and tomatoes; cover and reduce the heat to medium-low. Gently simmer for 25 minutes, or until the chicken is thoroughly cooked. Remove the pan from the heat.

2. Using a slotted spoon, remove the chicken to a plate. When it is cool enough to handle, shred the meat with a fork and return it to the soup. Return it to a simmer on medium heat. Add the greens and simmer for 5 minutes. Add the rice and lime juice; cook until the rice is heated, about 1 minute. Stir in the cilantro and green onions. Taste and season with salt.

3. Place the garnishes on a platter on the table. Ladle the soup into bowls and serve.

MEATLESS ALTERNATIVE Omit the chicken. Add 2 cups (about 1 pound) cubed extra-firm tofu in step 3.

NECTARINE

Nectarines are a fuzz-free subspecies of peaches, blessed with intoxicating fragrance and luxurious texture. Often their shape is more rounded than peaches and their flesh is a little denser. The white varieties have a very high degree of sweetness, while the yellow-fleshed varieties have a pleasing edge of tartness.

Recent analyses have added to the list of healthy phytochemicals cloaked in this juicy summer fruit. If a big bite of ripe nectarine fills you with a Zen-like joy, it might be more than the sweet reminiscence of summers past. Nectarines contain a compound called chlorogenate that French scientists found to have antianxiety effects.

NUTRITIONAL INFORMATION
(per 1 cup, sliced)

calories 63	sodium (mg) 0	vitamin A IUs 9%
fat calories 4	total carbohydrates (g) 15	vitamin C 13%
total fat (g) 0	fiber (g) 2	calcium 1%
sat fat (g) 0	sugars (g) 11	iron 2%
cholesterol (mg) 0	protein (g) 2	

CANCER PROTECTOR
The antioxidants in nectarines and other stone fruits have proven particularly specific for helping reduce the risks of cancer of the esophagus, head, and neck, according to scientists in Asia and at the National Institutes of Health.

B STRONG
Nectarines and other stone fruits are uniquely good sources of the vitamin niacin, also known as vitamin B_3. Niacin is involved in numerous metabolic functions, including blocking the development of low-density lipoproteins (the less desired cholesterol) that naturally helps increase the ratio of high-density lipoproteins (the more desired cholesterol).

AVAILABLE
May to September (United States), December to February (Chile)

KEEP IT FRESH
Deep red or maroon skin isn't necessarily a sign of ripeness. Look for fruit that gives to gentle pressure at the stem end (shoulders) and smells fragrant. Don't be shy; take a good whiff. Nectarines soften after harvest, so the texture can improve. But they do not ripen after they are picked, meaning that the sugar content and perfume do not substantially improve. To soften, leave them at room temperature for 2 to 4 days or use the brown bag method: Place them in a loosely sealed paper bag with an apple, banana, or pear at room temperature, out of direct sunlight. Refrigerate ripe fruit, unwashed and dry, loose in the crisper drawer for 7 to 9 days.

LAST-MINUTE PREP

Wash with cold water. Nectarines have very thin skin and usually do not require peeling. However, they can be peeled fairly easily with a paring knife. Or submerge in simmering water for about 1 minute (the riper it is, the less time it needs to simmer); refresh with cold water and slip off the skin by grasping it between a paring knife and your thumb, and pull it off in strips. To remove the pit, cut the fruit in half from top to bottom following the suture (seam). Twist halves in opposite directions and lift out the pit. If it is stubborn, use a spoon or a melon baller. If not using cut nectarines right away, rub them with lemon juice or dip them in a bowl of cold water augmented with a little fresh lemon juice.

QUICK COOK

Nectarines are often used raw but are also delicious cooked. Unlike peaches, nectarines can be cooked skin-on and the peel stays attached to the flesh. So simmer, poach, or use them in baked goods unpeeled if you like. Or grill them: Cut ripe (but not squishy) nectarines in half and remove the pits. Brush the cut sides with canola oil and grill them on medium heat until fairly dark marks form, about 2 to 3 minutes. Remove from the heat and lightly brush them with honey.

try it!

IN AN AMBROSIA UPDATE

Put 1½ cups fresh pineapple chunks in a medium bowl; add 1 unpeeled nectarine (pitted, cut into chunks) and 8 ounces low-fat peach yogurt. Gently toss. Top each serving with a good pinch of toasted flaked coconut.

IN SALAD, GRILLED AND SLICED

Grill 2 nectarines (see Quick Cook). In a small bowl, whisk together 2 tablespoons champagne vinegar and 3 tablespoons walnut oil and season with salt and pepper. In a large bowl, toss the dressing with 4 cups mixed baby greens. Divide the salad onto four plates. Slice the grilled nectarines and place them on top of each serving. Scatter ½ cup roasted, salted walnuts over the salads. Crumbled feta or blue cheese is an optional topping.

HOT-AND-SOUR MARKET-STALL STYLE

On a platter, arrange 2 ripe nectarines (pitted, cut into wedges), ½ jícama (peeled, cut into thin wedges), 2 Persian (baby) cucumbers (quartered lengthwise), 1 ripe avocado (pitted, cut into wedges or slices), and 2 limes (cut into wedges). In a small bowl, mix equal parts coarse salt and good-quality red chili powder. Instruct guests to sprinkle each portion with lime juice and some salt-chili mixture before eating.

Nectarine, Almond, and Blue Cheese Pita Pizzas

Crisp whole-grain pita breads are the tempting foundations for these fruit-nut pizzas. Browned sweet onion pulls the dish together, offering sweetness as well as a tantalizing aroma. The almonds play an important supporting role—both for flavor and crunch. Other nuts work well, too, including pistachios, hazelnuts, or walnuts.

Yields 8 servings

NUTRITIONAL INFORMATION
(per serving)

calories 170	sodium (mg) 270	vitamin A IUs 2%
fat calories 70	total carbohydrates (g) 21	vitamin C 4%
total fat (g) 8	fiber (g) 3	calcium 8%
sat fat (g) 2	sugars (g) 3	iron 6%
cholesterol (mg) 5	protein (g) 6	

⅓ cup whole almonds, unblanched

1 tablespoon extra-virgin olive oil

1 large sweet onion, such as Maui, cut into ¼-inch slices

1 large unpeeled nectarine, halved, cut into thin wedges

2 tablespoons balsamic vinegar

Freshly ground black pepper

Eight 4-inch whole-grain pita breads

½ cup crumbled blue cheese

1 tablespoon finely chopped fresh basil

1. Adjust an oven rack to the middle position and preheat the oven to 350 degrees F. Coarsely chop the almonds, leaving some only chopped in halves or thirds. Spread them on a rimmed baking sheet and bake until nicely browned, about 8 to 9 minutes. Set aside. Increase the oven temperature to 450 degrees F.

2. Heat the oil in a large nonstick skillet on medium-high heat; add the onion and cook, stirring occasionally, until it is tender and lightly browned, about 6 minutes. Add the nectarine wedges and cook until they are heated through, about 1½ minutes. Add the vinegar and season with pepper; cook until most of the liquid is gone and the onion is glazed, about 2 minutes.

3. Put the pitas on a large rimmed baking sheet and top with the nectarine mixture. Sprinkle them with the cheese and bake until the cheese melts and the pitas are crisp, about 10 to 15 minutes. Top with the nuts and basil.

Nectarine, Mango, and Black Bean Salsa

Not only do black beans taste wonderful in this salsa, but also they bring a good amount of nutrients to the table. One cup has about 15 grams of both protein and fiber. Grilled pork, chicken, or fish, as well as tofu or asparagus, perk up with a spoonful or two of this colorful mix. It is also scrumptious served atop brown rice or other cooked grains, such as farro or barley.

Yields 6 servings

NUTRITIONAL INFORMATION
(per serving)

calories 90	sodium (mg) 200	vitamin A IUs 20%
fat calories 5	total carbohydrates (g)....19	vitamin C 70%
total fat (g) 0	fiber (g) 4	calcium 2%
sat fat (g).........................0	sugars (g) 10	iron...............................4%
cholesterol (mg) 0	protein (g) 3	

1 ripe nectarine, diced

1 ripe mango, diced

½ red bell pepper, diced

½ hothouse cucumber, peeled and diced

1 cup canned black beans, drained and rinsed

1 jalapeño, seeded, veins removed, minced (*see Cook's Note*)

2 limes, juiced

3 tablespoons finely chopped fresh cilantro

Coarse salt (kosher or sea)

In a nonreactive bowl, such as glass or ceramic, combine all the ingredients. Gently toss with a rubber spatula. Allow the salsa to rest for 30 minutes at room temperature. Taste and adjust the seasoning as needed. Spoon over grilled chicken, fish, pork, or tofu. Or serve with toasted pita chips to use as dippers (*see Cook's Note*, page 327).

COOK'S NOTE Use caution when working with fresh chiles. Upon completion, wash your hands and work area thoroughly; do *not* touch your eyes or face.

Toasted Couscous Salad with Nectarines and Ricotta Salata

When ricotta cheese is salted and aged, it is called ricotta salata. The cheese is firm and good for grating or shaving. Its just-right saltiness offers the perfect flavor contrast for this couscous and nectarine salad. If you prefer, substitute other stone fruit for the nectarines. Apricots and plumcots as well as nectarines are especially delicious in this dish.

Yields 8 servings

NUTRITIONAL INFORMATION
(per serving)

calories ... 340	sodium (mg) ... 280	vitamin A IUs ... 15%
fat calories ... 170	total carbohydrates (g) ... 39	vitamin C ... 15%
total fat (g) ... 19	fiber (g) ... 7	calcium ... 8%
sat fat (g) ... 3	sugars (g) ... 8	iron ... 10%
cholesterol (mg) ... 5	protein (g) ... 9	

COUSCOUS

- 1½ teaspoons extra-virgin olive oil
- 1 cup whole-wheat couscous
- ⅛ teaspoon ground cumin
- ⅛ teaspoon ground cinnamon
- ⅛ teaspoon salt
- 1¼ cups boiling water

DRESSING

- 2½ tablespoons fresh lemon juice
- 1 teaspoon cider vinegar
- 1 teaspoon honey
- 1 teaspoon minced lemon zest
- Coarse salt (kosher or sea)
- Freshly ground black pepper
- ⅓ cup extra-virgin olive oil
- ½ medium red onion, finely diced
- 1 tablespoon finely chopped fresh mint

SALAD

- 2 ripe nectarines, halved and pitted
- ½ cup slivered almonds, toasted (*see Cook's Note*)
- 3 pitted dates, cut crosswise into ¼-inch slices
- 4 cups baby spinach
- 2 ounces ricotta salata cheese

1. To make the couscous: In a large, deep skillet, heat the oil on medium heat. Add the couscous and sprinkle the cumin, cinnamon, and salt on top. Cook, stirring occasionally, until the couscous lightly browns, about 4 minutes. Add the boiling water; stir and cover. Remove the skillet from the heat and let it sit for 12 minutes. Remove lid.

2. To make the dressing: In a small bowl or glass measuring cup with a handle, whisk together the lemon juice, vinegar, honey, and zest and season with salt and pepper. Whisk in the oil in a thin stream. Stir in the onion and mint.

3. To make the salad: Put the nectarine halves cut-side down on a cutting board. Cut each in half lengthwise. Cut each half crosswise into ⅜-inch slices.

4. Put the couscous in a large bowl and fluff it with a fork. Stir the dressing and add it to the couscous. Toss. Add the nectarines, almonds, and dates. Toss. Taste and adjust the seasoning as needed.

5. Divide the spinach between eight salad plates. Top with the couscous. Shave the ricotta on top (a vegetable peeler works well for this).

COOK'S NOTE To toast slivered almonds, place them in a single layer on a rimmed baking sheet. Bake in a 350-degree-F oven for 3 to 4 minutes, until lightly browned. Watch carefully because nuts burn easily.

OKRA

Don't wince. Okra can be downright delicious. If you avoid it because you don't like the texture, you've probably been cooking it wrong. Mucilaginous juices exude when okra are sliced and cooked in liquid. Quick-cooking them whole with dry heat keeps them in slime-free bliss.

Fresh okra needs just a flash in a hot sauté pan to keep it crisp and bright green and preserve its various nutrients or a light coat of oil—just a little—and some time on a grill. Its taste is a pleasant cross between green bean and eggplant, with an inviting trace of grassiness.

NUTRITIONAL INFORMATION
(per 1 cup raw, sliced)

calories 31	sodium (mg) 8	vitamin A IUs 7%
fat calories 1	total carbohydrates (g) 7	vitamin C 35%
total fat (g) 0	fiber (g) 3	calcium 8%
sat fat (g) 0	sugars (g) 1	iron 4%
cholesterol (mg) 0	protein (g) 2	

PROTEIN PRO
As one of civilization's oldest cultivated foods, okra has proven a significant plant source of protein and fiber for thousands of years. Each cup contains 2 grams protein, necessary for building tissues and creating the enzymes that power every action of the body.

SUPER FIBER
Okra also delivers 1 gram of fiber per ounce. As well as fiber's connection to heart health and the reduction of risk of certain cancers, the mucilaginous form of fiber in okra has been shown to reduce inflammation in the digestive tract associated with obesity and disease.

THINK OKRA
The phytochemicals rutin and quercetin concentrated from okra surprised researchers in a recent animal study at Mahasarakham University in Thailand by reducing cognitive deficit and having a neuroprotective effect.

AVAILABLE
Year-round with gaps in availability in late fall and early spring

KEEP IT FRESH
Look for tender pods that are 2 to 3 inches long, without discoloration or soft spots. They should be crisp. Test one; it should snap crisply when broken in half. Refrigerate okra, dry and unwashed, in a paper bag in the crisper drawer for up to 4 days.

LAST-MINUTE PREP

Wash with cold water and pat dry. Trim a tiny portion from the tip without piercing the interior and a small portion off the stem.

QUICK COOK

Breading with cornmeal then deep-frying is the choice of many cooks, but lightly coating okra with a little bit of oil and grilling it is a great alternative. Preheat a grill to medium heat. Thread the okra crosswise, placing 4 per slender bamboo skewer. Brush them with oil and season with coarse salt and pepper. Grill until they are caramelized (some spots will be lightly blackened). Or cook, oiled but unskewered, in a grill pan over medium heat, turning with tongs.

try it!

IN EGGS

In a bowl, lightly beat 4 eggs and 2 eggs whites and season with salt and pepper. Heat 1½ tablespoons extra-virgin olive oil in a medium nonstick skillet on medium-high heat. Add ¾ cup sliced okra and 1 green onion (sliced); cook until the onion starts to brown. Reduce the heat to medium-low. Add the eggs, and stir until the eggs are set. Serve over brown rice and top with tomato salsa.

WITH LEMONS AND CARROTS

Cut 12 ounces peeled carrots into ¼-inch slices on the diagonal; put them in a medium saucepan. Cut 1 lemon in half and squeeze the juice from one half into the pan. Cut the remaining half into thin slices and add it to the pan. Add ¼ cup water and a good pinch of salt. Bring them to a boil. Cover and reduce the heat to low. Simmer for 25 minutes; do not remove the lid, but shake the pan back and forth from time to time. Meanwhile, grill 8 ounces okra (see Quick Cook). Cut it into ¼-inch slices and toss it with the carrot-lemon mixture.

COOKED WITH GARLIC

Peel 2 large garlic cloves and cut them into thin crosswise slices. Heat 1 tablespoon canola oil in a large, deep skillet on medium-high heat. Add the garlic and cook until it is fragrant but not browned, about 45 seconds. Add 12 ounces whole okra and toss to coat. Cook on medium heat, shaking the pan frequently, until the okra is tender, about 5 minutes. Season with seasoned salt. If desired, top with crumbled crisp bacon.

Chopped Mediterranean Salad with Grilled Okra

Grilled okra gets a royal treatment in this classic Mediterranean salad. Oregano scents the dressing that tops a mixture of grilled okra, chopped lettuce, Provolone, garbanzo beans, and grape tomatoes. If you prefer, cook the okra in a hot grill pan on top of the stove instead of using the grill.

Yields 5 servings

NUTRITIONAL INFORMATION
(per serving, without salami)

calories 270	sodium (mg) 170	vitamin A IUs 80%
fat calories 160	total carbohydrates (g)....19	vitamin C 25%
total fat (g) 18	fiber (g) 6	calcium 8%
sat fat (g)...................... 3.5	sugars (g) 5	iron............................. 15%
cholesterol (mg) 10	protein (g) 9	

6½ ounces fresh medium okra
1 tablespoon extra-virgin olive oil
Coarse salt (kosher or sea)
Freshly ground black pepper

DRESSING
1 tablespoon red wine vinegar
2 teaspoons fresh lemon juice
2 teaspoons dried oregano
1 medium garlic clove, minced
¼ cup extra-virgin olive oil

SALAD
4 cups chopped iceberg
(*see Cook's Note*)
2 cups grape tomatoes, halved lengthwise
One 15-ounce can garbanzo beans, drained, rinsed
2 ounces Provolone cheese, diced

OPTIONAL 2 ounces salami, cut into ⅛-inch matchsticks

1. Preheat a grill to medium heat. Thread the okra crosswise, placing 4 per slender bamboo skewer. Brush them with the oil and season with salt and pepper. Grill until the okra are caramelized (some spots will be lightly blackened). Set aside to cool.

2. To make the dressing: In a small bowl or glass measuring cup with a handle, whisk together the vinegar, juice, oregano, and garlic. Season with salt and pepper. Whisk in the oil in a thin steam. Taste and adjust the seasoning as needed.

3. To make the salad: In a large bowl, combine the lettuce, tomatoes, beans, and cheese. If desired, add the salami. Stir the dressing and pour it over the salad. Toss. Cut the okra into ⅜-inch crosswise slices and add them to the salad. Toss.

COOK'S NOTE Use half romaine and half iceburg lettuce if you prefer.

Bulgur Pilaf with Grilled Okra and Corn

This bulgur-based concoction could charm even the most jaded palate. Grilled corn and okra give the dish a welcome hint of smokiness, and the skinny pieces of vermicelli offer a toothsome starchiness. A spinach salad is a pleasing accompaniment.

Yields 6 side-dish servings

NUTRITIONAL INFORMATION
(per serving)

calories 210	sodium (mg) 190	vitamin A IUs 6%
fat calories 80	total carbohydrates (g)....31	vitamin C 20%
total fat (g) 9	fiber (g) 7	calcium 4%
sat fat (g).....................2.5	sugars (g) 3	iron................................6%
cholesterol (mg) 10	protein (g) 6	

4½ ounces fresh medium okra

2 teaspoons extra-virgin olive oil

Coarse salt (kosher or sea)

Freshly ground black pepper

1 large ear corn, husked

PILAF

2⅓ cups fat-free, low-sodium chicken or vegetable broth

1½ tablespoons butter

1½ tablespoons extra-virgin olive oil

1 large yellow onion, chopped

½ cup 1-inch pieces vermicelli or fideo pasta

1 cup medium-grind bulgur (number 2 or number 3, see page 200)

Seasoned salt

2 tablespoons chopped fresh Italian parsley

1. Preheat a grill to medium heat. Thread the okra crosswise, placing 3 per slender bamboo skewer. Brush them with the oil and season with salt and pepper. Grill the okra and corn until they are caramelized (some spots will be lightly blackened). Set aside to cool. When the corn is cool enough to handle, cut the kernels off the cob.

2. To make the pilaf: Bring the broth to a boil in a small pot.

3. Put the butter and oil in a large saucepan with a tight-fitting lid over medium-high heat. Add the onion and cook until softened, stirring occasionally, about 4 to 5 minutes. Add the vermicelli and toss to coat; cook, stirring frequently, for 1 minute. Stir in the bulgur, and season with seasoned salt and pepper. Add the broth. Cover and reduce the heat to low. Simmer, covered, for 10 minutes, until the pasta is al dente.

4. Meanwhile, cut the okra into ⅜-inch crosswise slices.

5. Add the okra and corn to the bulgur mixture, but don't stir it in. Cover and remove the pan from the heat. Allow it to sit off the heat for 10 minutes. Toss. Taste and adjust the seasoning as needed.

Quick Pickled Okra and Carrots

Drained and coarsely chopped, these quick pickles are perfect atop tostadas and taco salads. Or leave whole and skewer them on a cocktail pick to use as a garnish for a Bloody Mary with attitude.

Yields 3 to 4 cups

NUTRITIONAL INFORMATION
(per tablespoon)

calories ...50	sodium (mg) ...530	vitamin A IUs ...100%
fat calories ...0	total carbohydrates (g)...13	vitamin C ...25%
total fat (g) ...0	fiber (g) ...2	calcium ...4%
sat fat (g)...0	sugars (g) ...10	iron...2%
cholesterol (mg) ...0	protein (g) ...1	

2¼ cups cider vinegar

½ cup agave syrup

1 tablespoon salt

8 ounces crinkle-cut carrot chips or 12 ounces carrots, peeled and cut into ½-inch diagonal slices

1 red onion, cut top to bottom into ¼-inch wedges

2 large jalapeños, cut into lengthwise eighths *(see Cook's Note)*

8 ounces fresh okra

1. In a large saucepan or Dutch oven, combine the vinegar, syrup, salt, and 3 cups water. Bring to a boil on high heat. Stir to combine. Add the carrots, onion, and jalapeños; stir and return the mixture to a boil.

2. Reduce the heat to medium to medium-low. Gently boil (rigorous bubbles around the edge, but none in the middle) until the carrots are tender-crisp, about 10 minutes. Add the okra and continue to gently boil for 1 minute. Pour everything into a heatproof nonreactive bowl. Let it cool completely. Cover and refrigerate for up to 2 weeks.

COOK'S NOTE Use caution when working with fresh chilies. Upon completion, wash your hands and work area thoroughly; do *not* touch your eyes or face.

ORANGE

Blood, Cara Cara, Navel, Valencia

Sweet oranges are the varieties most commonplace in American markets, not the sour Sevilles that are reserved primarily for marmalade production. Ambrosial without a doubt, sweet orange varieties yield irresistible sweet-tart flesh and juice: Cara Cara, navel, Valencia, and blood oranges are ones that are most readily available. The colored portion of the peel known as the zest (but not the bitter white pith beneath it) is edible, too. Oranges are practically synonymous with vitamin C, but these globes win awards for a lot more nutrition than that. Blood oranges, for example, are a good source of lycopene.

NUTRITIONAL INFORMATION
(per 1 cup raw sections of Valencia orange)

calories 88	sodium (mg) 0	vitamin A IUs 8%
fat calories 5	total carbohydrates (g).... 21	vitamin C 145%
total fat (g) 1	fiber (g) 5	calcium 7%
sat fat (g).........................0	sugars (g) 17	iron.................................1%
cholesterol (mg) 0	protein (g) 2	

HDL HELPER
The flavonoids in oranges help to raise the level of HDL (good) cholesterol, while its phytosterols work to block the uptake of cholesterol, leading to an overall decline in LDL (bad) cholesterol and total cholesterol. And the fiber in oranges brings another soldier to the fray in cholesterol control.

COUNTER INFLAMMATION EXPERT
Inflammation is a key component of a number of negative health states, including obesity, diabetes, and arterial disease. Oranges have a wealth of beneficial phytochemicals, such as flavonoids, flavonols, catechins, and other antioxidants (including vitamin C) that allay the inflammation caused by oxygen-damaging free radicals.

FIT, NOT FAT
By reducing inflammation, the beneficial components of oranges help the body regulate blood sugar and balance insulin and glucagon (two primary hunger and satiety hormones). They also boost metabolic control of lipid metabolism. Meanwhile, the glucose in oranges provides a one-two punch by its own sweet contribution to blood-sugar balance: A study in 2010 showed that glucose can diminish inflammation-triggered imbalances.

AVAILABLE
Blood oranges and Cara Cara oranges: domestic, peak December to March; imported, September

Navel oranges: December to March

Valencia oranges: February to November

KEEP IT FRESH

Look for oranges that feel heavy for their size, without soft spots. Skin color varies from variety to variety. Russeting (brown flecks) or green patches on the skin are fine. Dark maroon patches on the skin of blood oranges are an indication that the flesh will be deeply colored. Store oranges at cool room temperature for up to 1 week, or refrigerate loose for up to 3 weeks. Both the zest and juice can be frozen.

LAST-MINUTE PREP

Wash oranges with cold water.

TO CUT CITRUS FRUIT INTO SUPREMES (PEELED SEGMENTS)

Cut the top and bottom off through the white pith to reveal the flesh. Place the fruit cut-side down on a work surface. Following the contour of the fruit, cut off the peel and pith in strips with a sharp knife, starting at the top and cutting down. Working over a bowl (to collect juice), use a small sharp knife to cut parallel to each section's membrane, cutting toward the center. Repeat until all the sections are removed. Squeeze the "skeleton" membranes over the bowl to remove any remaining juice.

QUICK COOK

Oranges are most often eaten raw. The peel (without pith) can be candied or dried.

try it!

AS A MARINADE

Combine fresh orange juice with some fresh thyme leaves, seasoned salt, and a pinch of ground cumin; place in a shallow dish. Add fish fillets in a single layer. Cover with plastic wrap and refrigerate for 30 minutes, turning after 15 minutes. Grill the fish and top with peeled orange segments mixed with sliced green onion.

WITH LIQUEUR AND MINT

Place 3 peeled, sliced oranges on a large plate, slightly overlapping. In a small bowl, stir 1½ tablespoons orange liqueur with 2 tablespoons fresh orange juice or water; drizzle over the orange slices. Top with 3 tablespoons finely chopped fresh mint.

AS A DRESSING

Stir together ⅓ cup fresh orange juice with ½ teaspoon Dijon mustard and 1 tablespoon extra-virgin olive oil. Toss with chilled baby spinach leaves, using just enough dressing to generously coat the leaves. Sprinkle with coarse salt. Garnish the servings with peeled orange segments and toasted nuts.

Orange, Pomegranate, and Date Finale

A delicious trio of flavors tops this sliced orange dessert: honey-sweetened pomegranate molasses, chopped dates, and salted nuts. Syrupy-thick pomegranate molasses is made from concentrated pomegranate juice. It is sold in Middle Eastern markets and at many natural food stores. Tangerines and tangelos can be substituted for the oranges if desired.

Yields 8 servings

NUTRITIONAL INFORMATION
(per serving)

calories 100	sodium (mg) 25	vitamin A IUs 4%
fat calories 20	total carbohydrates (g).... 21	vitamin C 80%
total fat (g) 2	fiber (g) 3	calcium 4%
sat fat (g) 0	sugars (g) 17	iron 2%
cholesterol (mg) 0	protein (g) 2	

4 large navel or Cara Cara oranges, peeled, cut into ⅜-inch rounds

¼ cup chopped dates

1½ tablespoons honey

2 tablespoons pomegranate molasses

¼ cup chopped salted pistachios or mixed nuts

1½ tablespoons pomegranate seeds (arils)

OPTIONAL coarse salt (kosher or sea)

GARNISH 8 sprigs fresh mint or small handful microgreens

1. Lay the orange slices on a large platter, slightly overlapping them if needed. Top with the dates.

2. In a small bowl or glass measuring cup with a handle, whisk together the honey and molasses. Drizzle it on top of the oranges and dates. Top with the nuts and pomegranate seeds. If unsalted nuts are used, sprinkle on a tiny bit of coarse salt if desired. Garnish with sprigs of fresh mint or microgreens.

Iced Green Tea Dazzler with Orange and Ginger

The combination of fresh orange juice, green tea, and ginger is irresistible, especially when fizzy water comes into play. The base for the elixir can be prepared ahead and refrigerated for up to 10 days. At serving time, pour some in a tall glass, then add ice and sparkling water. Voilà—prepare to be dazzled!

Yields about 6 servings

NUTRITIONAL INFORMATION
(per serving)

calories 100	sodium (mg) 0	vitamin A IUs 0%
fat calories 0	total carbohydrates (g)... 26	vitamin C 8%
total fat (g) 0	fiber (g) 0	calcium 0%
sat fat (g) 0	sugars (g) 26	iron 0%
cholesterol (mg) 0	protein (g) 0	

¾ cup dark honey

2 tablespoons roughly chopped orange zest

1 tablespoon minced unpeeled fresh ginger

6 green tea bags

2 tablespoons fresh orange juice

Ice cubes

Sparkling water or club soda

GARNISH orange slices, halved

OPTIONAL GARNISH fresh mint sprigs

1. In a medium saucepan, combine 2 cups water with the honey, zest, and ginger. Bring them to a boil on medium-high heat. Reduce the heat and simmer for 8 to 10 minutes, stirring occasionally, until it gets fragrant. Remove from the heat and add the tea bags; cover and steep off the heat for 10 minutes.

2. Use the back of a spoon to push the tea bags against the sides of the pan to release any liquid. Remove the tea bags and let the liquid cool. Strain it through a fine-mesh sieve. Add the orange juice. The tea mixture may be refrigerated at this point for up to 10 days.

3. For each serving, place several ice cubes in a tall glass. Add ¼ cup tea mixture and top it off with either sparkling water or club soda. Garnish with a half slice of orange. If desired, garnish with a small sprig of mint.

Salmon with Orange and Fennel Salad

Fish and citrus make such a luscious team, since the acidity in the fruit makes the fish taste sweeter. Grilled salmon topped with a salad that showcases orange segments and thinly sliced fresh fennel is one mouth-watering example. Use either a heated grill pan or a barbecue to grill the salmon fillets, or, if you prefer, substitute grilled tofu.

Yields 4 servings

NUTRITIONAL INFORMATION
(per serving)

calories 390	sodium (mg) 115	vitamin A IUs 10%
fat calories 230	total carbohydrates (g)....16	vitamin C 90%
total fat (g) 26	fiber (g) 4	calcium 8%
sat fat (g)......................3.5	sugars (g) 8	iron................................10%
cholesterol (mg) 60	protein (g) 24	

Four 4-ounce skinless salmon fillets

Salt

Freshly ground black pepper

1 teaspoon ground fennel seed

2 large oranges, 1 zested and juiced; 1 cut into supremes (see page 230)

1 teaspoon Dijon mustard

2 tablespoons extra-virgin olive oil

1 small red onion, cut in half from top to bottom, thinly sliced

2 medium bulbs fresh fennel, untrimmed (about 20 ounces)

Canola oil or vegetable oil for brushing grill pan or grill

1 cup baby arugula

1. Place the salmon fillets in a single layer on a large plate. Season with salt, pepper, and the fennel seeds. If using a grill, preheat it to medium-high heat and clean the grate.

2. In a medium bowl, whisk together the zest, orange juice, and mustard, and season with salt and pepper. Whisk in the oil in a thin steam. Add the onion and toss. Set aside.

3. Trim off the dark green stalks and feathery fronds from the fennel bulbs. Roughly chop the fronds and set them aside for garnish. Quarter the bulbs lengthwise; cut out and discard the cores. Cut the quarters into very thin crosswise slices with a mandoline or a sharp knife. Add the fennel slices, chopped fronds, and orange sections to the vinaigrette. Gently toss.

4. If using a grill pan, heat it on medium-high heat. Brush the grill grate or pan with oil. Add the salmon, seasoned-side down. Grill about 5 minutes per side, or until just barely cooked through. Grilling times vary depending on the thickness of the fillets and heat of the grill.

5. Place the salmon on four dinner plates. Add the arugula to the fennel mixture and toss; spoon the salad over the salmon and serve.

MEATLESS ALTERNATIVE Instead of salmon, use marinated and grilled tofu (see page 112).

PAPAYA

Maradol, Red Caribbean, Strawberry

Cut a papaya lengthwise and enjoy the view. The brightly hued flesh—salmon pink, bright orange, or canary yellow—forms an eye-popping contrast to the shimmery black seeds that fill the core. Its aroma is pleasantly musky and the low-acid flesh is juicy and subtly sweet. A squeeze of lime or lemon juice gives it the perky edge it needs.

Papayas are a nutrition giant among fruits. The combination of vitamins and nutraceutical phytochemicals (plus high amounts of pectin fiber) put this tropical favorite on the health map for protection against disease and dysfunction.

NUTRITIONAL INFORMATION
(per 1 cup raw, cubed)

calories 55	sodium (mg) 4	vitamin A IUs 31%
fat calories 2	total carbohydrates (g)....14	vitamin C 144%
total fat (g) 0	fiber (g) 3	calcium 3%
sat fat (g).........................0	sugars (g) 8	iron.................................1%
cholesterol (mg) 0	protein (g) 1	

FOLATE FAVORITE
Papaya contains high amounts of folate, with one small fruit providing 15 percent of your daily needs. Folate helps protect unborn babies from neural tube defects and helps protect the cardio-vascular system from damage.

VITAMIN C STRENGTH
A small papaya also has more than one and a half times the daily vitamin C recommendation. Vitamin C builds collagen for healthy skin, helps regulate a number of enzymes, and has proven crucial to the immune system.

GESUNDHEIT!
Vitamin C turns out to have specific antihistamine effects, helping direct neutrophils, the cells that attack histamine compounds, toward their targets.

BURN NOTICE
The peppery seeds of the papaya serve multiple duties. They contain concentrated papain enzyme that helps break down proteins. Plus, when crushed, they can be used topically to soothe and heal burns.

AVAILABLE
Year-round

KEEP IT FRESH
Ripe fruit should give very slightly to pressure, something like a not-too-ripe avocado. Ripen papayas at room temperature or place them in a loosely sealed paper bag with an apple, banana, or pear at room temperature out of direct sunlight. Refrigerate ripe fruit, unwashed and dry, for up to 3 days.

LAST-MINUTE PREP

Wash with cold water. Cut the fruit in half lengthwise and scoop out the seeds using a spoon. The seeds are edible and have a peppery taste; they can be used whole in dressings for fruit-based salads or as a garnish. Use unpeeled halves as bowls for salads, or remove the skin with a paring knife or vegetable peeler and cut the flesh into strips, chunks, or dice.

QUICK COOK

Most often eaten raw, papaya can also be cooked. To grill, peel and seed a not-overly-ripe papaya and cut it into 2-inch chunks. Thread them on bamboo skewers and brush with canola oil. Sprinkle them lightly with a chili-salt mixture (coarse salt mixed in equal parts with pure chili powder) and grill on medium heat until they are lightly grill marked, about 3 to 4 minutes. Serve with brunch dishes or as an accompaniment to chili or Asian noodle dishes.

try it!

ATOP ASIAN SESAME NOODLES

Cook 8 ounces soba noodles according to package directions; drain. In a small bowl, combine 1½ tablespoons Asian (roasted) sesame oil, 2 tablespoons soy sauce, 1 teaspoon maple syrup, and pinch of dried red pepper flakes. Stir and toss with the noodles and 2 green onions (sliced). Top each serving with slices of peeled, seeded papaya.

IN A SIMPLE MUSHROOM-SPINACH SALAD

Heat 1 tablespoon extra-virgin olive oil in a medium skillet on medium-high heat. Add 6 ounces sliced (stemmed) shiitake mushrooms and cook until they are softened and lightly browned; set aside to cool. Toss the cooled mushrooms and any of their juices with 3 to 4 cups baby spinach and 1½ tablespoons balsamic vinegar. If the salad seems dry, add a little extra-virgin olive oil and toss. Season with salt and pepper. Top each serving with slices of fresh papaya.

AS A CONTAINER FOR FRUIT SALAD

Cut small papayas in half lengthwise. Scoop out the seeds and fill the centers with fresh fruit salad or seafood salad. Diners can scoop out some of the papaya flesh as they eat.

Sichuan-Style Tofu with Papaya and Green Onions

Papaya adds color and flavor to this sweet-sour-spicy Sichuan-themed dish. Only 2 teaspoons of tomato paste are used in this recipe, so what should you do with the leftover paste? Producers solved the problem a few years ago by packaging tomato paste in toothpaste-style tubes. Not all markets stock the handy tubes, but don't despair. Freeze leftover paste in 1-tablespoon portions in a small, zipper-style freezer bag, pressing out as much air as possible before sealing.

Yields 4 servings

NUTRITIONAL INFORMATION
(per serving)

calories 140	sodium (mg) 150	vitamin A IUs 6%
fat calories 70	total carbohydrates (g)....10	vitamin C 35%
total fat (g) 7	fiber (g) 1	calcium 6%
sat fat (g) 0.5	sugars (g) 5	iron..............................10%
cholesterol (mg) 0	protein (g) 9	

14 to 18 ounces firm tofu, drained

3 tablespoons fat-free, low-sodium chicken or vegetable broth

2 teaspoons balsamic vinegar

2 teaspoons tomato paste

1 teaspoon sodium-reduced soy sauce

1 teaspoon agave syrup

½ teaspoon cornstarch

¼ teaspoon dried red pepper flakes

1½ tablespoons canola oil

3 green onions, thinly sliced (including dark green stalks; reserve half for garnish)

¾ cup diced papaya

OPTIONAL FOR SERVING brown rice

1. Cut the tofu crosswise into 1¼-inch slices. Layer several paper towels on a rimmed baking sheet and arrange the tofu in a single layer. Top with 3 layers of paper towels and arrange a second baking sheet on top; place object on top to weight it, such as a bottle of wine or two medium cans. Let the tofu rest for 25 to 30 minutes to fully drain.

2. Meanwhile, combine the broth, vinegar, tomato paste, soy sauce, syrup, cornstarch, and pepper flakes in a small bowl or a glass measuring cup with a handle. Whisk to combine and set aside.

3. Cut the tofu into 1¼-inch cubes. Heat a large wok or large, deep skillet on medium-high heat. Add the oil; when it is hot, add the tofu and reduce the heat to medium. Cook for about 3 minutes on each side, or until the tofu is lightly browned, adding the onions in the last minute of cooking. Stir the sauce and add it to the tofu. Increase the heat to high and cook, stirring frequently, until the sauce clings, about 1 minute. Add the papaya and gently toss. Cook for 30 seconds more, then transfer the stir-fry to a platter or plates. Garnish with the remaining onions. If desired, accompany the stir-fry with cooked brown rice.

Honey-Glazed Salmon with Papaya and Spinach

A sweet-sour onion-spiked sauce brings out the best in fish or tofu. The sauce is a purée made with caramelized red onion augmented with a little brown sugar and champagne vinegar. The tasty topping is spooned over the fish or tofu before it goes under the broiler and forms a lightly browned crust. Papaya and fresh spinach provide a just-right contrast.

Yields 8 first-course servings

NUTRITIONAL INFORMATION
(per serving)

calories 160	sodium (mg) 60	vitamin A IUs 15%
fat calories 60	total carbohydrates (g)....13	vitamin C 45%
total fat (g) 7	fiber (g) 1	calcium........................4%
sat fat (g)........................2	sugars (g) 8	iron...............................6%
cholesterol (mg) 35	protein (g) 12	

1 pound skinless salmon fillet

Coarse salt (kosher or sea)

1½ tablespoons butter or soft tub margarine

⅓ cup diced red onion

2 tablespoons brown sugar

2 tablespoons champagne vinegar

1½ tablespoons honey

2 teaspoons extra-virgin olive oil

Freshly ground black pepper

6 cups baby spinach

1 papaya, cut into narrow strips

1. Adjust an oven rack to 6 to 8 inches below the broiler element. Preheat the broiler.

2. Cut the salmon crosswise into four servings. Line a heavy-duty rimmed baking sheet or the bottom of a broiler pan with aluminum foil. Place the salmon on the prepared pan in a single layer, leaving a little space between each fillet. Season with salt.

3. Melt the butter on medium-high heat in a small saucepan. Add the onion. Cook, stirring occasionally, until the onion is softened and just starting to brown slightly, about 5 minutes. Turn down the heat if the onion is over-browning. Remove the pan from the heat. Add the sugar and vinegar; stir until the sugar dissolves. Put the onion mixture in a blender. Blend until it is puréed, holding down the lid with a pot holder. Add the honey and oil; blend until thoroughly combined, about 20 seconds.

4. Pour the onion mixture over the salmon. Season it liberally with pepper. Broil for 7 to 9 minutes, or until the salmon is lightly browned on top and just barely cooked through. Cooking times will vary depending on the thickness of the salmon. The flesh should be uniformly just-barely opaque.

5. Divide the spinach between eight plates. Cut each fillet in half crosswise. Place a piece of salmon on of each plate. Garnish with the papaya.

MEATLESS ALTERNATIVE Instead of salmon, use 1 pound extra-firm tofu. Cut it into ½-inch crosswise slices. Prepare a pan as for the salmon. Pour the sauce on top of the tofu and broil until it is heated through and the tops are lightly browned, about 5 minutes. Watch it after 2 minutes to monitor the browning.

Papaya with Roasted Grapes and Shaved Parmesan

Roasting grapes with olive oil and fresh thyme gives them condensed sweetness along with a luscious herbal note. Team them with ripe papaya, and the dish pairs perfectly with rich game or pork. The texture and taste are positively exquisite.

Yields 6 servings

NUTRITIONAL INFORMATION
(per serving)

calories 250	sodium (mg) 620	vitamin A IUs 30%
fat calories 130	total carbohydrates (g) ... 25	vitamin C 140%
total fat (g) 14	fiber (g) 3	calcium 20%
sat fat (g) 3.5	sugars (g) 18	iron 6%
cholesterol (mg) 10	protein (g) 9	

- 10 ounces red seedless grapes, stemmed
- 1½ tablespoons extra-virgin olive oil
- 1 teaspoon coarse salt (kosher or sea)
- 1 teaspoon chopped fresh thyme or rosemary
- 1 large shallot, thinly sliced
- 2 teaspoons seasoned rice vinegar
- 4 cups mixed baby greens or baby spinach
- 2 small ripe or 1 large papaya, cut into ¾-inch slices
- 3 ounces Parmesan cheese, shaved
- ½ cup walnut halves, toasted (*see Cook's Note*)

1. Preheat the oven to 475 degrees F. Put the grapes on a rimmed baking sheet and drizzle them with the oil (or enough to nicely coat them); season with the salt and thyme. Toss to coat. Roast for 10 minutes. Add the shallot, scattering it over the grapes. Roast an additional 5 to 10 minutes, or until the grapes are soft inside and slightly crisp and wrinkled on the outside. Some grapes may burst. Remove the pan from the oven and allow it to cool for 5 minutes.

2. Add the vinegar to the baking sheet and use a metal spatula to scrape up any pan drippings.

3. Arrange the greens on a platter, spreading them out to form an even layer. Fan the papaya slightly overlapping on top of the greens. Spoon the grape mixture on top of the papaya, including any pan juices. Top with the Parmesan and walnuts.

COOK'S NOTE To toast walnuts, place them in a single layer on a rimmed baking sheet. Bake in a 350-degree-F oven for 4 to 6 minutes, until lightly browned. Watch carefully because nuts burn easily.

PASSION FRUIT

The word that best describes passion fruit's personality is "vibrant." The no-snooze flavor profile combines the perfume of tropical fruit with the perky flavor of citrus. It's a blend of banana, pineapple, and guava, mixed with lime.

Inside the wrinkled purple rind, BB-size black seeds dot the pulp. They are as crisp as a tortilla chip. Some prefer to strain the seeds from the yolk-colored pulp; others appreciate the crunch and leave them in.

A long list of healthful benefits resides inside the inedible, egg-shaped shell. Vitamins, fiber, iron, and potassium abound in the juicy pulp.

NUTRITIONAL INFORMATION
(per 1 cup, raw)

calories 229	sodium (mg) 66	vitamin A IUs 60%
fat calories 14	total carbohydrates (g)... 55	vitamin C 118%
total fat (g) 2	fiber (g) 25	calcium........................ 3%
sat fat (g)........................0	sugars (g) 26	iron.............................. 21%
cholesterol (mg) 0	protein (g) 5	

ATTENTION MEN
Passion fruit is a great source of lycopene, which a number of studies have suggested helps prevent prostate cancer.

EYES HAVE IT
Lycopene also is part of the carotenoid complex that keeps eyes healthy by protecting the retina and keeping the lenses clear. And as a good source of vitamin A, passion fruit provides a double-carotenoid punch to further keep vision function sharp.

TUMMY SOOTHER
Extracts of passion fruit displayed antiulcer abilities in a recent Indian study, and multiple studies point to anti-inflammatory action from compounds in the fruit. Passion fruit studies on animals with diabetes indicated an ability to help lower blood sugar and facilitate improved blood flow. And if soothing the tummy isn't enough, some researchers discovered evidence of antianxiety capabilities in passion fruit's phytochemical compounds.

AVAILABLE
February to June (New Zealand), August to December (United States)

KEEP IT FRESH

Look for fruits with wrinkled skin; the wrinkles are a sign of ripeness. Ripen those with smooth skin by placing them out of direct sunlight at room temperature, turning them occasionally. Refrigerate ripe fruit loosely enclosed in a plastic bag for up to 1 week.

LAST-MINUTE PREP

Wash with cold water and dry. Cut the fruit in half through the equator. Using a small spoon, scoop the seeds, pulp, and juice from the shell. Discard the shell. Strain the pulp through a medium-mesh sieve or leave the seeds in; they have the consistency of pomegranate seeds (arils).

try it!

AS A GARNISH

Enjoy the crunch; spoon unstrained passion fruit over panna cotta, custard, or yogurt.

IN COMPOUND BUTTER

In a food processor, combine 3 tablespoons strained passion fruit and ½ cup chilled butter; refrigerate thoroughly. Spoon a small knob atop hot grilled shellfish or asparagus. Leftover butter mixture can be frozen

IN BUBBLY

Pour chilled Prosecco into champagne glasses. Add 1 teaspoon strained passion fruit and 1 teaspoon pomegranate juice to each; stir.

Warm Cheesy Pudding with Passion Fruit and Blueberries

Big, bright, and sassy flavors make this special-occasion dessert irresistible. Passion fruit and blueberries bring their vibrant sweet-tart flavors to balance the richness of the creamy cheeses. Mascarpone, that oh-so-rich Italian-style cream cheese, teams with goat cheese to bake into a warm pudding-like base for the fruit topping.

Yields 6 servings

NUTRITIONAL INFORMATION
(per serving)

calories 210	sodium (mg) 170	vitamin A IUs 10%
fat calories 100	total carbohydrates (g)....21	vitamin C 6%
total fat (g) 11	fiber (g) 1	calcium 6%
sat fat (g)...........................6	sugars (g) 13	iron.................................6%
cholesterol (mg) 145	protein (g) 8	

Butter for greasing pan

5 tablespoons soft goat cheese
   (2½ ounces)

4 tablespoons mascarpone (2 ounces)

5 tablespoons sugar

4 eggs, separated

1 teaspoon minced orange zest

½ teaspoon vanilla extract

¼ cup potato starch (*see Cook's Note*)

⅛ teaspoon salt

2 ripe (wrinkled) passion fruit

¾ cup fresh blueberries

OPTIONAL 2 teaspoons honey

1. Adjust an oven rack to the middle position. Preheat the oven to 375 degrees F. Grease a 9-inch glass pie pan with butter.

2. Put the goat cheese, mascarpone, 3 tablespoons of the sugar, the yolks, zest, and vanilla in a food processor. Whirl until smooth and well combined. Add the starch and process until well mixed.

3. In the bowl of an electric mixer, beat the egg whites on medium speed until foamy. Add the salt and increase the speed to high. Beat until soft peaks form. Continue beating, adding the remaining 2 tablespoons sugar, 1 teaspoon at a time. Beat until they are glossy and stiff. Add one-fourth of the meringue to the cheese mixture. Pulse 1 or 2 times to partially incorporate it. Using a rubber spatula, scrape the cheese mixture into the remaining meringue. Gently fold them together. Spoon it into the prepared pie pan and smooth the top with a spatula. Bake until the surface turns golden brown, about 16 to 17 minutes. Place the pan on a wire rack to cool for about 15 minutes (the pudding will flatten slightly).

4. Meanwhile, cut each passion fruit in half and scoop out the seeds and pulp into a small bowl. Add the blueberries and gently toss, breaking up the passion fruit pulp. If desired, sweeten the fruit mixture with honey.

5. Spoon the warm pudding onto six rimmed dessert plates. Top with the fruit mixture so that some of the fruit goes on top and some is spooned on the side. Serve.

COOK'S NOTE Potato starch is used as a thickener for sauces, soups, and stews. It is sold at natural food stores and many supermarkets, where it is often stocked in the kosher or gluten-free sections.

Crunchy Passion Fruit Sweeties

Dollops of honeyed yogurt provide mouthfeel luxury in these snazzy desserts. There is a considerable amount of chewy crunch to contrast that silkiness when passion fruit pulp (with the seeds), granola, and toasted pistachios are layered into the mix. The desserts are best assembled just before serving. Have all the components ready, and they can be put together without any hassle.

Yields 6 small servings

NUTRITIONAL INFORMATION
(per serving)

calories 160	sodium (mg) 90	vitamin A IUs 2%
fat calories 40	total carbohydrates (g)... 23	vitamin C 4%
total fat (g) 4.5	fiber (g) 2	calcium......................... 6%
sat fat (g)......................1.5	sugars (g) 17	iron............................... 2%
cholesterol (mg) 5	protein (g) 8	

3 ripe (wrinkled) passion fruit

2 cups plain low-fat Greek-style yogurt

¼ cup honey

½ cup granola

¼ cup coarsely chopped toasted salted pistachios

1. Cut each passion fruit in half and scoop the seeds and pulp into a small bowl.

2. In another small bowl, stir to combine the yogurt and honey.

3. Set six small stemmed bowls or glasses on the counter. Divide half of the yogurt mixture between them. Divide two-thirds of the passion fruit between the bowls or glasses and top with the granola. Spoon the remaining yogurt on top, then add the remaining passion fruit. Sprinkle on the nuts and serve.

For an easier approach, serve in shallow bowls, and instead of layering, top granola with yogurt and surround with passion fruit.

Passion Fruit Dressing

Chipotle chiles are ripe jalapeños that have been dried and smoked. Most often, they are sold in small cans packed in a tomato-based adobo sauce. Teaming the chipotles with strained passion fruit pulp results in a sweet-spicy dressing that harmonizes well with grilled tofu, fish, chicken, or pork. Or try it as a luscious addition to fruit salads or coleslaw.

Yields about 1 cup

NUTRITIONAL INFORMATION
(per 2 tablespoons)

calories 20	sodium (mg) 0	vitamin A IUs 4%
fat calories 0	total carbohydrates (g) 5	vitamin C 10%
total fat (g) 0	fiber (g) 1	calcium 0%
sat fat (g) 0	sugars (g) 3	iron 2%
cholesterol (mg) 0	protein (g) 0	

6 ripe (wrinkled) passion fruit

1 chipotle chile (canned in adobo sauce)

1 tablespoon white wine vinegar

2 teaspoons agave syrup

½ teaspoon adobo sauce (from the can of chipotles)

1. Cut each passion fruit in half and scoop out the seeds and pulp; strain and discard the seeds.

2. Put the strained pulp in a blender. Add the chipotle, vinegar, syrup, and adobo. Cover and whirl until smooth.

PEACH

Ripe peaches are a regal blend of buttery flesh, summery perfume, and run-down-your-arm juice. Few fruits can compete with their distinctive sweet-tart flavor profile.

Similar to the nutrition profiles of their cousins nectarines and plums, peaches have vitamins and minerals accompanied by phytochemical compounds. These have scientists looking at stone fruits with new respect.

BONES ABOUT IT
Results of a University of Oklahoma study show that the phenolic and flavonoid compounds found in stone fruits are "highly effective in modulating bone mass" and can even contribute to the reversal of previous bone loss.

NUTRITIONAL INFORMATION
(per 1 cup, sliced)

calories ... 60	sodium (mg) ... 0	vitamin A IUs ... 10%
fat calories ... 3	total carbohydrates (g) ... 15	vitamin C ... 17%
total fat (g) ... 0	fiber (g) ... 2	calcium ... 1%
sat fat (g) ... 0	sugars (g) ... 13	iron ... 2%
cholesterol (mg) ... 0	protein (g) ... 1	

CHILL OUT
Some of the concentrated phytochemicals in peach peels could support the neurotransmitter actions that regulate mood and help bring on a sense of calm, while the aroma of a ripe peach has ranked as one of the more emotionally soothing smells in aromatherapy.

NO PAIN, NO PAIN
Peach aromas also have demonstrated analgesic effects, reducing the feeling of pain, lifting depression, and creating a sense of well-being. As a mineral-rich, high-water, high-fiber, low-acid fruit, peaches help soothe the digestive system and maintain hydration.

AVAILABLE
Yellow flesh and white flesh: peak mid-May to September (United States) or December to February (Chile)
Saturn: May to August (United States)

KEEP IT FRESH
Fragrance is a key sign of ripeness, so take a whiff at the stem end. It should smell fragrant. A rosy blush on the skin isn't necessarily a sign of ripeness. The fruit should give to gentle pressure at the stem end. The texture can improve after harvest, but the sugar content and perfume do not substantially improve. To soften, leave peaches at room temperature for 2 to 4 days or use the brown bag method: Place them in a loosely sealed paper bag with an apple, banana, or pear at room temperature out of direct sunlight. Refrigerate ripe fruit, unwashed and dry, loose in the crisper drawer for 7 to 9 days.

LAST-MINUTE PREP

Wash with cold water. If peeling, use a paring knife to cut away the skin, or submerge it in simmering water for about 1 minute; the riper it is, the less time it needs to simmer. Refresh with cold water. Slip off the skin by grasping it between a paring knife and your thumb, and pull it off in strips. To remove the pit, cut the fruit in half from top to bottom following the suture (seam). Twist the halves in opposite directions and lift out the pit. If it is stubborn, pry it out with the tip of a teaspoon, a grapefruit spoon, or melon baller. If you are not using cut peaches right away, rub them with lemon juice or dip in a bowl of cold water augmented with a little fresh lemon juice.

QUICK COOK

Peaches are often used raw but are also delicious cooked in sweet or savory dishes. Most often they are peeled when cooked because their skin loosens when heated in liquids. To quickly grill them, cut ripe (but not squishy) unpeeled peaches in half along the seam, twist to separate, and remove the pits. Brush the cut sides with canola oil and grill them on medium heat until fairly dark marks form, about 2 to 3 minutes. Remove them from the heat and lightly brush the cut sides with a mixture of equal parts honey and balsamic vinegar.

try it!

GRILLED ON ARUGULA SALAD

Roll a log of goat cheese in coarsely chopped toasted pecans; refrigerate. Brush the cut side of halved, pitted peaches with a bit of canola oil. Grill them cut-side down until nicely marked. Drizzle the cut sides with a little honey and season with salt and pepper. Toss baby arugula with enough extra-virgin olive oil to lightly coat it. Season with fresh lemon juice and toss. Serve the grilled peaches atop the arugula and garnish with slices of nut-coated goat cheese.

FANNED DESSERT-STYLE

Make a berry sauce by melting ¾ cup all-fruit, seedless blackberry spread in a small saucepan over medium heat, about 1 minute. Stir in 2 tablespoons fresh lemon juice and ½ teaspoon minced unpeeled ginger; remove from the heat. Peel 3 peaches; cut them into ⅜-inch wedges. Cut 12 hulled strawberries into lengthwise slices. Spoon the sauce on six plates, tilting to spread the sauce. Fan the peach slices on each plate and top with the strawberry slices. Garnish with fresh mint.

IN FRUIT SALAD HEAVEN

Combine peeled, sliced peaches with peeled, sliced mangoes and red grapes. Gently toss the fruit and top each serving with a dollop of lime yogurt.

Peachy Oatmeal with Bittersweet Chocolate Bits

Hot oatmeal soaks up the flavorful juices as peach slices gently heat on its surface. Chopped bittersweet chocolate comes to the party, adding its richness by melting into the warm cereal. What a way to start the day!

Yields 4 servings

NUTRITIONAL INFORMATION
(per serving)

calories 300	sodium (mg) 120	vitamin A IUs 10%
fat calories 45	total carbohydrates (g)... 52	vitamin C 8%
total fat (g) 5	fiber (g) 6	calcium 20%
sat fat (g)........................1	sugars (g) 23	iron..............................15%
cholesterol (mg) 5	protein (g) 12	

2½ cups nonfat milk

Pinch salt

2 cups quick-cooking oatmeal

1½ tablespoons agave syrup

1 teaspoon vanilla extract

2 tablespoons chopped bittersweet chocolate

2 ripe peaches, cut into thin slices

1. Combine the milk and salt in a medium saucepan on medium-high heat. Bring them to a boil. Stir in the oatmeal, syrup, and vanilla. Reduce the heat to medium and cook, stirring frequently, until the mixture is thickened, about 4 minutes.

2. Divide the oatmeal between four shallow bowls. Top with the chocolate, pushing some of the bits down with the back of a spoon. Add the peach slices and serve.

Summertime Composed Tomato and Peach Salad

Pairing tomatoes with peaches may seem like an odd match at first glance. But remember, tomatoes are fruit, and they have a pleasingly sweet edge if harvested when ripe. Tomatoes with peaches and pesto are an inspired combination.

Yields 8 servings

NUTRITIONAL INFORMATION
(per serving)

calories 150	sodium (mg) 390	vitamin A IUs 40%
fat calories 100	total carbohydrates (g).....11	vitamin C 25%
total fat (g) 11	fiber (g) 3	calcium..........................8%
sat fat (g)....................2.5	sugars (g) 8	iron.................................4%
cholesterol (mg) 5	protein (g) 4	

PESTO

- 1 cup (loosely packed) fresh basil leaves, plus extra for garnish
- 1/3 cup extra-virgin olive oil
- 1/3 cup freshly grated Parmesan cheese
- 2 medium garlic cloves, peeled
- 2 tablespoons balsamic vinegar
- 1 teaspoon coarse salt (kosher or sea)
- 1/8 teaspoon dried red pepper flakes

SALAD

- 4 cups mixed baby greens
- 3 large ripe beefsteak tomatoes, cut into wedges
- 3 large ripe peaches or nectarines, cut into wedges (*see Cook's Note*)

1. To make the pesto: In a food processor, combine the basil, oil, Parmesan, garlic, vinegar, salt, and pepper flakes. Whirl until smooth.

2. To make the salad: Spread the greens on a platter. Place the tomato wedges in rows cut-sides up, leaving a space between them. Stir the pesto and drizzle it over the tomatoes. Place the peach wedges, cut-sides up, between the tomato wedges. Garnish with extra basil sprigs and serve.

COOK'S NOTE Many peaches in the marketplace have been mechanically "brushed" to remove their exterior fuzz, so they almost feel as smooth as a nectarine. If you are using fuzzy peaches, you may prefer to peel off the tickle before cutting them into wedges.

Poached Peaches in White Wine

On a hot summer day, chilled peaches afloat in sweet wine is a tempting finale to a lunch or dinner. Poaching works best if the peaches are slightly under-ripe: not rock hard, but with flesh that yields reluctantly when pressed at the stem end.

Yields 6 servings

NUTRITIONAL INFORMATION
(per serving)

calories 110	sodium (mg) 0	vitamin A IUs 6%
fat calories 0	total carbohydrates (g).... 21	vitamin C 10%
total fat (g) 0	fiber (g) 1	calcium 0%
sat fat (g)..........................0	sugars (g) 18	iron...............................2%
cholesterol (mg) 0	protein (g) 1	

¼ cup agave syrup

2 tablespoons fresh lime juice

3 large peaches, peeled, cut into ½-inch wedges (about 4 cups; *see Cook's Note*)

1 cup sweet wine, such as Beaumes de Venise or Sauternes

GARNISH 6 sprigs fresh mint

1. Combine the syrup, juice, and ⅓ cup water in a large saucepan. Stir to combine and add the peach wedges. Gently toss them with a rubber spatula. Bring them to a boil on high heat; cover and reduce the heat to medium-low. Gently simmer for 3 to 5 minutes, until the peaches are tender when pierced with the tip of a knife, but not falling apart. Let them cool.

2. Add the wine to the peaches and gently stir. Cover and refrigerate. Serve in small bowls or stemmed goblets; garnish each serving with a sprig of fresh mint.

COOK'S NOTE Rather than using the submerging method for removing the skin, peel them with a vegetable peeler (a serrated blade on a swivel-bladed peeler works very well).

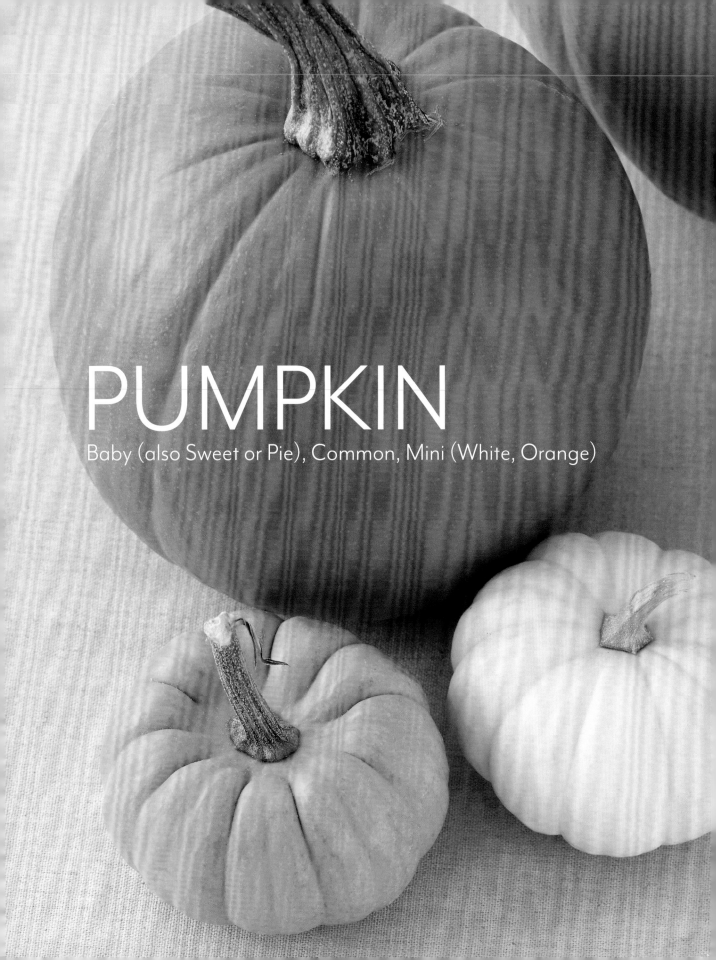

PUMPKIN

Baby (also Sweet or Pie), Common, Mini (White, Orange)

The earthy nuttiness of pumpkin is often enhanced with aromatic spices such as cinnamon, clove, ginger, and nutmeg. Together the flavor-packed team is the centerpiece for a wide variety of both sweet and savory dishes. The deep carroty-orange hue offers visual allure as well, to everything from pies and tarts to pasta sauces and soups.

Baby pumpkins, also labeled "sweet" or "pie," have thicker walls and are the best variety to use for purées. Common pumpkins make showy containers for baking stews and soups. For baking individual servings, mini pumpkins are the best container choice.

Pumpkins are rich in cancer-protective antioxidants, loaded with energy-giving complex carbohydrates, and replete with health-boosting vitamins and minerals—including potassium. In fact, 1 cup of pumpkin has about 20 percent more potassium than a banana.

NUTRITIONAL INFORMATION
(per 1 cup raw common pumpkin, cubed)

calories	30	sodium (mg)	0	vitamin A IUs	35%
fat calories	0	total carbohydrates (g)	8	vitamin C	15%
total fat (g)	0	fiber (g)	less than 1	calcium	2%
sat fat (g)	0	sugars (g)	5	iron	6%
cholesterol (mg)	0	protein (g)	1		

HEALTHY VIEWING

Pumpkin is one of the most concentrated sources of the carotenoid compounds important to health, especially eye health. For vitamin A alone, pumpkin has almost twice the amount as carrots. While the vitamin A works on protecting corneas from cataracts and a condition called xeropthalmia, which causes damage due to drying, two other carotenoids, lutein and zeaxanthin, are absorbed in the retina and protect against age-related macular degeneration, a leading cause of blindness. The lycopene also helps vision health by protecting against diabetic retinopathy.

ROUGH SHELL, SOFT SKIN

In addition to the vitamin A, pumpkin has lots of vitamins C and E, too. All three help make for soft and supple skin. The vitamin C is important for building the collagen that keeps skin structure tight, while the super-antioxidant vitamin A protects against damage from the sun and pollutants. Vitamin E is integral to every cell, helping form the lipid layer that keeps cells intact. These vitamins are important for immunity in general, so you feel good on the inside while you look good on the outside.

ADDITIONAL BONUS

Pumpkin seeds are a good source of omega-3 fatty acids—1 ounce has nearly 4 grams, as well as iron and zinc, which are minerals vital to circulatory health, vitality, and immunity.

AVAILABLE

September to November

KEEP IT FRESH

Store whole pumpkins at room temperature for up to 1 month out of direct sunlight. Refrigerate purée airtight up to 1 week, or freeze up to 3 months in a zipper-style freezer bag (press out air before sealing).

LAST-MINUTE PREP

Wash with cold water. Prep directions vary depending on how the pumpkin is used. Many recipes instruct that the top is cut about 1½ inches below the stem end and removed; the seeds and fibers are removed with a sturdy spoon.

HOW TO ROAST SEEDS

Scoop seeds from the pumpkin and place them in a colander. Run cold water over the seeds and use your fingers to rigorously squish them back and forth, removing the pulp in the process. Drain well. Spread the seeds on two clean dish towels; rub to dry them. It is important that the seeds are dry to roast properly. Preheat the oven to 350 degrees F. For 2 cups of seeds: Toss them in a bowl with 2 tablespoons extra-virgin olive oil, plus either 2 teaspoons ground fennel seed or 1 tablespoon minced dried rosemary or 1 teaspoon ground cardamom combined with ½ teaspoon ground nutmeg. Add coarse salt to taste. Spread the seeds in a single layer on a rimmed baking sheet. Bake 10 to 12 minutes, or until they turn golden. Spread them on paper towels and cool; use as a snack or atop salad or soup.

TO MAKE PUMPKIN PURÉE

Adjust an oven rack to the lower third of the oven; preheat the oven to 375 degrees F. Wash a baby pumpkin (also called "pie" or "sweet") with cold water. Dry. Place it on a cutting board on its side. Cut through the "equator" using a sturdy knife. Use a sturdy spoon to remove the seeds and fiber. Coat a rimmed baking sheet with nonstick cooking spray. Place the pumpkin halves cut-side down on the sheet. Roast for 35 to 40 minutes, or until the pumpkin is fork tender. Remove it from the oven. The skin should be a little loose. When it is cool enough, use a paring knife to pull off and discard the skin. Place the flesh in a food processor and whirl until it is smooth and puréed. If using other pumpkin varieties, the purée may be watery. In that case, drain the purée in a coffee filter for a few minutes to remove excess moisture.

try it!

IN SOUP WITH A SWEET-SPICY EDGE

Warm 1 tablespoon butter and 1 tablespoon olive oil in a 4- or 6-quart saucepan or Dutch oven on medium heat. Add 1 medium onion (chopped); cook until it is softened. Add ½ teaspoon ground cinnamon, ½ teaspoon ground cardamom, and 2 teaspoons dried red pepper flakes; cook for 1 minute, stirring occasionally. Add 3 cups chopped carrots, 6 cups fat-free low-sodium chicken or vegetable broth, and 1 cup water; bring them to a boil, partially cover, and reduce the heat to low. Simmer for 25 minutes. Add 2 cups pumpkin purée; simmer for 5 minutes. Process the soup in batches in a food processor or blender, using caution (hold down the lid with a pot holder). Season with salt and pepper; if needed, add ½ teaspoon additional dried red pepper flakes. Garnish each serving with a pinch of finely chopped Italian parsley and a dollop of plain fat-free Greek-style yogurt.

PANCAKES À LA PUMPKIN

An appealing blend of spices makes these pancakes so delicious that toppings are optional. In a small bowl, stir together 1 cup all-purpose flour, 3 tablespoons light brown sugar, 1½ teaspoons baking powder, 1½ tablespoons pumpkin pie spice, ½ teaspoon ground cinnamon, and ¼ teaspoon salt. In a food processor, combine 1 cup nonfat milk, ⅓ cup pumpkin purée, 1 tablespoon canola oil, and 1 large egg. Pulse 3 times. Add the dry ingredients; pulse 6 to 8 times, or until thoroughly blended. Coat a griddle or nonstick skillet with nonstick spray and heat on medium heat. Add ¼ cup batter for each pancake. Turn when the edges are cooked and bubbles appear. When they are cooked through, after 1 to 1½ minutes, remove the pancakes.

ROASTED AND TOASTED

Roast a baby ("sweet" or "pie") pumpkin as in To Make Pumpkin Purée (page 257). Wearing oven mitts, turn the halves cut-side up; cut them into quarters and season with salt and freshly ground black pepper. In a small bowl, combine ½ cup panko (Japanese bread crumbs) with 1 tablespoon extra-virgin olive oil and ¾ teaspoon chopped fresh thyme; scatter them over the pumpkin. Adjust an oven rack to 8 to 10 inches below the broiler element; preheat the broiler. Broil until the tops are browned and crisp, about 2 minutes. Watch carefully because bread crumbs burn easily.

Pasta with Roasted Pumpkin, Basil, and Walnuts

Roasted pumpkin purée is delicious tossed with pasta and fresh herbs. Topped with both toasted walnuts and Parmesan cheese, the dish is augmented with a garnish of tasty pumpkin wedges made delicious with fresh orange juice and a generous sprinkle of orange zest and freshly ground black pepper. You can reserve the pumpkin seeds you remove in step 1 for roasting (see page 257), if you wish.

Yields 12 side-dish servings

NUTRITIONAL INFORMATION
(per serving, without optional oil)

calories 200	sodium (mg) 300	vitamin A IUs 90%
fat calories 50	total carbohydrates (g) 31	vitamin C 20%
total fat (g) 6	fiber (g) 4	calcium 10%
sat fat (g) 1.5	sugars (g) 3	iron 8%
cholesterol (mg) 5	protein (g) 8	

One 3-pound baby (sweet or pie) pumpkin

Nonstick vegetable oil cooking spray

¼ cup fat-free, low-sodium chicken or vegetable broth

1 orange, zested and juiced

3 tablespoons finely chopped fresh basil

1 teaspoon balsamic vinegar

Salt

Freshly ground black pepper

14 ounces corkscrew-style whole-grain or multi-grain pasta, such as rotini or fusilli

½ cup walnut pieces, toasted (*see Cook's Note, page 240*)

OPTIONAL GARNISH extra-virgin olive oil or pumpkin seed oil

OPTIONAL dried red pepper flakes

½ cup grated Parmesan cheese

1. Adjust an oven rack to the lower third of the oven. Preheat the oven to 375 degrees F. Cut the pumpkin in half through the equator using a sturdy knife. Use a sturdy spoon to remove the seeds and fiber. Coat a rimmed baking sheet with nonstick cooking spray. Place the pumpkin halves cut-side down on the sheet. Roast for 35 to 40 minutes, or until the pumpkin is fork tender. Remove it from the oven. The skin should be a little loose. When it is cool enough, use a paring knife to pull off and discard the skin.

2. Bring a large pot of salted water to a boil.

3. Half of the pumpkin will be puréed for the sauce and the other half used as a garnish. Cut each half into wedges. Place half of the wedges in a food processor fitted with the metal blade. Add the broth, zest, half the juice, 2 tablespoons of the basil, and the vinegar. Season with salt and pepper; purée until smooth.

4. Drizzle the remaining orange juice over the pumpkin wedges still on the rimmed baking sheet. Sprinkle with the remaining basil and season well with salt and pepper.

5. Cook the pasta in the boiling salted water until it is al dente (following the package directions). Drain the pasta, reserving ⅓ cup of the cooking water. Toss the pasta and puréed pumpkin together in a large bowl. Add the reserved pasta water and toss again. Taste for seasoning.

6. Heap the pasta on a large platter. Scatter the walnut pieces on top. If desired, drizzle with a little extra-virgin olive oil and sprinkle with pepper flakes. Arrange the pumpkin wedges around the edge of the pasta. Top the pasta with the Parmesan and serve immediately.

Succotash-Stuffed Roast Pumpkin

Pumpkins make gorgeous edible containers. The soft interior flesh is spooned up along with the tasty filling, leaving the skin behind. In this recipe, a reduced-fat twist on succotash is the stuffing. It teams beautifully with the sweet starchiness of pumpkin. Because it is showy, serve the stuffed pumpkin at the table. With each serving, scoop up a good-size portion of pumpkin to accompany the succotash. If you have any succotash leftovers, they are well-suited as a component in a broth-based soup.

Yields 8 to 10 servings

NUTRITIONAL INFORMATION
(per serving, with ¼ cup pumpkin)

calories 170	sodium (mg) 50	vitamin A IUs 170%
fat calories 70	total carbohydrates (g)... 20	vitamin C 20%
total fat (g) 8	fiber (g) 3	calcium 6%
sat fat (g) 1.5	sugars (g) 3	iron 10%
cholesterol (mg) 5	protein (g) 6	

One 3-pound baby (sweet or pie) pumpkin
Salt
Freshly ground black pepper

VINAIGRETTE

1½ tablespoons white wine vinegar

3 tablespoons extra-virgin olive oil

8 large fresh basil leaves, minced

SUCCOTASH

1 tablespoon extra-virgin olive oil

1 tablespoon unsalted butter

1 cup hominy, drained

1½ cups corn kernels

1 cup frozen shelled edamame or lima beans, thawed, patted dry

One 15-ounce can red beans, rinsed, and drained

OPTIONAL FOR SERVING brown rice or wild rice

1. Adjust an oven rack to the lower third of the oven. Preheat the oven to 400 degrees F. Using a sturdy knife, cut off a pumpkin "lid" (cutting about 1 inch from the top). Use a sturdy spoon to remove the fibers and seeds. If desired, reserve the seeds for roasting (see page 257). Season the inside of the pumpkin with salt and pepper. Wrap the exterior and cut edges and lid separately with aluminum foil. Reposition the lid on the pumpkin and place it on a baking pan (not glass). Put it in the oven and add about ½ inch of hot water to the pan. Bake until the pumpkin's interior is fork tender but not mushy, about 1 hour and 15 minutes. Check halfway through baking; add more water to the pan if needed. Cautiously remove the pan from the oven. Using pot holders or oven mitts, remove the pumpkin to a serving platter.

2. Meanwhile, make the vinaigrette: In a small bowl or glass measuring cup with a handle, whisk the vinegar and season it with salt and pepper. Whisk in the oil in a thin stream. Stir in the basil; set aside.

3. To make the succotash: In a large, deep skillet, heat the oil and butter on high heat. When the butter melts, add the hominy and corn. Cook, stirring occasionally, until they are lightly browned, about 5 minutes. If the mixture starts popping and sending kernels out of the skillet, reduce the heat to medium. Add the edamame and red beans. Add the vinaigrette and stir to combine. Cook until heated through, 2 to 3 minutes. Taste and adjust the seasoning if needed.

4. When cool enough to handle, remove the foil from the pumpkin and lid. Fill the pumpkin with the succotash and replace the lid. Because the pumpkin is full, it is easier to scoop the first 2 or 3 servings of pumpkin from the interior of the lid. If desired, accompany the succotash and pumpkin with rice.

Individual Pumpkin Pies in the Shells

These nutrient-packed individual pies are baked in mini pumpkins instead of piecrust. Diners can spoon up filling along with a little baked pumpkin to boost the nutritional benefits. Whipped cream and baked piecrust leaves are optional.

Yields about 12 to 15 servings

NUTRITIONAL INFORMATION
(per serving, without optional garnishes)

calories 80	sodium (mg) 60	vitamin A IUs 180%
fat calories 0	total carbohydrates (g)....16	vitamin C 10%
total fat (g) 0	fiber (g) 1	calcium 8%
sat fat (g)........................0	sugars (g) 12	iron..............................6%
cholesterol (mg) 0	protein (g) 3	

12 to 15 **mini pumpkins**
(*see Cook's Notes*)

3 **egg whites**

1½ **cups pumpkin purée or one 15-ounce can solid pack pumpkin (not pumpkin pie mix)**

One **12-ounce can evaporated fat-free milk**

½ **cup sugar**

1½ **teaspoons pumpkin pie spice**

½ **teaspoon ground cinnamon**

½ **teaspoon vanilla extract**

⅛ **teaspoon salt**

OPTIONAL GARNISH 1 cup heavy cream, whipped to soft peaks; baked piecrust leaves (*see Cook's Notes*)

1. Preheat the oven to 425 degrees F. Cut off the top ½- to 1-inch of each pumpkin. Scoop out the seeds, strings, and enough flesh to leave ½ inch of flesh on the sides and bottom. Set aside.

2. Put the egg whites in the bowl of an electric mixer; beat until frothy (tiny bubbles form). Add the pumpkin, milk, sugar, pie spice, cinnamon, vanilla, and salt. Beat to combine, scraping down the sides of the bowl as needed.

3. Fill each pumpkin to ¼ inch below the top edge. Place them in a baking dish (or two, if necessary), without crowding. Add about 1 inch of hot water to the bottom of each dish. Bake for 25 minutes. Reduce the heat to 350 degrees F; bake 35 to 45 minutes more, or until set. The filling should be puffy when it comes out of the oven but will fall as it cools. Let the pies cool 20 minutes before serving. If desired, top each serving with a dollop of whipped cream and a piecrust leaf.

COOK'S NOTES Mini pumpkins are smaller than a softball. They are squatty and deeply fluted and hold about ¼ cup filling. "Baby" pumpkins are slightly larger, usually softball size, and will also work well in this recipe. They will hold about ½ cup filling.

To make piecrust leaves, cut out leaf shapes from rolled-out pie dough with a sharp knife or cookie cutter. Use the back of the knife to create deep veins in the leaves. Place the leaves in a single layer on a nonstick baking sheet. Bake in a 350-degree-F oven until nicely browned, about 4 to 6 minutes.

RAPINI

also Broccoli Raab

With stalks more slender than those found on broccoli, rapini is topped with spiky, jagged-edged leaves and compact, tightly closed buds. More mature buds open into yellow blossoms, which are edible, too. It has a no-snooze flavor profile with a pleasing bitterness that can be tamed with cooking and well-planned ingredient partners. Chile, garlic, or ginger complement its assertive side, as do creamy pasta, grains with dried fruit, or caramelized onion. Although rapini is a broccoli cousin, it is a lot more nutrient-packed. It has three times the calcium, vitamin A, and niacin, plus almost twice the folate, vitamin C, and vitamin E.

NUTRITIONAL INFORMATION
(per 1 cup raw, chopped)

calories	9	sodium (mg)	13	vitamin A IUs	21%
fat calories	2	total carbohydrates (g)	1	vitamin C	13%
total fat (g)	0	fiber (g)	1	calcium	4%
sat fat (g)	0	sugars (g)	0	iron	5%
cholesterol (mg)	0	protein (g)	1		

PLAN B FOR PAIN
With fewer than 60 calories per cup after cooking, rapini offers a wealth of B vitamins, including thiamin, riboflavin, and niacin, as well as heart-healthy folate. It turns out that B vitamins, especially riboflavin, can help alleviate the pain of migraines. A Dutch study noted that riboflavin was particularly effective on tension migraines in children. And niacin has been shown to lessen wound pain in some adults.

GREEN OMEGA
A cup of rapini is a surprisingly good source of omega-3 fatty acids, delivering more than 200 milligrams per cup. Omega-3s are thought to protect the body from heart disease and cancer while lowering the risk of cognitive decline and alleviating depression, arthritis pain, and inflammation.

AVAILABLE
Year-round

KEEP IT FRESH
Look for rapini that smells fresh, without yellowed leaves or soft spots. Stalks should be firm and buds compact. Refrigerate rapini, unwashed, stored loose in a plastic bag, for 3 to 5 days.

LAST-MINUTE PREP
Wash with cold water. Trim off a small portion at the base of the stems. Most often rapini is cut into 1- or 2-inch lengths before it is cooked.

QUICK COOK

Bring several cups of salted water to a boil in a large, deep skillet or 4-quart saucepan on high heat. Add 1 or 2 bunches of rapini (trimmed, cut into 2-inch lengths). Cook just until they are tender-crisp, 3 to 5 minutes. Drain in a colander; refresh with cold water. If desired, toss the rapini with quick Asian dressing: Combine 3 tablespoons sodium-reduced soy sauce with 3 tablespoons rice vinegar, 1 teaspoon agave syrup, 1 teaspoon roasted sesame oil, and a drop or two of Asian hot sauce.

try it!

SMOTHERED IN RED ONIONS

Slice 2 medium red onions. Heat 2 tablespoons extra-virgin olive oil in a large, deep skillet on medium-high heat; add the onions and cook until they are softened and starting to brown. Reduce the heat to medium and cook until they are nicely caramelized. Toss in 1 bunch blanched rapini (see Quick Cook). Season with salt and freshly ground black pepper. Drizzle a little balsamic vinegar around each serving.

IN RICE-BASED SOUP

Soften 1 medium onion (coarsely chopped) in 2 teaspoons oil in a large saucepan on medium-high heat. Add 1 cup sliced mushrooms, ¾ cup coarsely chopped rapini, a pinch of dried red pepper flakes, and 1 cup shredded or thinly sliced carrots; cook 3 to 4 minutes, stirring occasionally. Add 4 cups fat-free low-sodium vegetable broth and bring to a simmer. Reduce to medium and cook until the rapini is tender-crisp, about 4 minutes. Add 1½ cups cooked brown rice and ½ teaspoon dried thyme. Season with garlic salt plus a small splash of balsamic vinegar.

IN STIR-FRIES

Add some 1-inch blanched rapini pieces to a vegetable-based stir-fry dish during the last minute of cooking.

Rapini and Barley Salad

If you like the flavor of brown rice, you will undoubtedly appreciate the earthy, nutty taste and alluring chewiness of barley. Rapini adds its signature spark to this salad, the flavor profile balanced with sweet raisins and toasted almonds. Served on a big platter, this dish is great for a buffet table or picnic.

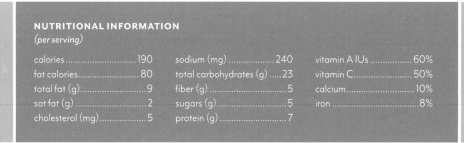

Yields 10 servings

NUTRITIONAL INFORMATION
(per serving)

calories 190	sodium (mg) 240	vitamin A IUs 60%
fat calories 80	total carbohydrates (g) 23	vitamin C 50%
total fat (g) 9	fiber (g) 5	calcium 10%
sat fat (g) 2	sugars (g) 5	iron 8%
cholesterol (mg) 5	protein (g) 7	

¼ cup golden raisins

1 cup pearl barley

Salt

10 ounces rapini

½ cup slivered almonds, toasted
(*see Cook's Note*)

3 tablespoons extra-virgin olive oil

4 tablespoons fresh lemon juice

Freshly ground black pepper

6 cups mixed baby greens

½ cup grated Parmesan cheese

GARNISH 6 small lemon wedges

1. Put the raisins in a small bowl; cover them with hot water and set aside.

2. In a large saucepan, combine the barley, 3½ cups water, and a pinch of salt. Bring them to a boil on high heat. Stir and cover; reduce the heat to low. Gently simmer until the barley is tender, about 30 minutes. Drain and cool for 10 minutes.

3. Bring a large saucepan three-fourths full of water to a boil on high heat. Cut the rapini in 1-inch pieces. Blanch it until tender-crisp, about 3 to 5 minutes. Drain it in a colander. Run cold water over the rapini and shake the colander to remove excess water.

4. Put the barley and rapini in a large bowl. Add the almonds and sprinkle the oil on top; toss. Drain the raisins and add them; toss. Sprinkle with lemon juice and toss. Season with salt and pepper and let rest for 10 minutes.

5. Mound the baby greens on a platter in an even layer. Top with the barley mixture. Sprinkle the top with the cheese. Place the lemon wedges on a separate plate for optional use.

COOK'S NOTE To toast slivered almonds, place them in a single layer on a rimmed baking sheet. Bake in a 350-degree-F oven for 3 to 4 minutes, or until lightly browned. Watch carefully because nuts burn easily.

Rapini with Caramelized Onions and Brown Rice

There are several brands of brown rice blends in the marketplace. When cooked, they have a lovely earthiness that teams well with rapini. One example is a blend of long-grain brown, nutty Wehani, and black Japonica rice. Brown rice generally triples in volume when cooked, but brown rice blends often yield a little less, varying from brand to brand. Figure that approximately 1½ cups raw brown rice blend will yield 4 cups when cooked.

Yields 6 servings

NUTRITIONAL INFORMATION
(per serving)

calories 220	sodium (m) 35	vitamin A IUs 120%
fat calories 40	total carbohydrates (g)... 37	vitamin C 150%
total fat (g) 4.5	fiber (g) 3	calcium 6%
sat fat (g) 0.5	sugars (g) 3	iron 8%
cholesterol (mg) 0	protein (g) 7	

1½ tablespoons extra-virgin olive oil

1 large yellow onion, cut into ⅜-inch slices

OPTIONAL ½ teaspoon sugar

2 large garlic cloves, thinly sliced

1¼ pounds rapini, cut into 2-inch pieces

¼ teaspoon dried red pepper flakes

Salt

Freshly ground black pepper

1½ cups uncooked brown rice blend

GARNISH 2 tablespoons minced fresh Italian parsley

1. Heat the oil in a large deep skillet on medium-high heat. Add the onion and toss to coat it with the oil. Cook until it starts to soften and turn brown. Reduce the heat to medium-low. If desired, add the sugar. It helps the onion to caramelize, but it will brown without it; it will just take a little longer. Cook until the onion is nicely browned, stirring occasionally, about 15 minutes, adding the garlic 3 to 4 minutes before the end of cooking.

2. Meanwhile, put a large pot of salted water on high heat. When it is boiling, add the rapini. Cook until it is tender-crisp, about 3 to 5 minutes. Drain it well in a colander. Add it to the onion. Add dried red pepper flakes and toss. Season with salt and pepper.

3. Divide the rice between six bowls. Spoon the rapini mixture over the rice, garnish with the parsley, and serve.

Spaghetti with Rapini, Artichokes, and Grape Tomatoes

It's easy to understand why Italians are so crazy about rapini. It adds such an irresistible and interesting edge to pasta dishes. If you like the idea of adding a little more sweet starchiness to the dish, stir in 1 cup of fresh or frozen peas when adding the olives in step 3.

Yields 6 first-course servings

NUTRITIONAL INFORMATION
(per serving)

calories 330	sodium (mg) 150	vitamin A IUs 110%
fat calories 60	total carbohydrates (g)... 52	vitamin C 130%
total fat (g) 7	fiber (g) 8	calcium 15%
sat fat (g)...................... 1.5	sugars (g) 5	iron............................. 15%
cholesterol (mg) 5	protein (g) 13	

- 1 pound rapini, cut into 2-inch pieces
- 12 ounces dry whole-wheat spaghetti
- 1½ tablespoons extra-virgin olive oil
- ½ medium red onion, coarsely chopped
- 2 large garlic cloves, thinly sliced
- ½ cup dry white wine
- Salt
- Freshly ground black pepper
- 1 cup frozen artichoke hearts, defrosted, patted dry, and quartered
- ½ cup pitted green olives, drained and quartered lengthwise
- 1½ cups halved grape tomatoes
- ¼ cup grated Parmesan cheese
- ½ cup fresh basil leaves

1. Bring a large pot of salted water to a boil on high heat. Add the rapini and cook until it is tender-crisp, about 3 to 5 minutes. Remove it with a slotted spoon; drain well and set it aside. Bring the water back to a boil.

2. Add the spaghetti to the water and cook until it is al dente (following the package directions). Drain well, reserving ¾ cup of the cooking water.

3. Heat 1 tablespoon of the oil in a large, deep skillet on medium heat. Add the onion and garlic; cook, stirring occasionally, until they are softened, about 3 minutes. Add the wine and increase the heat to medium-high. Cook until the wine evaporates, about 3 minutes. Season with salt and pepper. Add the artichokes and toss; cook until they start to brown a little. Add the olives and 1 cup of the tomatoes; cook, stirring occasionally, until the tomatoes start to break up a little, about 3 minutes. Add the remaining tomatoes, rapini, and spaghetti and toss.

4. Off the heat, toss the pasta with the cheese and remaining ½ tablespoon oil. Tear the basil into small pieces and add. Toss the mixture with enough of the reserved cooking water to make a creamy consistency. Taste and adjust the seasoning if needed. Serve.

RASPBERRY

Tiny juice sacs surround each raspberry's hollow interior. Sweet with tart overtones, the plump berries are delicate and highly perishable. Their vibrant flavor can enliven many dishes. Drop a few raspberries on a serving of so-so applesauce, and ordinary becomes enticing. Add a few to a pancake, and dull becomes dynamic.

Of all the berries, raspberries are in the top tier for minerals, vitamins, and powerful antioxidants called proanthocyanins.

NUTRITIONAL INFORMATION
(per 1 cup, raw)

calories 64	sodium (mg) 1	vitamin A IUs 1%
fat calories 7	total carbohydrates (g)....15	vitamin C 54%
total fat (g) 1	fiber (g) 8	calcium 3%
sat fat (g).........................0	sugars (g) 5	iron..............................5%
cholesterol (mg) 0	protein (g) 1	

SEEING RED
Red berries such as raspberries are loaded with vitamins C, E, and K, plus folate, iron, potassium, and manganese. Manganese helps bones in three ways for the structure of the bone matrix, for the bone-cell growth process, and to work with the enzymes that drive bone growth and density.

FIBER FANTASTIC
While all types of produce act as excellent fiber sources, raspberries have some of the highest concentrations of the ingredient; nearly one-fifth of the berry by weight is made up of digestive fiber. This means raspberries pack a lot of satiety, heart health, and digestive health into a very little package.

A HAPPIER PANCREAS
In a recent study, scientists at the University of Oklahoma Health Sciences Center and the University of Texas Health Science Center discovered that extracts of raspberry actually helped inhibit the cellular death process in pancreatic cancer, blocking the growth, feeding, and proliferation of cancer cells.

AVAILABLE
Year-round

KEEP IT FRESH

Select berries that are free of mold and discoloration. If packaged, make sure that berries move freely when the container is tilted; avoid containers in which the berries stubbornly stick together, as they are probably moldy. They are highly perishable and should be eaten as soon as possible. Store, unwashed, refrigerated in a single layer on a paper towel–lined shallow dish or rimmed pan. Raspberries freeze well, but their texture becomes mushy when defrosted (thus they are best used in cooked dishes or puréed). To freeze, place them in a single layer on a rimmed baking sheet; when frozen, transfer them to an airtight plastic container.

LAST-MINUTE PREP

Place the berries in a sieve or colander; rinse lightly with cold water. Place them on a paper towel to absorb excess water.

QUICK COOK

Raspberries are most often eaten raw. To make a sauce to serve with game, place 1 cup (packed) fresh raspberries in a small saucepan with 3 tablespoons water, 1½ tablespoons agave syrup, and 1 teaspoon minced orange zest. Cook on medium-high heat until the sauce thickens, stirring frequently, about 10 minutes. Strain through a medium-mesh sieve and discard the debris left behind. Spoon onto the plate next to cooked game.

try it!

IN CHAMPAGNE

Place fresh raspberries in wine glasses or champagne flutes. Pour chilled champagne over the berries. Eat the raspberries; drink the champagne.

IN BERRY-ORANGE LEMONADE

Combine ½ cup raspberries, ⅓ cup blackberries, 1 cup water, and 3 cups ice cubes in a large pitcher. Add ⅓ cup agave syrup and 1½ cups fresh lemon juice. Stir to break up the berries. Add 1½ cups fresh orange juice and 1 lemon (thinly sliced, seeded); stir. Taste and add more water and/or agave if needed.

IN PANCAKES

Drop a few raspberries onto whole-wheat pancakes just before turning them over, pressing the berries down a little with a spatula. Turn and complete the cooking.

Raspberry Pie with Graham Crust

Raspberries make a big impression in this tempting pie. The crust is made with graham flour—whole-wheat flour that is much more nutritious than graham crackers (which contain sweeteners and fat). Whole-wheat graham flour is sold in natural food stores and supermarkets with large natural foods specialty sections. If you can't find it, substitute graham cracker crumbs.

Yields 12 small servings

NUTRITIONAL INFORMATION
(per serving)

calories 220	sodium (mg) 20	vitamin A IUs 8%
fat calories 110	total carbohydrates (g)... 25	vitamin C 8%
total fat (g) 13	fiber (g) 1	calcium 4%
sat fat (g) 8	sugars (g) 10	iron 4%
cholesterol (mg) 60	protein (g) 4	

CRUST

Butter for greasing pan

- 1 cup whole-wheat graham flour
- ½ cup unbleached all-purpose flour
- ¼ cup sugar
- ½ teaspoon minced lemon zest
- 10 tablespoons (1¼ sticks) unsalted butter, melted and cooled slightly

FILLING

- 1 cup fat-free milk
- 4 tablespoons sugar
- 3 tablespoons unbleached all-purpose flour
- 2 eggs
- 2 tablespoons unsalted butter, at room temperature
- 1½ teaspoons vanilla extract

TOPPING

- 2½ cups fresh raspberries

OPTIONAL GARNISH 2 tablespoons powdered sugar

1. Adjust an oven rack to the middle position and preheat the oven to 350 degrees F. Lightly butter the bottom and sides of a 9-inch glass pie plate.

2. To make the crust: In a medium bowl, stir together the graham flour, all-purpose flour, sugar, and zest. Gradually add the butter, stirring until moist crumbs clump together. Press the dough into the prepared pie pan, pushing it into an even layer on the bottom and up the sides. Bake for 20 minutes, or until it is golden brown. Cool it on a rack.

3. To make the filling: Combine the milk and 2 tablespoons of the sugar in a small saucepan. Bring them to a boil on medium heat. Meanwhile, whisk together the remaining 2 tablespoons sugar and the flour in a medium bowl. Whisk in the eggs one at a time. When the milk comes to a boil, off heat, whisk about one-third of it into the egg mixture. Return the milk mixture to low heat and whisk in the egg mixture in a thin stream, whisking constantly until the pastry cream thickens and comes to a boil. Boil, stirring constantly, for about 30 seconds. Remove from the heat and whisk in the butter and vanilla.

4. Transfer the filling to a glass or ceramic bowl and cover it with plastic wrap, pressing down the plastic wrap so it rests on the surface. Chill.

5. To assemble: Spread the fully cooled filling into the cooled crust, spreading it to make an even layer. Pile the raspberries on top. If you want a sweeter dessert, put the powdered sugar in a small sieve and shake it back and forth over the top of the berries.

Poached Pears with Raspberries in Rosé Syrup

The poach-steep method makes fresh pears irresistible, especially if they are served garnished with fresh raspberries. In this recipe, the poaching mixture is an alluring combination of wine and orange juice, augmented with herbs, spices, and zest. The pears can be prepared 2 days before serving. They turn a lovely reddish brown, a color that gets deeper with increased steeping in the chilled poaching brew.

Yields 8 servings

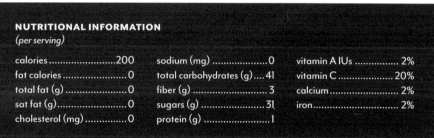

NUTRITIONAL INFORMATION
(per serving)

calories 200	sodium (mg) 0	vitamin A IUs 2%
fat calories 0	total carbohydrates (g)....41	vitamin C 20%
total fat (g) 0	fiber (g) 3	calcium 2%
sat fat (g)..................0	sugars (g) 31	iron..............................2%
cholesterol (mg) 0	protein (g) 1	

1	small orange
2½	cups rosé wine
⅔	cup agave syrup
1	bay leaf
One	3-inch-long cinnamon stick
4	ripe pears
1½	cups fresh raspberries

GARNISH 8 small sprigs fresh mint

OPTIONAL FOR SERVING crisp cookies

1. Using a swivel-bladed vegetable peeler, remove two 2-inch-wide strips of orange zest. In a nonreactive large pan or Dutch oven, combine the zest strips, wine, syrup, bay leaf, and cinnamon stick. Bring to a boil on high heat. Cover and reduce the heat to low; simmer gently for 15 minutes.

2. Meanwhile, peel the pears, leaving the stems attached. Add the pears to the wine mixture, arranging them on their sides and maneuvering them so they are all lying in the poaching liquid. Cover and place the pan on high heat; bring it to a boil. Reduce the heat to medium-low and simmer for 15 to 20 minutes, turning the pears halfway through cooking. They should be fork tender but not falling apart. Use a large slotted spoon to remove the pears. Simmer the poaching liquid until it is reduced by about one-third and thickened.

3. Cut the pears in half from top to bottom. Remove the cores (a melon baller is helpful for this). Return the pears to the syrup. Cover and refrigerate them for several hours or overnight.

4. Place the pear halves cut-side up in shallow bowls. Strain the syrup and spoon it over the pears. Place the raspberries on top. Garnish with the fresh mint. Pass cookies, if desired.

Raspberries with Yogurt and Chocolate Meringue Cookies

Chocolate and red berries are mouthwatering partners. These simple meringue cookies, enhanced with unsweetened cocoa powder, nest in a mixture of raspberries and strawberries coated with raspberry coulis. The coulis is a sauce made by straining puréed raspberries. The cookies can be prepared up to 5 days in advance of serving and stored airtight at room temperature.

Yields 8 servings, plus about 13 leftover cookies

NUTRITIONAL INFORMATION
(per serving)

calories 170	sodium (mg) 80	vitamin A IUs 10%
fat calories 15	total carbohydrates (g)... 37	vitamin C 40%
total fat (g) 1.5	fiber (g) 1	calcium.......................15%
sat fat (g)........................1	sugars (g) 26	iron..............................2%
cholesterol (mg) 5	protein (g) 5	

3 large egg whites, at room temperature (*see Cook's Note*)

⅛ teaspoon cream of tartar

¾ cup granulated sugar

3 tablespoons unsweetened cocoa powder

2½ cups fresh raspberries

¼ cup agave syrup, plus more if needed

1¼ cups sliced fresh strawberries

4 cups vanilla low-fat yogurt

OPTIONAL TOPPINGS 2 tablespoons powdered sugar; 8 sprigs fresh mint

1. Adjust the oven racks to the upper and lower thirds of the oven. Preheat the oven to 375 degrees F. Line two baking sheets with parchment paper.

2. Put the egg whites in the bowl of an electric mixer. Beat on medium speed until foamy. Add the cream of tartar and increase the speed to high. When soft peaks form, add the sugar ¼ cup at a time; beat until the whites are stiff and glossy. Put the cocoa powder in a sieve and shake it over the whites to distribute it gently. Gently fold it in until just barely blended.

3. Drop the meringue by tablespoonfuls onto the prepared sheets, placing them 1½ inches apart. Bake for 20 to 25 minutes, or until the cookies are dry, rotating the sheets halfway through the baking. Carefully peel the cookies from the parchment and let them cool thoroughly on a wire rack.

4. Put 1 cup of the raspberries and the syrup in a blender or food processor. Pulse to purée; strain and discard the debris in the sieve. In a nonreactive bowl, such as glass or ceramic, combine the sauce, remaining 1½ cups raspberries, and the strawberries; gently toss. Taste and add additional syrup if needed for sweetness.

5. Divide the yogurt between eight small bowls. Top with the berries. Place a cookie on top of each serving, pushing it down slightly so that it rests in the berries and yogurt. If desired, put the powdered sugar in a sieve and shake it over the top of each dessert and garnish each serving with a small sprig of fresh mint.

COOK'S NOTE To bring cold eggs to room temperature, submerge them in a bowl of warm water for 5 minutes. Dry the eggs before use.

RED
CURRANTS

Arranged in grape-like clusters on scrubby stems, red currants have translucent bright red skin and an assertive tart flavor. The drooping clusters grow on bushes and are harvested and packed still attached to the stem.

The tiny orbs' tart taste makes them a great choice for jelly or preserves to accompany game, lamb, or poultry. Used raw as a garnish, they are delicious as well as vividly colored. Leave a few attached on the stem to accompany desserts or fancy-up a cheese platter. Off the stem, toss them in mixed green salads tamed with creamy blue cheese and dressed with vinaigrette sweetened with a little honey or agave syrup.

The Zante currant, sometimes labeled "currant," is a small, dried seedless Black Corinth grape; it is not a dried red currant.

NUTRITIONAL INFORMATION
(per 1 cup raw)

calories 63	sodium (mg) 1	vitamin A IUs 1%
fat calories 2	total carbohydrates (g) 15	vitamin C 77%
total fat (g) 0	fiber (g) 5	calcium 4%
sat fat (g) 0	sugars (g) 8	iron 6%
cholesterol (mg) 0	protein (g) 2	

IMMUNE-BUILDING C
Just 1 cup of red currants delivers about the same amount of vitamin C as one small orange, which is about three-fourths of your daily requirement of C.

PROTECTOR AND DEFENDER
The antioxidant compounds called anthocyanins abound in currants. These have cancer-protective activity as well as anti-inflammation capacity.

DEPRESSION FIGHTER
Currants also have comparatively large amounts of an uncommon omega-6 fatty acid called gamma linolenic acid (GLA). GLA has strong anti-inflammatory properties as well as related analgesic properties. In fact, recent studies showed that for some people the effect matches drugs like ibuprofen or aspirin for conditions such as arthritis. The berries also contain monoamine oxidase inhibitors and have been investigated as effective agents against certain forms of mild depression. GLA has shown similar potentials. All this in a package that comes in at a mere 18 calories per ounce!

AVAILABLE
March to July; late November to December

KEEP IT FRESH
Look for berries with shiny, bright red skin, avoiding any that are mushy or moldy. Refrigerate them unwashed. They are highly perishable; super-fresh currants can be refrigerated up to 5 days, but for the safest bet, use as soon as possible.

LAST-MINUTE PREP
Rinse them with cold water and gently pat dry with a kitchen cloth or paper towels. If using currants off the stem, a dinner fork is a handy tool; use the tines to loosen the berries from the stems.

try it!

IN A GAME-FRIENDLY SAUCE

Cut dark green stalks from a large leek. Cut the remaining white and light green parts in half lengthwise. Wash and place them cut-side down on a work surface; cut them into thin slices. In a large saucepan, combine the leeks; 1 teaspoon extra-virgin olive oil, and ⅓ cup sugar; cook on medium-high heat, stirring to dissolve the sugar. Add 8 ounces stemmed fresh red currants, 1 sprig fresh rosemary, and ¼ cup vegetable broth or dry white wine. Bring it to a boil; reduce the heat to medium. Simmer until the sauce is slightly thickened, about 15 minutes. Add 1½ tablespoons balsamic vinegar and season with salt and pepper. Taste the sauce; if additional sweetening is needed, add honey or agave syrup. Allow the sauce to cool. Remove the rosemary sprig. Serve the sauce with lamb, venison, pork, or grilled tofu.

WITH CHOCOLATE CAKE

For a beautiful garnish, place a sprig of fresh red currants next to a thin slice of flourless chocolate cake and accompany it with whipped cream.

IN MAPLE SYRUP

Just before serving pancakes or waffles, heat some maple syrup. Add a handful of stemmed fresh red currants and gently stir; spoon them over pancakes or waffles.

Bread Pudding with Kumquat-Currant Topping

This special-occasion dessert is redolent of spices reminiscent of winter holidays and festive with colorful fresh currants and kumquats. To reduce the calorie count, serve smaller portions and accompany each serving with mixed fresh berries sweetened with a drizzle of dark honey or agave syrup.

Yields 8 servings

NUTRITIONAL INFORMATION
(per serving)

calories 310	sodium (mg) 220	vitamin A IUs 4%
fat calories 50	total carbohydrates (g) ... 58	vitamin C 15%
total fat (g) 6	fiber (g) 5	calcium 15%
sat fat (g) 1.5	sugars (g) 43	iron 15%
cholesterol (mg) 60	protein (g) 8	

Eight ½-inch slices rustic whole-wheat bread

Nonstick cooking spray

2 cups 2% milk

½ cup (packed) dark brown sugar

½ cup golden raisins

2 eggs, lightly beaten

1½ teaspoons vanilla extract

1 teaspoon pumpkin pie spice

1 teaspoon ground cinnamon

TOPPING

1 tablespoon canola or vegetable oil

1 cup kumquats, cut crosswise into ¼-inch slices and large seeds removed

½ cup golden raisins or dried cherries

½ cup stemmed fresh red currants

¼ cup (packed) dark brown sugar

¾ teaspoon ground cinnamon

1. If the bread isn't slightly dry, allow it to sit out at room temperature for 6 to 8 hours to dry out a little.

2. Adjust an oven rack to the middle position. Preheat the oven to 350 degrees F. Generously coat an 8-inch square baking dish with nonstick spray.

3. Trim the crust from the bread and cut it into ½-inch cubes. Put them in a large bowl; add the milk, sugar, raisins, eggs, vanilla, pie spice, and cinnamon. Toss to combine and allow it to rest for 10 minutes, tossing halfway through.

4. Pour the mixture into the prepared dish. Put it in a larger dish on the oven rack and add enough hot water to the outside dish to come halfway up the side of the smaller dish. Bake for 1 hour, or until a knife inserted in the center comes out clean. Set it on a cooling rack.

5. Make the topping: Heat the oil in a medium, heavy-bottomed saucepan on medium-high heat. Add the kumquats and raisins; cook 2 to 3 minutes, stirring occasionally, until the raisins start to soften. Reduce the heat to medium; add the currants, sugar, and cinnamon. Cook until the sugar melts, about 1 minute. Add ¾ cup water and cook until the sauce gets syrupy, about 8 minutes, gently stirring occasionally.

6. Cut the pudding into portions and place them in shallow bowls. Spoon the sauce on top. Serve.

Southwestern-Style Cherry and Currant Slaw

Fresh red currants and sweet cherries give this tangy slaw a sweet-sour spark (most cherries sold in the marketplace are sweet, because most of the sour cherries are used by canneries). This colorful mélange is delicious served with grilled fish or poultry. Or for a vegetarian option, serve it with wild rice augmented with some chopped cilantro and toasted pine nuts.

Yields 8 side-dish servings

NUTRITIONAL INFORMATION
(per serving)

calories 220	sodium (mg) 45	vitamin A IUs 80%
fat calories 60	total carbohydrates (g) ... 39	vitamin C 130%
total fat (g) 7	fiber (g) 11	calcium 8%
sat fat (g) 1	sugars (g) 22	iron 10%
cholesterol (mg) 0	protein (g) 5	

1 medium green cabbage, cored, and shredded

2 pounds fresh cherries, pitted and halved

1 medium jícama, peeled and cut into sticks ¾ by ⅛ by ⅛ inch

3 medium carrots, peeled and shredded

½ medium red onion, finely diced

½ cup chopped fresh cilantro

¼ cup stemmed fresh red currants

¼ cup pine nuts, lightly toasted
(*see Cook's Notes*)

DRESSING

⅓ cup fresh lime juice
(*see Cook's Notes*)

1 jalapeño, seeded and minced
(*see Cook's Notes*)

1 teaspoon lime zest

¼ teaspoon chili powder

Coarse salt (kosher or sea)

GARNISH 1 medium, ripe avocado, peeled, sliced, and coated with fresh lime juice

1. In a large bowl, combine the cabbage, cherries, jícama, carrots, onion, cilantro, and currants. Set aside.

2. To make the dressing: In a small bowl, whisk together the lime juice, jalapeño, zest, and chili powder; season with salt. Pour the dressing over the cabbage mixture; add the pine nuts and gently toss. Garnish each serving with avocado slices.

COOK'S NOTES To toast pine nuts, place them in a small skillet on medium-high heat. Shake the skillet to redistribute the nuts so they won't overbrown on one side. Cook until they are lightly browned. Watch carefully because nuts burn easily.

Use caution when working with fresh chiles. Upon completion, wash your hands and work area thoroughly; do *not* touch your eyes or face.

Remove the zest from limes before juicing them.

Polenta with Fresh Currants and Raisins

Creamy polenta takes a sweet-tart turn when fresh red currants and raisins come to the party. It is delicious served alongside game, lamb, or grilled tofu. Or try it served with a mixture of wild mushrooms that have been sautéed in a little extra-virgin olive oil and tumbled with minced fresh basil.

Yields 6 side-dish servings

NUTRITIONAL INFORMATION
(per serving)

calories ... 180	sodium (mg) ... 480	vitamin A IUs ... 2%
fat calories ... 40	total carbohydrates (g) ... 30	vitamin C ... 10%
total fat (g) ... 5	fiber (g) ... 1	calcium ... 8%
sat fat (g) ... 3	sugars (g) ... 6	iron ... 4%
cholesterol (mg) ... 15	protein (g) ... 5	

1 teaspoon kosher salt

1 cup polenta or yellow cornmeal or corn grits

1½ tablespoons unsalted butter or soft tub margarine

¼ cup grated Parmesan cheese

⅓ cup raisins

Freshly ground black pepper

¾ cup stemmed fresh red currants

1. In a deep 6-quart pan or Dutch oven, bring 3½ cups water to a boil on high heat. Stir in the salt.

2. Gradually stir in the polenta using a long-handled wooden spoon (to prevent burns). Reduce the heat and gently simmer, stirring often, until the polenta is al dente (following the package directions), 20 to 25 minutes.

3. Stir in the butter and cheese. Mix in the raisins and season with pepper. Gently fold in the currants. Serve immediately.

ROMAINE

The outer leaves of romaine lettuce have crunchy spines. They make juicy, noisy counterpoints to the quiet tender leaves that surround them. Work your way to the heart, and the dissimilarity diminishes. Rather than a deep green color, smaller leaves are celery green and the spines are quieter. The heart has a mild flavor profile with a touch of sweetness.

We know it best as the Caesar salad lettuce, but the versatility of romaine is well established. And it has great nutritional benefits for its ultra-low-calorie impact.

NUTRITIONAL INFORMATION
(per 1 cup raw, chopped)

calories	8	sodium (mg)	4	vitamin A IUs	55%
fat calories	1	total carbohydrates (g)	2	vitamin C	19%
total fat (g)	0	fiber (g)	1	calcium	2%
sat fat (g)	0	sugars (g)	1	iron	3%
cholesterol (mg)	0	protein (g)	1		

GREENS FOR BLUES
As with all leafy greens, romaine lettuce is a rich source of the B vitamin folate, which is good for heart health and bone health. Multiple studies have suggested a link between low folate status and depression. Two cups of romaine provides about one-third of your daily folate requirement.

B IS ALSO FOR BONE
Romaine has B vitamins beyond folate. It's a good source of thiamin, riboflavin, and B_6. The B group of vitamins performs thousands of functions in the body. They are often overlooked for their contribution to bone metabolism, both through lowering blood homocysteine levels (associated with hip fractures) and by participating in numerous enzyme functions related to bone metabolism. And romaine is a super source of vitamin K, another bone-building nutrient.

EYES ON LETTUCE
Lettuces such as romaine are good sources of lutein and zeaxanthin, phytochemicals related to vitamin A and crucial for protecting the retina and staving off macular degeneration (a leading cause of blindness in older adults).

AVAILABLE
Year-round

KEEP IT FRESH
Look for heads of romaine that look crisp and are free of soft spots or discoloration. Wash before storage. If grilling (or if you want to keep the leaves attached at the root end for a salad), cut the head in half lengthwise, using a plastic lettuce knife if available; leave the leaves attached at the root end. Otherwise, cut them off at the root end. Submerge the romaine in a large bowl or tub of cold water. If they're very dirty, the leaves may require two rinses. Drain them in a colander; wrap the damp leaves loosely in a clean kitchen towel, and tuck them into a plastic bag. Partially close the bag and refrigerate for up to 5 days.

LAST-MINUTE PREP

None, except if using in tossed salads. In that case, gently tear the leaves into bite-size pieces.

QUICK COOK

Grill romaine just long enough to create marks on the cut side; do not thoroughly cook it. Use 2 well-chilled hearts of romaine that have been cut in half lengthwise with the root end left intact (see Keep It Fresh). Brush the cut sides with extra-virgin olive oil. On a very hot grill, place the romaine cut-side down. Grill just until it is lightly charred, about 5 to 20 seconds, depending on the heat of the grill. Place the romaine on a platter, cut-side up, and cut off the bottom core. Drizzle with Ceasar dressing and garnish, if desired, with shelled roasted sunflower seeds.

try it!

GRILLED WITH MEYER LEMONS

Cut a Meyer lemon in half and brush the cut sides with extra-virgin olive oil and honey; season with salt and pepper. When grilling well-chilled halves of hearts of romaine (see Quick Cook), add the lemon halves to the grill, cut-side down. Grill them until they are deeply marked. When they're cool enough to handle, squeeze the juice from the lemon over the grilled romaine. Top with crumbled goat cheese.

WITH BEETS AND TANGERINES

Shred romaine and place it on a platter. Top with bite-size roasted beets (cooled and quartered or halved), tangerine sections, and slivers of red onion. Drizzle with extra-virgin olive oil and tangerine juice. Season with salt and pepper. Top with toasted pine nuts and thinly sliced fresh basil.

WITH FENNEL AND RADISH SALAD

Thinly slice 3 or 4 radishes and 1 trimmed and cored bulb of fresh fennel. Put them in a bowl and top with enough vinaigrette to generously coat. Coarsely chop 1 heart of romaine; add it to the bowl, along with 1 tablespoon minced fresh Italian parsley, 1 tablespoon minced fennel fronds, and ¼ cup small cubes feta cheese. Toss; taste and adjust the seasoning as needed. Garnish with pitted black olives, such as kalamata.

Huevos Rancheros with Salsa Verde and Romaine Salad

Sure they are often served for breakfast, but huevos rancheros make great dinners, too. A romaine salad is refreshing and offers a welcome bit of crunch to contrast the creaminess of the beans and eggs. Offer bottles of hot sauce for diners to use if they want a spicier hit.

Yields 4 servings

NUTRITIONAL INFORMATION
(per serving)

calories 330	sodium (mg) 430	vitamin A IUs 50%
fat calories 80	total carbohydrates (g)... 43	vitamin C 6%
total fat (g) 9	fiber (g) 9	calcium 25%
sat fat (g) 3	sugars (g) 1	iron............................. 20%
cholesterol (mg) 15	protein (g) 21	

2 teaspoons extra-virgin olive oil

2 teaspoons fresh lime juice

Coarse salt (kosher or sea)

Freshly ground black pepper

2 green onions, thinly sliced (including dark green stalks)

2 radishes, thinly sliced

2½ tablespoons chopped fresh cilantro

2 cups thinly sliced hearts of romaine

One 15-ounce can pinto beans, drained, rinsed, well drained again

½ cup salsa verde, store-bought or homemade (see page 105)

8 corn tortillas

Nonstick vegetable oil cooking spray

¾ cup shredded low-fat pepper Jack cheese

8 egg whites

1. Preheat the oven to 400 degrees F.

2. In a medium bowl, combine the oil and lime juice and season them with salt and pepper. Add the onions, radishes, and cilantro; toss. Add the romaine, but wait to toss it until after the eggs are cooked.

3. In a small bowl, combine the beans and salsa verde; toss.

4. Coat both sides of the tortillas with cooking oil spray and place them in pairs on a rimmed baking sheet (each pair should overlap by about 3½ inches). In the middle of each overlapping pair, place about ⅓ cup bean mixture. Top with 2 tablespoons cheese. Bake until they are hot and the cheese melts, about 9 minutes.

5. Meanwhile, coat a large nonstick skillet with cooking oil spray and place it on medium heat. Lightly beat the egg whites and add them to the skillet. Cook, without stirring, for about 1½ minutes, or until they are almost set. Turn and finish cooking them, about 45 seconds.

6. Transfer each pair of tortillas to a separate plate and top each with some eggs; season with salt and pepper. Toss together the romaine mixture. Top the eggs with the romaine and remaining 1 tablespoon cheese for each serving.

Romaine with Toasted Nuts and Seeds

Toasted nuts and seeds add an appealing crunch factor and turn this dish into a more substantial salad that will serve deliciously as a light lunch as well as a first course. If desired, the mixture of almonds, pumpkin seeds, sesame seeds, and pepper flakes can be toasted a day in advance.

Yields 4 first-course servings

NUTRITIONAL INFORMATION
(per serving)

calories 200	sodium (mg) 360	vitamin A IUs 90%
fat calories 170	total carbohydrates (g).....4	vitamin C 10%
total fat (g) 19	fiber (g) 2	calcium 8%
sat fat (g).......................4	sugars (g) 1	iron................................8%
cholesterol (mg) 10	protein (g) 6	

- 3 tablespoons whole skin-on almonds
- 1 tablespoon pumpkin seeds
- 1½ teaspoons sesame seeds
- Pinch dried red pepper flakes
- 3 tablespoons extra-virgin olive oil
- 1½ tablespoons fresh lemon juice
- 1 teaspoon balsamic vinegar
- Coarse salt (kosher or sea)
- Freshly ground black pepper
- 3½ cups bite-size pieces romaine
- ¾ cup coarsely chopped fresh dill
- ¾ cup coarsely chopped fresh basil
- ½ cup coarsely chopped fresh cilantro
- 1½ ounces chilled goat cheese, pinched into small nuggets

1. Coarsely chop the almonds, leaving many only chopped in halves or thirds. Place a plate next to the stove. In a medium, deep skillet, combine the almonds, pumpkin seeds, sesame seeds, and pepper flakes. Toast them on medium-high heat, shaking the handle almost constantly, until the sesame seeds are lightly browned, 1 to 2 minutes. Spread the mixture on the plate to cool.

2. In a small bowl or glass measuring cup with a handle, whisk together the oil, juice, and vinegar and season with salt and pepper.

3. In a large bowl, combine the romaine and herbs; toss. Stir the dressing and pour it over the salad; toss to combine. Add the nut mixture and toss. Divide the salad between four salad plates. Top with the cheese and serve.

Romaine Salad Crowned with Harissa Carrots

Carrots are generally sweeter if you buy them with the green stalks attached. Because they have increased natural sweetness, they harmonize in a lovely way with the spicy heat of harissa, a chile paste that is often used in North African cuisines. Serve these sweet-hot carrots as a topping for a simple chopped romaine salad.

Yields 8 side-dish servings

NUTRITIONAL INFORMATION
(per serving)

calories 130	sodium (mg) 190	vitamin A IUs 270%
fat calories 8	total carbohydrates (g).....11	vitamin C 15%
total fat (g) 10	fiber (g) 3	calcium....................... 4%
sat fat (g)......................1.5	sugars (g) 7	iron.............................. 4%
cholesterol (mg) 0	protein (g) 1	

CARROTS

- ½ teaspoon ground cumin
- 8 medium carrots, peeled, cut into ¾-by-⅛-by-⅛-inch matchsticks
- ¼ cup fresh lemon juice
- 2 teaspoons harissa (*see Cook's Note*)
- ½ teaspoon coarse salt (kosher or sea)
- 1½ tablespoons extra-virgin olive oil

VINAIGRETTE

- 3 tablespoons fresh lemon juice
- 1 tablespoon maple syrup

Salt to taste

Freshly ground black pepper

- ¼ cup extra-virgin olive oil
- 2 tablespoons diced dates
- 1 medium garlic clove, minced

- 6 cups chopped romaine

1. To make the carrots: Sprinkle the cumin in a small skillet. Toast it over medium-low heat, until it is fragrant and darker in color, 2 to 3 minutes. Remove it from the heat and set aside.

2. Bring a medium saucepan or Dutch oven half full of water to a boil on high heat. Add the carrots and cook until they are tender-crisp, about 1 to 2 minutes. Drain well. In a medium-large bowl, whisk together the lemon juice, harissa, toasted cumin, and the salt. Add the carrots and toss. Set the carrots aside to cool to room temperature. Add the oil and toss. Taste and adjust the seasoning as needed.

3. To make the vinaigrette: In a small bowl, whisk together the lemon juice and syrup and season with salt and pepper. Add the oil in a thin stream, whisking constantly. Stir in the dates and garlic. Set aside.

4. Put the romaine in a medium-large bowl. Stir the vinaigrette and pour it over the romaine; toss well. Divide the salad between eight plates. Top with the carrots and serve.

COOK'S NOTE Harissa is a North African chile paste that is often packaged in toothpaste-type tubes, but it is also available in jars. Look for it at natural food stores, stores that carry imported specialty foods, and some supermarkets.

SAVOY
CABBAGE

Savoy cabbage offers delicate flavor as well as a stunning appearance, its green ruffled leaves crisscrossed with white veining. Cabbage is in the same plant family as Brussels sprouts, cauliflower, and broccoli. They are classified together as cruciferous vegetables because their flowers have four petals that resemble a cross.

They are nutrient-packed rascals, excellent sources of fiber and vitamins A, B (especially folate and riboflavin), C, and K.

NUTRITIONAL INFORMATION
(per 1 cup raw, shredded)

Calories 19	sodium (mg) 20	vitamin A IUs 14%
fat calories 1	total carbohydrates (g).....4	vitamin C 36%
total fat (g) 0	fiber (g) 2	calcium 2%
sat fat (g).......................0	sugars (g) 2	iron.............................. 2%
cholesterol (mg) 0	protein (g) 1	

CELL PROTECTION
One family of healthful phytochemicals found in abundance in savoy cabbage is glucosinolates. These beneficial, water-soluble elements are known to protect cells from the damage that can lead to cancer. In animal studies, they help prevent development of tumors in the liver, colon, pancreas, and breast tissues. Newer research shows glucosinolates to be effective anti-inflammatory agents as well as activators of enzymes called histone deacetylase inhibitors, which have been used as mood stabilizers and antiseizure medications.

REPAIR JOB
Another class of phytochemicals in savoy are indoles. They can actually stimulate repair of DNA in a cell that's already been damaged—another way to protect the body against cancer.

AVAILABLE
Year-round

KEEP IT FRESH
Look for cabbage heads without discoloration or soft spots and those that seem heavy for their size, with crisp leaves. Refrigerate them dry and unwashed, in a plastic bag in the crisper drawer, up to 2 weeks.

LAST-MINUTE PREP
Remove the first layer of leaves if they are discolored or wilted. Wash the exterior with cold water and shake to remove excess water. Cut the cabbage into quarters from top to bottom, then cut away and discard the solid white core. If shredding, place the flat side on a cutting surface and cut crosswise into narrow shreds about the width of a pencil.

QUICK COOK

Overcooked or cooked in too much liquid, savoy cabbage takes on an unpleasant sulfur smell. The crispness turns soggy, and the spicy-sweet taste turns bland.

Stir-fry, quick-braise, or steam savoy for the best results. To quick braise, quarter, core, and shred a head of savoy cabbage. In a large, deep skillet, heat 1 tablespoon extra-virgin olive oil on medium-high heat. Add ⅓ cup fat-free low-sodium vegetable or chicken broth, ½ teaspoon fresh thyme, and the cabbage. Bring them to a simmer; cover and cook on medium heat, tossing occasionally, until the cabbage is wilted, about 8 minutes (add a little more broth if the pan goes dry). Season with salt and pepper; sprinkle with 1½ tablespoons chopped fresh parsley.

try it!

WITH FARRO AND WALNUTS

Toss equal volumes of quick-braised savoy cabbage (see Quick Cook) and cooked farro. Drizzle with a little extra-virgin olive oil, and add some toasted walnut pieces. Toss and season with fresh lemon juice and salt.

RAW, HOT-AND-SOUR STYLE

In a large bowl, stir together 3 tablespoons rice vinegar with 2 teaspoons Asian sesame oil, 1 tablespoon sodium-reduced soy sauce, 1½ teaspoons minced fresh ginger, and a pinch of dried red pepper flakes. Add 3 cups shredded savoy cabbage (if long, chop it into bite-size pieces), 1 ripe mango (diced), and 4 green onions (trimmed, cut crosswise into thin slices, including dark green stalks). Toss and season with salt and pepper.

IN GREEN PASTA

Shred ½ head savoy cabbage, then coarsely chop it. Quick-braise it until wilted (see Quick Cook); drain if any liquid remains. Toss the cabbage with 1 pound cooked (al dente) spinach pasta (small shells or penne), 1 cup (cooked and shelled) edamame, 1 cup corn kernels (fresh or thawed frozen), 2 tablespoons extra-virgin olive oil, and ¼ cup chopped fresh basil. Season with garlic salt, pepper, and fresh lemon juice.

Sautéed Peppers with Savoy, Raisins, and Quinoa

Bell peppers are pleasantly herbal without even a hint of capsaicin, the compound that produces heat in other members of the pepper family. Green bell peppers have the most distinct flavor profile; they are grassy with a gentle spicy finish. Red, orange, or yellow bell peppers are milder, with a sweeter note. Here the sweet red and yellow bells team with savoy cabbage and raisins to make a colorful vegetarian medley to top red quinoa.

Yields 8 side-dish servings

NUTRITIONAL INFORMATION
(per serving, without cheese)

calories 130	sodium (mg) 230	vitamin A IUs 4%
fat calories 10	total carbohydrates (g)...26	vitamin C 100%
total fat (g) 1.5	fiber (g) 3	calcium 4%
sat fat (g).........................0	sugars (g) 10	iron.............................10%
cholesterol (mg) 0	protein (g) 4	

1 cup dry red quinoa

3 tablespoons extra-virgin olive oil

2 red bell peppers, cored, seeded, and cut into ¼-inch strips

2 yellow bell peppers, cored, seeded, and cut into ¼-inch strips

½ cup golden raisins, coarsely chopped

1 teaspoon fennel seeds

Coarse salt (kosher or sea)

Freshly ground black pepper

1 cup coarsely chopped savoy cabbage

1½ teaspoons balsamic vinegar

OPTIONAL GARNISH crumbled feta cheese

1. Combine the quinoa with 2 cups water in a small saucepan. Bring it to a boil on high heat. Cover and decrease the heat to medium-low. Simmer until the quinoa is tender and the water is absorbed, about 15 minutes. Gently stir and set it off heat, covered.

2. Meanwhile, heat the oil in a large, deep skillet on medium-high heat. Add the peppers and toss to coat. Cook, stirring occasionally, for 5 minutes. Add the raisins and fennel seeds and season with salt and pepper. Cook until the peppers are softened, about 4 minutes. Add the cabbage and vinegar. Stir to combine and cook until the cabbage is limp, about 4 minutes.

3. Divide the quinoa between eight small bowls. Taste the pepper mixture and adjust the seasoning with vinegar, salt, and/or pepper. Spoon the cabbage mixture over the quinoa. If desired, top each serving with some feta cheese. Serve.

Ribollita

This version of the hearty Tuscan soup calls for a generous amount of savoy cabbage. It lends an earthy sweetness that balances beautifully with the other vegetables and cannellini beans. It is traditional to add stale bread to the soup during the last few minutes of cooking. If you prefer a straight vegetable-bean concoction, you can omit the bread and reduce the amount of liquid added in step 7. It won't be ribollita, but it will be a delicious vegetable-bean soup.

Yields 10 to 12 servings

NUTRITIONAL INFORMATION
(per serving)

calories 140	sodium (mg) 220	vitamin A IUs 80%
fat calories 15	total carbohydrates (g)... 26	vitamin C 30%
total fat (g) 1.5	fiber (g) 6	calcium.........................8%
sat fat (g)..........................0	sugars (g) 4	iron.............................10%
cholesterol (mg) 0	protein (g) 6	

Two   15-ounce cans cannellini beans, undrained

1½ tablespoons olive oil

5 celery stalks with leaves, coarsely chopped

4 medium-large carrots, peeled and coarsely chopped

2 medium red onions, coarsely chopped

¼ cup coarsely chopped fresh Italian parsley

2 garlic cloves, minced

One   14½-ounce can diced tomatoes, drained

4 cups coarsely chopped savoy cabbage

8 slices stale rustic bread, such as ciabatta or whole-wheat baguette, about 1 inch thick

Coarse salt (kosher or sea)

Freshly ground black pepper

OPTIONAL ¼ teaspoon dried red pepper flakes

OPTIONAL GARNISH extra-virgin olive oil

1. In a food processor, purée the contents of one can of the beans; set it aside. Rinse the other can of beans and set it aside.

2. Heat the oil in a large pan or Dutch oven on medium heat. Add the celery, carrots, onions, parsley, and garlic. Cook for 15 to 20 minutes on low heat, or until the vegetables soften, stirring occasionally.

3. Add the tomatoes and stir to combine. Simmer for 5 minutes. Add the whole beans and cabbage. Add enough water to generously cover the ingredients. Bring them to a boil on high heat. Reduce the heat to medium-low and simmer for 30 minutes, until the vegetables are soft.

4. Add the bean purée to the soup. Stir to combine. Add enough boiling water to make the soup a liquid consistency. The exact amount of liquid will vary; you need to balance the liquid with the bread. The soup should be very thick after the bread is added, but there should be some broth as well.

5. Stir in the bread and season with salt and pepper. If desired, add the pepper flakes. Simmer for 4 minutes, or longer if you wish the bread to further dissolve into the soup. If you wish, stir in a drizzle of extra-virgin olive oil, or use it as a garnish on top of the soup after it has been ladled into individual bowls.

Savoy Stir-Fry with Brown Rice

A vegetable-based stir-fry gets a flavor boost when served atop cilantro-spiked brown rice. The herbal, chewy rice lends a nuttiness that is especially welcoming to the cabbage and baby bok choy in the mix.

Yields 8 servings

NUTRITIONAL INFORMATION
(per serving)

calories ... 230	sodium (mg) ... 330	vitamin A IUs ... 80%
fat calories ... 60	total carbohydrates (g) ... 39	vitamin C ... 50%
total fat (g) ... 6	fiber (g) ... 5	calcium ... 10%
sat fat (g) ... 0.5	sugars (g) ... 3	iron ... 8%
cholesterol (mg) ... 0	protein (g) ... 6	

1½ cups uncooked brown rice

1 pound baby bok choy, quartered lengthwise, washed

2½ tablespoons canola oil or vegetable oil

2 large garlic cloves, minced

1 pound savoy cabbage, quartered, cored, thinly sliced

1 medium carrot, peeled, cut into matchsticks

½ teaspoon salt

½ teaspoon Asian sesame oil

Freshly ground black pepper

1½ tablespoons chopped fresh cilantro

1 teaspoon toasted sesame seeds (*see Cook's Note*)

1. Cook the rice according to the package directions.

2. Meanwhile, cut the bok choy quarters into ½-inch crosswise strips. Set them next to the stove with the remaining prepared ingredients.

3. Heat a wok or large, deep skillet on high heat. Add the oil and swirl to coat the bottom and sides. When the oil is hot, add the garlic and stir-fry it for 5 seconds. Add the cabbage, carrot, and salt; stir-fry for 2 to 3 minutes. Add the bok choy and stir-fry until it is limp and tender-crisp, about 3 minutes. Toss with the sesame oil. Taste and add more salt or sesame oil if needed.

4. Mix the rice with the cilantro and season it with salt and pepper. Divide it between eight bowls. Top with the stir-fried vegetables. Garnish with the toasted sesame seeds and serve.

COOK'S NOTE Toasted sesame seeds are sold at some supermarkets and most Asian markets. Or, if you prefer, you can toast them. Place them in a small skillet on medium-high heat. Shake the handle to redistribute the seeds, cooking until they are lightly browned. Remove from the heat and let cool.

SNO PEA

also Snow Pea, Chinese Pea

Not to be confused with sugar snap peas, sno peas are flat with discernable bumps where immature peas reside inside the edible pods. Sugar snaps are plumper and most often a little shorter. Sno peas are a colorful addition to soup, salad, or stir-fry, or as part of a raw vegetable platter served with dips or cheeses. They have a sweet flavor profile and a high degree of crunch.

Sno peas bring some heavy-hitting nutrition to the table replete with fiber, vitamins, and nutraceutical components.

NUTRITIONAL INFORMATION
(per 1 cup raw, chopped)

calories 41	sodium (mg) 4	vitamin A IUs 21%
fat calories 2	total carbohydrates (g) 7	vitamin C 98%
total fat (g) 0	fiber (g) 3	calcium 4%
sat fat (g) 0	sugars (g) 4	iron 11%
cholesterol (mg) 0	protein (g) 3	

THINK CLEARLY
One phytochemical in sno peas, coumestrol, protects astrocyte brain cells from amyloid-beta peptide plaque. This is the type of plaque that builds up in people with Alzheimer's disease.

SWEET AND LOW
In spite of their sweetness, sno peas help manage blood sugar. Chemicals called saponins, which have anti-inflammatory and antioxidant power, act with the very high fiber and the resistant starch in the peas to balance sugar metabolism.

METAL TO THE PEDAL
The bright little peas are amazing mineral storehouses, with lots of iron, magnesium, calcium, manganese, copper, selenium, and potassium.

AVAILABLE
Year-round

KEEP IT FRESH
Avoid sno peas with cracks, wilting, discoloration, or soft spots. Refrigerate them, unwashed, in a perforated bag in the crisper drawer for 4 to 6 days.

LAST-MINUTE PREP

Rinse with cold water and drain. Snap the stem end and pull toward the opposite end to remove any strings. Some sno pea varieties are stringless, so if you are having difficulty finding and removing a string, it is likely that you have a string-free variety.

QUICK COOK

Place trimmed peas in boiling, lightly salted water; boil until they are tender-crisp, about 1 minute. Drain them in a colander; refresh with cold water. To steam, place trimmed peas in a steamer basket over (but not touching) boiling water; cover and cook for 1 to 2 minutes, or until they are just tender-crisp.

WITH CARROTS

Peel 3 carrots and cut them into thin slices on the diagonal. Trim and string 4 ounces sno peas. Cut each in half crosswise on the diagonal. Bring a large saucepan of water to a boil on high heat. Add the carrots and cook until they are tender-crisp, about 2½ minutes. Add the sno peas and cook until they are tender-crisp, about 45 to 60 seconds more. Toss the vegetables with 1 tablespoon minced fresh Italian parsley or basil and 1 tablespoon soft tub margarine. Season with seasoned salt.

ADDED TO CHICKEN NOODLE SOUP

Trim and string sno peas; cut them into 1-inch lengths. Drop the pieces into simmering noodle soup; heat long enough to cook the sno peas just until tender-crisp, 1 to 2 minutes.

WITH GINGER SAUCE

Trim and string 8 ounces sno peas; blanch them in boiling water until they are tender-crisp, about 1 minute. Drain. In a small bowl, stir together ¼ cup soy sauce, 2½ tablespoons unseasoned rice vinegar, 1 teaspoon agave syrup, and 2 teaspoons minced ginger. Put the drained sno peas in a bowl or on a platter and spoon the sauce on top.

Sno Pea and Bok Choy Soup

This tasty soup is a great way to use up leftovers. It is tempting studded with chunks of cooked steak or roast, but if you prefer, omit the meat and add cubes of extra-firm tofu. The first step calls for cooking a small amount of brown rice. If you have leftover cooked rice, whole grain noodles, or orzo, omit step 1 and use up what you have. Maybe this dish should be dubbed "Leftover Soup with Fresh Vegetables."

Yields 4 servings

NUTRITIONAL INFORMATION
(per serving)

calories 220	sodium (mg) 240	vitamin A IUs 50%
fat calories 40	total carbohydrates (g)... 35	vitamin C 70%
total fat (g) 4.5	fiber (g) 5	calcium 6%
sat fat (g) 1	sugars (g) 6	iron............................. 15%
cholesterol (mg) 15	protein (g) 10	

⅔ cup raw brown rice

1½ teaspoons minced lemon zest

4 cups fat-free, low-sodium beef or vegetable broth

5 ounces sno peas, cut diagonally into 1-inch pieces

1 head baby bok choy, quartered lengthwise, cut crosswise into ¾-inch slices

½ red bell pepper, cut into ¾-by-⅛-by-⅛-inch matchsticks

¾ cup ½-inch-wide strips thinly sliced cooked roast beef or steak, or 1 cup ½-inch cubes extra-firm tofu

⅔ cup sliced green onions (including half of dark green stalks; save remaining stalks for garnish)

1½ tablespoons minced unpeeled fresh ginger

1½ tablespoons seasoned rice vinegar

2 teaspoons Asian (roasted) sesame oil

1. Cook the rice according to the package directions. Gently stir the zest into the rice and set aside.

2. In a large saucepan, bring the broth to a boil on high heat. Reduce it to medium heat. Add the peas, bok choy, and bell pepper; simmer for 1 minute. Add the beef, onions, and ginger; remove from the heat. Cover and allow it to rest off heat for 1 minute.

3. Stir the vinegar and sesame oil into the soup. Taste and adjust the seasonings as needed. Mound the rice in four bowls. Ladle the soup on top. Garnish with the reserved onion stalks.

Sno Peas with Yellow Potatoes, Caramelized Shallots, and Tarragon Pesto

Caramelizing whole shallots makes them earthy sweet—the perfect partners for bright green sno peas and Baby Dutch Yellow potatoes. This makes an appealing side dish with roast chicken or pork but can become the meal when paired with a spinach or kale salad. Be sure to dress the vegetables while they're still warm to infuse them with the lively scent of fresh tarragon.

Yields 6 servings

NUTRITIONAL INFORMATION
(per serving)

calories 240	sodium (mg) 0	vitamin A IUs 10%
fat calories 130	total carbohydrates (g)... 23	vitamin C 70%
total fat (g) 15	fiber (g) 2	calcium 4%
sat fat (g).........................2	sugars (g) 3	iron.............................10%
cholesterol (mg) 0	protein (g) 5	

6 medium shallots, peeled

6 small (pee-wee) Baby Dutch Yellow potatoes or red potatoes

6 tablespoons extra-virgin olive oil

Coarse salt (kosher or sea)

Freshly ground black pepper

¼ cup (packed) fresh tarragon

2 tablespoons chopped fresh Italian parsley

2 tablespoons slivered almonds

1 tablespoon grated Asiago or Parmesan cheese

8 ounces sno peas, strings removed

1. Preheat the oven to 350 degrees F. Toss the shallots and potatoes in a bowl with 2 tablespoons of the oil; season with salt and pepper. Transfer the shallots to a medium baking dish or ovenproof skillet and cover with aluminum foil. Roast them for 20 minutes. Remove the foil and add the potatoes. Bake for 20 minutes longer, until both are tender.

2. Put the tarragon, parsley, and almonds in a food processor; process until they are minced. With the motor running, add the remaining 4 tablespoons oil in a thin steam. Add the cheese and process until blended. Set aside.

3. Bring a medium saucepan three-fourths full of water to a boil on high heat. Add the peas and cook until they are tender-crisp, about 1 to 2 minutes. Drain.

4. Add the peas and pesto to the shallots and potatoes; gently toss. Serve.

Sno Pea Stir-Fry with Radishes and Almonds

For the best results, even this very simple dish requires standard stir-fry protocols. Before you begin to cook, make sure all the ingredients are cut, measured, and ready to go. Line them up next to the stove. Heat the wok or skillet before you add the oil, unless you are using one that has a nonstick surface. In that event, heat the pan with the oil in it.

Yields 4 servings

NUTRITIONAL INFORMATION
(per serving, without rice)

calories 100	sodium (mg) 180	vitamin A IUs 20%
fat calories 60	total carbohydrates (g).....9	vitamin C 80%
total fat (g) 7	fiber (g) 3	calcium 6%
sat fat (g).................... 0.5	sugars (g) 4	iron.............................10%
cholesterol (mg) 0	protein (g) 3	

- 1 tablespoon sodium-reduced soy sauce
- 1 tablespoon seasoned rice vinegar
- 1 teaspoon Asian (roasted) sesame oil
- 1/8 teaspoon dried red pepper flakes
- 1 tablespoon canola oil
- 1 tablespoon minced unpeeled fresh ginger
- 1 large garlic clove, minced
- 10 ounces sno peas, strings removed
- 3/4 cup trimmed and quartered (lengthwise) radishes
- 3 green onions, cut into 1/2-inch pieces on the diagonal (including dark green stalks)
- 2 tablespoons slivered almonds, toasted (*see Cook's Note*)

OPTIONAL 1 teaspoon toasted sesame seeds; cooked brown rice

1. In a small bowl, combine the soy sauce, vinegar, sesame oil, and pepper flakes; stir to combine and set aside.

2. Heat a wok or large deep skillet on high heat. Add the canola oil and tilt to cover the bottom and sides. When the oil is hot, but not smoking, add the ginger and garlic. Cook, stirring, for about 30 seconds; do not let them brown. Add the peas, radishes, and onions. Cook, stirring frequently, until the peas and onions are tender-crisp, about 2 to 4 minutes. Add the sauce and toss to combine. Remove from the heat.

3. Add the almonds and, if using, the sesame seeds. Toss and serve over cooked brown rice, if desired.

COOK'S NOTE To toast slivered almonds, place them in a single layer on a rimmed baking sheet. Bake in a 350-degree-F oven for 3 to 4 minutes, or until lightly browned. Watch carefully because nuts burn easily.

SUGAR
SNAP PEA

Plump, crescent-shaped sugar snap peas maintain their sweet crunchiness and bright green color when cooked just long enough to make them barely tender. Still crisp, both the pods and the rows of peas that line their interiors are welcome additions to hot or cold savory dishes.

Just like their sno pea cousins, sugar snap peas carry an impressive array of nutrients.

POD FOR THE HEART

As a great source of B vitamins, sugar snaps provide plenty of pantothenic acid (vitamin B_5), without which we could not metabolize the very food we eat. For example, B_5 has been shown to lower blood triglycerides and low-density lipoproteins for healthier blood cholesterol, making it a benefit to cardiovascular health.

NUTRITIONAL INFORMATION
(per 1 cup raw, chopped)

calories 41	sodium (mg) 4	vitamin A IUs 21%
fat calories 2	total carbohydrates (g)..... 7	vitamin C 98%
total fat (g) 0	fiber (g) 3	calcium 4%
sat fat (g) 0	sugars (g) 4	iron 11%
cholesterol (mg) 0	protein (g) 3	

LOOSEN UP

Researchers have been following evidence that pantothenic acid can improve symptoms of arthritis such as joint stiffness and pain, especially in people with rheumatoid arthritis.

STOKE IT UP

Coumestrol, a phytoestrogen phytochemical in snap peas, could be the perfect companion to grilled meats. In a 2009 study by the Instituto Naçional de Salud Pública in Cuernavaca, Mexico, coumestrol blocked the action of nitrates and nitrites (found in grilled and cured meats) and inhibited the growth of cancerous cells in the stomach.

AVAILABLE

Year-round

KEEP IT FRESH

Look for pods that are bright green without any sign of shriveling or soft spots. Snap one in half; it should sound crisp and make a popping noise. Refrigerate unwashed snap peas in a perforated bag in the crisper drawer for up to 8 days.

LAST-MINUTE PREP

Rinse with cold water. Some snap pea varieties have strings, and some don't. Frequently they have strings on both top and bottom. If serving them hot, remove the strings before cooking. If serving them cold, remove the strings when they're cool enough to handle; they are often easier to remove when cooked. Either cooked or raw, snap off the stem end, breaking it toward the side of the pod rather than the bottom or top; pull toward the opposite end of the pod, dragging the strings still attached to the broken stem portion.

QUICK COOK

Brief steaming renders pods crisp and bright green. To steam, place sugar snap peas in a steamer basket over (but not touching) boiling water; cover and cook for about 2 to 3 minutes, or until they are tender-crisp.

try it!

WITH PISTACHIOS AND CHOPPED DRIED CRANBERRIES

Steam 2 cups sugar snap peas until crisp-tender; when they're cool enough to handle, remove the strings. Heat 1 tablespoon extra-virgin olive oil in a medium skillet. Add the peas and season with salt and pepper. Add 2 tablespoons chopped dried cranberries or cherries and 2 tablespoons chopped pistachios; toss and cook until everything is heated through.

IN SOUP

Bring 6 cups vegetable broth to a simmer on medium heat in a large saucepan or Dutch oven. Add 2 cups sliced button mushrooms; cover and simmer on medium-low for 10 minutes. Add 2 cups sugar snap peas (strings removed, each halved crosswise), and 6 ounces extra-firm tofu (cut into ½-inch dice). Simmer until the peas are tender-crisp, 2 to 3 minutes. Stir in 2 green onions (thinly sliced).

SAUTÉED WITH CORN AND TOMATOES

Remove strings from 1 cup sugar snap peas. In a large deep skillet, heat 1 tablespoon extra-virgin olive oil on medium-high heat. Add the peas and cook, stirring occasion-ally, for 1 minute. Add 1 cup raw corn kernels, ½ cup halved grape tomatoes, and 2 green onions (sliced, including dark green stalks). Cook, stirring occasionally, until everything is heated through, about 2 to 4 minutes.

Sugar Snap Peas with Warm Sesame Vinaigrette

This side dish may steal the show. Served slathered with a vinegar-spiked dressing, the blanched peas and watercress mixture is garnished with toasted sesame seeds. Serve it over cooked brown rice or on its own, as an accompaniment to grilled meat or tofu.

Yields 4 side-dish servings

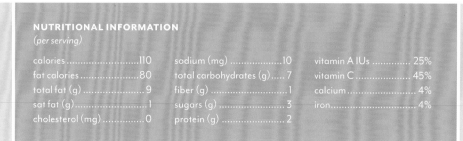

NUTRITIONAL INFORMATION
(per serving)

calories	110	sodium (mg)	10	vitamin A IUs	25%
fat calories	80	total carbohydrates (g)	7	vitamin C	45%
total fat (g)	9	fiber (g)	1	calcium	4%
sat fat (g)	1	sugars (g)	3	iron	4%
cholesterol (mg)	0	protein (g)	2		

12 ounces sugar snap peas

1 bunch watercress (2 to 3 ounces), tough stems removed

2 tablespoons canola oil

3 large shallots, thinly sliced crosswise

2 tablespoons seasoned rice vinegar

1½ teaspoons Asian (roasted) sesame oil

Coarse salt (kosher or sea)

GARNISH 2 teaspoons toasted sesame seeds
(see Cook's Note)

1. Add about 4 cups water to a large pan. Bring it to a boil on high heat. Add the peas and blanch until they are tender-crisp, 30 to 60 seconds. Drain and refresh them with cold water; if present, remove the strings when they are cool enough to handle. Toss the peas with the watercress in a medium bowl.

2. Heat the canola oil in a large saucepan or Dutch oven on medium-high heat. Add the shallots and reduce the heat to medium-low. Cook until the shallots are lightly browned, 10 to 12 minutes. Add the vinegar and sesame oil and season with salt; cook until they are heated through, about 15 to 25 seconds. Add the pea mixture and toss; cook just until everything is heated through, about 30 seconds. Serve it topped with the sesame seeds.

COOK'S NOTE Toasted sesame seeds are sold at some supermarkets and most Asian markets. Or, if you prefer, you can toast them. Place them in a small skillet on medium-high heat. Shake the handle to redistribute the seeds, cooking until they are lightly browned. Remove from the heat and let cool.

White Bean Bruschetta with Sugar Snap Peas

Cannellini beans—those large white kidney beans that are so popular in Italian cuisine—make creamy spreads to use as appetizers. Here, the earthy mash is augmented with a little extra-virgin olive oil along with vinegar, parsley, basil, red onion, and tomato. It can be prepared several hours in advance and stored airtight in the refrigerator. It travels well, making this an ideal recipe for picnics.

Yields 8 servings

NUTRITIONAL INFORMATION
(per serving)

calories 180	sodium (mg) 250	vitamin A IUs 8%
fat calories 45	total carbohydrates (g)... 28	vitamin C 20%
total fat (g) 5	fiber (g) 4	calcium 4%
sat fat (g).......................... 1	sugars (g) 2	iron.............................. 15%
cholesterol (mg) 0	protein (g) 7	

Sixteen ½-inch slices whole-wheat baguette, such as sourdough wheat

2 to 3 tablespoons extra-virgin olive oil (*see Cook's Notes*)

⅛ teaspoon coarse salt (kosher or sea)

16 sugar snap peas

One 15-ounce can cannellini beans, undrained (*see Cook's Notes*)

1 Roma tomato, cored, finely diced

3 tablespoons minced fresh Italian parsley

2 tablespoons finely chopped red onion

1 tablespoon minced fresh basil

1 teaspoon white wine vinegar

Salt to taste

Freshly ground black pepper

OPTIONAL 2 ounces thinly sliced prosciutto, cut into ¼-inch strips

1. Adjust an oven rack to about 8 to 10 inches below the broiler element. Preheat the broiler. Arrange the bread in a single layer on a rimmed baking sheet. Brush both sides lightly with oil, using 1 to 2 tablespoons of the oil. Broil until the bread is brown on the outside edges but slightly soft in the center. Turn, sprinkle with the salt, and repeat broiling until the bread is lightly toasted.

2. Add about 4 cups water to a large saucepan. Bring it to a boil on high heat. Add the peas and blanch until they are tender-crisp, 30 to 60 seconds. Drain and refresh them with cold water. If they are present, remove strings when the peas are cool enough to handle.

3. Put the beans in a medium bowl; mash them to a coarse consistency with a fork. Add the remaining 1 tablespoon oil, the tomato, parsley, onion, basil, and vinegar. Season with salt and pepper and stir to combine. Taste and adjust the seasoning as needed.

4. If using, top each toasted bread with 1 or 2 prosciutto strips. Top each toast with a spoonful of the bean mixture. Garnish each with a sugar snap pea.

COOK'S NOTES If you prefer to eliminate the oil, toast the bread without brushing it with olive oil.

Canned beans can be salty, so use caution when adding salt in step 3; none may be needed.

Snap Pea and Wild Mushroom Salad

Warm bacon dressing is a classic partner for salads made with sturdy greens. Here, the vinaigrette showcases Canadian bacon, a leaner choice than standard bacon. The warm dressing brings out the best in the romaine and fresh basil, as well as the sugar snap peas and wild mushrooms. For a meatless alternative, simply omit the Canadian bacon.

Yields 6 first-course servings

NUTRITIONAL INFORMATION
(per serving)

calories 250	sodium (mg) 480	vitamin A IUs 90%
fat calories 130	total carbohydrates (g) ... 23	vitamin C 20%
total fat (g) 14	fiber (g) 4	calcium 6%
sat fat (g) 2.5	sugars (g) 4	iron 10%
cholesterol (mg) 10	protein (g) 15	

CROSTINI

- ¾ teaspoon minced fresh rosemary
- 2 teaspoons extra-virgin olive oil
- Six ⅜-inch slices narrow whole-wheat baguette
- 4 ounces Canadian bacon

DRESSING

- 1 large shallot, minced
- 2 tablespoons sherry vinegar or champagne vinegar
- 2 tablespoons fresh orange juice or tangerine juice
- 1 teaspoon finely minced orange or tangerine zest
- Coarse salt (kosher or sea)
- Freshly ground black pepper
- 2 tablespoons extra-virgin olive oil
- ¼ cup chopped fresh chives
- 4 fresh sage leaves, chopped

SALAD

- 1½ tablespoons extra-virgin olive oil
- 2 cups sugar snap peas, strings removed, cut in half crosswise
- 12 ounces mixed fresh wild mushrooms, such as chanterelle, shiitake, and porcini, quartered lengthwise
- 6 cups bite-size pieces romaine lettuce, including thick outer leaves
- ¼ cup (packed) fresh basil leaves (if large, tear them in half)
- ¼ cup pine nuts, toasted (*see Cook's Note*)

1. Adjust an oven rack to the middle position; preheat the oven to 350 degrees F.

2. Make the crostini: Combine the rosemary and oil in a small bowl. Using a pastry brush, lightly brush both sides of the bread with the oil mixture and arrange it in a single layer on a rimmed baking sheet. Bake until it is crisp and lightly browned, about 5 minutes.

3. Using the same brush and any remaining oil, lightly coat a skillet that is large enough to hold the bacon in a single layer. Brown the bacon on both sides on medium-high heat; cut it into narrow strips and set aside.

4. To make the dressing: In a small bowl or a glass measuring cup with a handle, stir together the shallot, vinegar, juice, and zest; season with salt and pepper. Add the oil in a thin stream, whisking constantly. Stir in the herbs. Taste and adjust the seasoning.

5. To make the salad: Heat the oil in a large, deep skillet on medium-high heat. Add the peas and mushrooms. Cook, stirring occasionally, until the mushrooms start to brown and soften and the peas are tender-crisp. Add the dressing and toss. Remove from the heat.

6. Put the lettuce and basil in a large bowl. Add the still-warm mushroom mixture and toss. Add the bacon and pine nuts; toss. Season with salt and/or pepper as needed. Divide the salad between six salad plates. Top each salad with a crostini and serve.

COOK'S NOTE To toast pine nuts, place them in a small skillet on medium-high heat. Shake the skillet to redistribute the nuts so they won't overbrown on one side. Cook until lightly browned. Watch carefully because nuts burn easily.

SPINACH

Eaten raw, emerald-green spinach leaves are crisp and refreshing, a welcome addition to salads or sandwiches. They become creamy and delicious when cooked and are satisfying on their own or used as a tasty bed beneath protein-rich entrées. Cooking is quick and easy, once you get over the somewhat disappointing fact that what starts out as a mountain ends up as a hill.

There are loads of good things in spinach: an abundance of antioxidants (beta carotene and lutein), folic acid, and vitamins (C, K, and thiamine). A variety of minerals are also present: iron, calcium, potassium, and zinc.

NUTRITIONAL INFORMATION
(per 1 cup, raw)

calories 7	sodium (mg) 24	vitamin A IUs 56%
fat calories 1	total carbohydrates (g) 1	vitamin C 14%
total fat (g) 0	fiber (g) 1	calcium 3%
sat fat (g) 0	sugars (g) 0	iron............................... 5%
cholesterol (mg) 0	protein (g) 1	

IRON GIANT

Spinach is well known as one of the richest plant sources of iron and calcium. One cup of cooked spinach has more than one-third of your daily iron needs and one-quarter of the calcium requirement. It was previously thought that a common plant constituent called oxalate prevented uptake of these crucial bone, blood, and heart minerals. A subsequent study, however, shows that more of the minerals are absorbed than originally believed.

BELLY GOOD

Spinach contains a type of fat compound called glycoglycerolipids. While they help the plant convert light to food in photosynthesis, scientists recently discovered that these components protect the delicate cells lining the digestive system from the type of damage and inflammation that can lead to cancer.

GOOD STUFF BONANZA

Spinach has plenty of the derivatives of the antioxidant carotenoid, specifically lutein and zeaxanthin for eye health and lycopene for skin health and prostate protection. Spinach also is a great plant source of omega-3 oils, with each cup carrying 166 milligrams of the health powerhouse. And when it comes to vitamin K, crucial to blood and bone health and nerve protection, a 1-cup serving has more than 1,100 percent of your daily needs.

AVAILABLE

Year-round

KEEP IT FRESH

Spinach leaves should smell fresh and be bright green and free of wilting, soft spots, or discoloration. Loose spinach can be refrigerated up to 2 days, dry and unwashed, in a plastic bag. Or, for longer storage, wash it just before refrigeration. If the leaves are large, break off the stems by pinching them at the base of the leaf before washing. Swish leaves in a large bowl or tub of cold water. Repeat if necessary until the water is clean and free of grit. Drain in a colander. Wrap the spinach in a clean towel or paper towels and place it in a partially closed plastic bag. Refrigerate it in the crisper drawer for up to 3 days. If buying washed baby spinach leaves in a sealed cellophane or plastic bag, refrigerate them for up to 2 days.

LAST-MINUTE PREP

If stored unwashed, wash as directed in Keep It Fresh.

QUICK COOK

Put 4 to 5 cups baby spinach leaves in a microwave-safe bowl. If they are dry, sprinkle a tiny bit of water over the surface. Cover with a microwave-safe plate. Microwave on high power for 2 to 3 minutes, or until the leaves are hot and just barely wilted. Toss them with a little balsamic vinegar and soft-tub margarine or butter. Season with salt and pepper.

try it!

WITH RUSTIC MASHED SPUDS

Cook 2 pounds peeled potatoes (such as Yukon Gold or russet) in boiling water until they are fork tender. Meanwhile heat ½ cup evaporated milk and 1½ tablespoons butter or soft tub margarine in a medium saucepan to a simmer; cover and set aside. Drain the potatoes. Add 3 to 4 cups (about 4 ounces) baby spinach to the hot milk mixture; toss, cover, and let it sit for 1 minute. Add the mixture to the potatoes, reserving some of the liquid; mash, adding the reserved liquid until the desired consistency is reached. Season with salt and pepper.

IN OMELET OR LASAGNA FILLING

Cook ½ onion (chopped) in 1 teaspoon oil in a medium nonstick skillet on medium-high heat until it is starting to brown. Add 5 ounces baby spinach (coarsely chopped), 1 garlic clove (minced), and 1 tablespoon water. Cook, stirring frequently, until the spinach wilts. Drain the spinach mixture in a sieve, gently pressing down with the back of a large spoon. Add as an additional layer in your favorite lasagna recipe or as a filling in omelets.

IN BLENDER ASIAN DRESSING

Cook spinach as directed for an omelet filling, doubling the recipe. To make dressing, add 2 tablespoons toasted, cooled sesame seeds to a blender. Whirl until they are ground. Add 3 tablespoons peanut oil, 2 tablespoons seasoned rice vinegar, 1½ tablespoons soy sauce, 1 teaspoon Asian (roasted) sesame oil, and ⅛ teaspoon salt. Whirl to combine. Spoon the dressing over the cooked spinach. If desired, sprinkle additional toasted sesame seeds on each serving.

Southwest Spicy Pork Tenderloin–Spinach Salad

Southwest-themed ingredients give this salad a spicy edge. It's served alongside thin slices of pork tenderloin seasoned with a mixture of spices before it is roasted. Pork tenderloin is surprisingly lean; a 3-ounce serving has about 130 calories (the same as skinless chicken breast) and only 3 grams of fat.

Yields 8 servings

NUTRITIONAL INFORMATION
(per serving)

calories 220	sodium (mg) 830	vitamin A IUs 60%
fat calories 70	total carbohydrates (g)....19	vitamin C 50%
total fat (g) 8	fiber (g) 7	calcium 4%
sat fat (g)...................... 1.5	sugars (g) 3	iron............................ 20%
cholesterol (mg) 50	protein (g) 21	

SALAD

- 1 tablespoon cumin seeds
- 2 teaspoons kosher salt
- 1½ teaspoons coarsely ground black pepper
- 1 teaspoon dried thyme or 1 tablespoon fresh thyme
- ½ teaspoon dried red pepper flakes
- 1¼ pounds well-trimmed pork tenderloin
- 2 teaspoons extra-virgin olive oil
- 6 cups baby spinach
- 5 cups mixed baby greens
- 1½ cups canned black beans, drained, rinsed
- 1 red bell pepper, diced
- 12 grape tomatoes, halved lengthwise
- 1 avocado, diced
- 1 cup cubed jícama

DRESSING

- ¼ cup low-fat buttermilk
- 3 tablespoons fat-reduced mayonnaise
- 2 tablespoons finely chopped fresh cilantro
- 1 tablespoon finely chopped fresh Italian parsley
- 1 teaspoon garlic salt
- ¼ teaspoon onion powder

1. Adjust an oven rack to the middle position. Preheat the oven to 425 degrees F.

2. To make the salad: Put the cumin seeds in a mini-processor and process until they are finely ground or place in a zipper-style plastic bag and pound with a mallet or pot. Add the salt, pepper, thyme, and pepper flakes, and process until everything is roughly ground. You will use about half this mixture for the tenderloins, the rest can be stored airtight (for 2 weeks if using fresh thyme, up to 3 months for dried thyme).

3. Put the tenderloin in a small roasting pan. Rub it with the oil and sprinkle on a thin coating of the herb mixture (on all sides), using about half the mixture. Roast it for 10 minutes. Reduce the heat to 350 degrees F and roast for 20 to 25 minutes more, or until the internal temperature reaches 155 in the thickest part of the tenderloin. Set it aside to cool.

4. Combine the spinach and baby greens in a large bowl. Add the beans, bell pepper, tomatoes, avocado, and jícama.

5. To make the dressing: In a small bowl or glass measuring cup with a handle, whisk together the buttermilk, mayonnaise, cilantro, parsley, garlic salt, and onion powder. Add them to the spinach mixture and toss.

6. Cut the tenderloin into thin crosswise slices. Divide it between eight plates, place the salad mixture next to the meat, and serve.

MEATLESS ALTERNATIVE Omit the pork. Add 1 cup canned garbanzo beans, drained, rinsed, in step 4. Garnish the salad with shredded pepper Jack cheese.

Mushrooms with Spinach

Spinach salad studded with raw, wafer-thin mushroom slices is a classic cold dish. Those key elements translate beautifully in this warm version. No vinaigrette is needed—only a good squeeze of fresh lime juice to add a spark of acidity. If you like, top each serving with shaved Parmesan cheese.

Yields 6 servings

NUTRITIONAL INFORMATION
(per serving without rice)

calories 100	sodium (mg) 240	vitamin A IUs 20%
fat calories 60	total carbohydrates (g)....10	vitamin C 8%
total fat (g) 7	fiber (g) 2	calcium 4%
sat fat (g)........................ 2	sugars (g) 3	iron................................ 8%
cholesterol (mg) 5	protein (g) 4	

1 tablespoon butter

2 tablespoons plus 2 teaspoons extra-virgin olive oil

2 pound cremini mushrooms, cut lengthwise into ½-inch slices (including stems)

1 large garlic clove, minced

2 tablespoons chopped fresh thyme

6 cups (loosely packed) baby spinach leaves

Coarse salt (kosher or sea)

Freshly ground black pepper

OPTIONAL 5 cups cooked brown rice tossed with salt, pepper, and 1 tablespoon minced fresh Italian parsley

GARNISH 6 lime wedges

1. In a large, deep skillet, melt the butter with 2 tablespoons of the oil over medium-high heat. Add the mushrooms and cook until they are golden brown. Remove the mushrooms from the pan.

2. Return the pan to medium-high heat and add the remaining 2 teaspoons oil. Add the garlic and thyme; cook until the garlic is softened, but not browned, about 40 to 50 seconds. Add the spinach and cook until it is wilted, tossing occasionally, about 2 minutes. Toss in the mushrooms and season with salt and pepper.

3. If using the rice, divide it between six bowls. Top with the mushroom-spinach mixture. Accompany each bowl with a lime wedge for squeezing.

Rotini with Spinach, Almonds, and Prosciutto

Large pieces of toasted unblanched (skin-on) almonds provide robust crunch and nutty flavor to this pasta. Teaming them with a fresh tarragon-spiked spinach mixture and prosciutto makes this dish irresistible.

Yields 8 side-dish servings

NUTRITIONAL INFORMATION
(per serving)

calories 240	sodium (mg) 230	vitamin A IUs 4%
fat calories 70	total carbohydrates (g)...34	vitamin C 0%
total fat (g) 7	fiber (g) 4	calcium.......................6%
sat fat (g).....................2.5	sugars (g) 3	iron.............................8%
cholesterol (mg) 15	protein (g) 9	

⅓ cup whole skin-on almonds

12 ounces whole-grain rotini

6 cups baby spinach

¾ cup fat-free, low-sodium chicken or vegetable broth

½ cup reduced-fat sour cream

1¾ ounces thinly sliced prosciutto, finely chopped

1½ tablespoons butter or soft tub margarine

1½ teaspoons minced fresh tarragon

Freshly ground black pepper

1. Adjust an oven rack to the middle position and preheat the oven to 350 degrees F.

2. Coarsely chop the almonds, leaving some only chopped in halves or thirds. Spread them on a rimmed baking sheet and toast them in the oven until they are nicely browned, about 8 to 9 minutes. Set aside.

3. Bring a large pan three-fourths full of salted water to a boil on high heat. Cook the pasta until it is al dente (following the package directions). Drain.

4. Meanwhile, in a large, deep skillet, combine the spinach, broth, sour cream, prosciutto, butter, and tarragon; season with pepper. Bring the mixture to a boil on medium-high heat, stirring occasionally, until the spinach wilts. Add the pasta and almonds. Toss well. Taste and add more pepper, if desired.

MEATLESS ALTERNATIVE Omit the prosciutto. After tasting the dish at the end of step 4, season with salt and, if desired, a pinch of dried red pepper flakes.

STRAWBERRY

The natural sweetness of juicy ripe strawberries makes them perfect candidates for quick-to-prepare dishes. Whether they are used in a sweet or savory recipe, it doesn't take much time or effort to turn these ruby-red jewels into palate pleasers. Uncomplicated approaches showcase their flavor the best, making the cook's job easy.

Filled with vitamins, minerals, and phytonutrients, 1 cup of strawberry slices has as much vitamin C as a cup of orange juice, half again as much fiber as a slice of whole-wheat bread, and about as much folate as 1 cup of green beans.

NUTRITIONAL INFORMATION
(per 1 cup raw halves)

calories 49	sodium (mg) 2	vitamin A IUs 0%
fat calories 4	total carbohydrates (g)....12	vitamin C 149%
total fat (g) 0	fiber (g) 3	calcium 2%
sat fat (g).........................0	sugars (g) 7	iron.............................. 3%
cholesterol (mg) 0	protein (g) 1	

LOW PRESSURE
With all those benefits, the fact that they could help control blood pressure is strawberry icing on a health-filled cake. Combined studies investigating health risks of more than 150,000 men and women found that those who ate diets high in anthocyanins, especially from strawberries and blueberries, enjoyed a lower chance of developing hypertension.

ELLAGIC ACID HERO
In addition to scoring big on cancer-protective and disease-preventing anthocyanins, strawberries are very high in ellagic acid. It aids blood sugar control and fat-burning qualities.

AVAILABLE
Year-round

KEEP IT FRESH
Select berries that are highly colored without soft spots, discoloration, or mold. If they are boxed, tilt the container to see if the berries move. If they stick together, it is a sign that they are moldy. Ripe strawberries are highly perishable, and are best consumed within 2 days. Refrigerate, dry and unwashed, on a shallow pan lined with paper towels.

LAST-MINUTE PREP
Rinse briefly with cold water. Remove the leaves and stem (hull) with the point of a small knife or the pointed end of a swivel-bladed vegetable peeler or strawberry huller. Use them whole, halved, or sliced.

QUICK COOK

Most often strawberries are used raw, but to make a warm strawberry sauce to serve atop whole-wheat pancakes or cooked wheat berries (or cooled and served over cottage cheese or yogurt), place 1 pound ripe, hulled strawberries in a food processor. Pulse until some of the berries are puréed and others are chopped. Pour them into a saucepan on medium heat; cook them on medium heat, stirring frequently, until they are just heated through. Stir in 1½ teaspoons lemon juice, ½ teaspoon ground cinnamon, and 2 tablespoons maple syrup.

try it!

IN VINAIGRETTE

In a food processor, combine 2 cups sliced strawberries with 3 tablespoons agave syrup and 3 tablespoons raspberry vinegar. Whirl until smooth. Toss with mixed baby greens, toasted slivered almonds, slivers of red onion, and quartered strawberries, adding just enough dressing to coat the leaves.

IN A PROTEIN SHAKE

In a blender, combine 1 cup ice, 1 tablespoon whey powder, ½ teaspoon vanilla extract, ½ banana, 1 cup sliced strawberries, and ½ cup plain nonfat yogurt. Blend for 2 to 3 minutes.

WITH TARRAGON AND BALSAMIC

In a medium bowl, combine 3 tablespoons agave syrup, 1 teaspoon balsamic vinegar, and 1 teaspoon minced fresh tarragon; stir to combine. Add 3 cups halved strawberries and gently toss.

Heirloom Tomato Salad with Strawberries and Goat Cheese

Tomatoes and strawberries are an alluring match, especially if both are perfectly ripe. Heirloom tomatoes, available in a wide variety of sizes, shapes, and colors, are especially good here. Often it's advantageous to cut them into wedges rather than slices; that way you can more easily cut around little hard brown spots or divots.

Yields 6 servings

NUTRITIONAL INFORMATION
(per serving)

calories 110	sodium (mg) 55	vitamin A IUs 25%
fat calories 70	total carbohydrates (g).....9	vitamin C 80%
total fat (g) 8	fiber (g) 3	calcium 4%
sat fat (g)..................... 2.5	sugars (g) 6	iron.............................. 4%
cholesterol (mg) 5	protein (g) 3	

- 1½ pounds ripe heirloom tomatoes
- 2 cups sliced ripe strawberries
- 2 tablespoons extra-virgin olive oil
- 2 teaspoons minced shallot
- 1 tablespoon red wine vinegar
- Coarse salt (kosher or sea)
- Freshly ground black pepper
- 2 ounces goat cheese, crumbled
- ½ cup microgreens

1. Depending on the size and shape of the tomatoes, cut them into wedges or slices. If you have a variety of sizes and shapes, it is fine to have some sliced and some in wedges. Arrange them on a platter or six salad plates.

2. Put 1 cup of the strawberries in a blender. Add 2 tablespoons water; whirl until puréed. Stop the motor if necessary to redistribute the berries to purée the entire batch. Add the oil, shallot, and vinegar and season with salt and pepper. Whirl until blended. Taste and adjust the seasoning.

3. Scatter the remaining 1 cup berries over the tomatoes. Drizzle the dressing on top. Scatter the cheese and microgreens on top, and serve.

Chocolate Sorbet Ringed with Sliced Strawberries

Bittersweet chocolate sorbet is a dessert every cook should have in their recipe arsenal. It is easy to prepare and irresistibly creamy. But most of all, it is extremely versatile because it pairs beautifully with almost any fruit. This recipe makes about 3¼ cups of sorbet. If you prefer, serve smaller portions and increase the amount of fresh fruit, using the frozen chocolate sorbet as a garnish.

Yields 6 servings

NUTRITIONAL INFORMATION
(per serving)

calories 290	sodium (mg) 0	vitamin A IUs 0%
fat calories 60	total carbohydrates (g)...55	vitamin C 50%
total fat (g) 7	fiber (g) 3	calcium 2%
sat fat (g)....................3.5	sugars (g) 46	iron................................10%
cholesterol (mg) 0	protein (g) 3	

- ½ cup sugar
- ½ cup agave syrup
- 3 ounces bittersweet chocolate, chopped
- ⅔ cup Dutch-processed (alkalized) unsweetened cocoa powder
- 1½ teaspoons vanilla extract
- 2 cups sliced ripe strawberries

1. Combine 2 cups water with the sugar and syrup in a heavy-bottomed medium saucepan. Whisk to combine and bring them to a boil on medium-high heat, stirring frequently. Remove the pan from the heat and add the chocolate; whisk until the chocolate melts and the mixture is smooth.

2. Put the cocoa in a sieve and shake to sift it into a medium bowl. Whisk the chocolate-sugar mixture into it a little at a time. Whisk in the vanilla. Let the mixture cool to room temperature. Cover with plastic wrap, pressing the wrap onto the surface of the chocolate mixture. Refrigerate for at least 1 hour or up to 6 hours.

3. Whisk the mixture and process it in an ice-cream machine according to the manufacturer's instructions. Transfer the sorbet to a plastic bowl with a lid; cover the surface with plastic wrap. Cover the container with the lid and freeze for several hours. Move the sorbet to the refrigerator for 15 minutes before serving for easier scooping.

4. Scoop the sorbet into six small bowls and spoon the strawberries around the edge of each scoop.

Cold Berry-Cherry Dessert Soup

On a hot summer day, chilled fruit-based soup is a dessert that is both refreshing and enticing. And it's easy on the cook because the dish can be prepared in the cool of the day, as much as 24 hours in advance of serving. Rather than using it as a finale, it can stand in as a passed appetizer, served in individual shot glasses garnished with a fresh strawberry.

Yields 10 servings

NUTRITIONAL INFORMATION
(per serving)

calories 120	sodium (mg) 5	vitamin A IUs 0%
fat calories 0	total carbohydrates (g)... 23	vitamin C 45%
total fat (g) 0	fiber (g) 2	calcium..........................2%
sat fat (g)........................0	sugars (g) 18	iron..............................2%
cholesterol (mg) 0	protein (g) 2	

- 1½ cups Beaujolais or other light, fruity red wine
- ½ lemon
- ⅓ cup agave syrup
- 5 black peppercorns
- One 2- to 3-inch cinnamon stick
- 1 pound sweet cherries, pitted and halved
- 2 cups sliced ripe strawberries
- 1 cup raspberries, fresh or frozen
- 1½ teaspoons kirsch

TOPPING
- ½ cup plain fat-free Greek-style yogurt mixed with 1 teaspoon dark honey

1. In a large nonreactive pan, combine the wine and 1¼ cups water. Using a swivel-bladed vegetable peeler, remove wide strips of lemon zest; add them to the wine mixture and set the lemon aside. Add the syrup, peppercorns, and cinnamon stick. Bring everything to a boil on high heat, stirring occasionally; reduce the heat to medium-low and simmer for 5 minutes.

2. Add the cherries and bring them to a simmer on high heat. Reduce the temperature to medium-low and simmer for 10 minutes, or until the cherries are tender. Strain the mixture. Discard the zest, peppercorns, and cinnamon; reserve the cherries. Return the liquid to the pan.

3. Add the strawberries and raspberries to the pan. Bring them to a simmer on high heat; reduce the heat to medium-low and simmer for 3 minutes. Add half of the reserved cherries. Process the mixture in batches in a blender (use caution and hold down the lid with pot holder). Strain, pressing down the fruit with the back of a large spoon or rubber spatula. In a pan or bowl, combine the strained mixture, kirsch, and remaining reserved cherries; let cool. Cover and refrigerate thoroughly, 4 to 24 hours.

4. Taste the soup. If desired, add a little fresh lemon juice. Ladle the chilled soup into small bowls, top with a small spoonful of sweetened yogurt, and serve.

SUMMER SQUASH

Crookneck, Straightneck, Pattypan, Sunburst, Zucchini

Fast growing and prolific, both yellow and green varieties of summer squash are the darlings of home gardeners. They grow quickly, producing fruit in only 40 to 50 days. Their shapes and colors are beguiling—some with uniform scalloped edges, others with swan-like necks or blimp-shaped builds. Their flesh is tender and delicately mild, a taste and texture that lends itself to an endless variety of dishes.

Summer squashes pack in fiber, most B vitamins, vitamin C, and the minerals calcium, manganese, magnesium, potassium, phosphorous, copper, and zinc. They also have certain phytochemicals that show some unique abilities.

NUTRITIONAL INFORMATION
(per 1 cup raw, sliced)

calories ...18	sodium (mg) ...2	vitamin A IUs ...5%
fat calories ...2	total carbohydrates (g) ...4	vitamin C ...32%
total fat (g) ...0	fiber (g) ...1	calcium ...2%
sat fat (g) ...0	sugars (g) ...2	iron ...2%
cholesterol (mg) ...0	protein (g) ...1	

DIABETES FIGHTER
There's a very good reason not to peel squash. Researchers in India, looking at extracts in the peel of summer squashes (especially the yellow crookneck variety), found that they countered the effects of diabetes on blood glucose levels, insulin levels, and total cholesterol, including triglycerides and HDLs, LDLs, and VLDLs.

LOVE YOUR LIVER
The same Indian scientists found that the chemicals in those squash peels can protect the liver from alterations in lipid peroxidation, which is a mechanism of cellular injury used as an indicator of oxidative stress in cells and tissues.

COUGH CONTROL
Certain compounds in some summer squash showed cough-suppressant abilities. The molecular structure and shape of pectin-like polysaccharides seemed to work directly on the smooth muscles of the airway.

AVAILABLE
Year-round

KEEP IT FRESH
Look for summer squash that is free of discoloration or soft spots, nicks, or shriveling. Avoid those that are overgrown, as they can have woody interiors and a bitter flavor. Refrigerate them dry and unwashed in the crisper drawer for up to 4 days.

LAST-MINUTE PREP

Wash with cold water. Trim the ends.

QUICK COOK

Grilling summer squash gives it a marvelous taste. Simply trim the ends and cut the squash into ½-inch slices on the diagonal. Toss the slices in a bowl with minced garlic, chopped fresh rosemary or thyme, and enough extra-virgin olive oil to lightly coat the slices. Add seasoned salt and freshly ground pepper. Grill over medium heat in a single layer, 3 to 4 minutes per side, or until it is just barely tender, placing the slices at an angle to the grill grates. If grilling whole baby varieties, a grill basket is a necessity. If desired, top the squash with grated hard cheese, crumbled soft cheese, or, if you prefer, toasted pine nuts. Summer squash can also be grilled in a grill pan on a stovetop.

try it!

WITH PESTO CHICKEN BREASTS

In a large, deep nonstick skillet, heat 1 tablespoon extra-virgin olive oil on medium-high heat. Add 4 skinless, boneless chicken breasts. Cook on medium heat for 4 to 5 minutes. Turn them over and add 2½ cups diced zucchini around the chicken; season with salt and pepper and cook, occasionally tossing the squash, until the chicken is opaque throughout and the squash is tender-crisp. Meanwhile, drain 1½ tablespoons prepared pesto sauce in a sieve to remove excess oil; spread the pesto over the chicken and serve it with the squash. For a vegetarian version, pan-fry diced zucchini in a little olive oil and toss with drained prepared pesto.

IN ENCHILADAS VERDE

Instead of chicken or shrimp, add diced summer squash (sautéed until tender-crisp in a bit of canola oil) to enchilada filling along with corn kernels and reduced-fat shredded pepper Jack cheese.

Chilled Curried Summer Squash Soup

Any summer squash variety can be used in this versatile soup. The recipe calls for yellow crookneck and zucchini, but the scalloped-edged pattypan (green) or sunburst (yellow) would be delicious, too. Serve it hot or cold, and adjust the amount of spiciness by using either a mild or hot curry powder. The brown rice in the mix lends a toothsome quality to the puréed soup, leaving a tiny bit of bite to the texture.

Yields 8 servings

NUTRITIONAL INFORMATION
(per serving)

calories 80	sodium (mg) 400	vitamin A IUs 4%
fat calories 5	total carbohydrates (g)....14	vitamin C 20%
total fat (g) 0.5	fiber (g) 1	calcium 10%
sat fat (g).........................0	sugars (g) 8	iron................................4%
cholesterol (mg) 0	protein (g) 4	

SQUASH PICKLES

2½ medium crookneck yellow squash, ends trimmed, unpeeled

¼ cup seasoned rice vinegar

1 tablespoon minced fresh mint, plus extra for garnish

SOUP

2 medium zucchini, ends trimmed, unpeeled

3½ cups fat-free, low-sodium chicken broth or vegetable broth

1 small white onion, finely chopped

3 tablespoons uncooked brown rice

2 teaspoons curry powder

1½ teaspoons minced unpeeled fresh ginger

½ teaspoon dry mustard

1 cup fat-free evaporated milk

1 teaspoon coarse salt (kosher or sea)

1 teaspoon freshly ground black pepper

4 tablespoons plain fat-free Greek-style yogurt

1. To make the squash pickles: Using the narrow end of 1 yellow squash, cut it crosswise into very thin slices (use a mandoline if you have one) and place them in a small bowl. Toss them with the vinegar and mint. Cover and refrigerate for at least 4 hours or up to 2 days.

2. To make the soup: Cut the remaining squash and the zucchini into thin slices and put them in a medium pan. Add the broth, onion, rice, curry powder, ginger, and dry mustard. Stir to submerge the rice. Bring everything to a boil on high heat; reduce the heat to medium-low and simmer for 20 minutes, or until the squash is tender.

3. Purée the mixture in batches in a blender or food processor; use caution if using a blender (hold the lid down with a pot holder). Stir the milk, salt, and pepper into the soup. Taste and add more salt and/or pepper as needed. Cover and refrigerate the soup for 3 to 4 hours, or up to 2 days.

4. Pour the squash pickles into a strainer. Divide the soup between eight bowls. Top each with a dollop of yogurt, a couple of squash pickles, and a pinch of minced mint.

Roasted Vegetable Dip with Pita Chips

Roasting vegetables gives them sweet earthiness, bringing out delicious flavors without requiring much fuss. To make the dip, you pulse them in a food processor just enough for some vegetables to be puréed, while others are in tiny pieces. Accompany the dip with sturdy pita chips and an assortment of olives.

Yields 12 servings

NUTRITIONAL INFORMATION
(per 2-tablespoon serving, without pita chips)

calories 25	sodium (mg) 20	vitamin A IUs 20%
fat calories 5	total carbohydrates (mg).. 4	vitamin C 20%
total fat (g) 0	fiber (g) 1	calcium 2%
sat fat (g) 0	sugars (g) 3	iron 2%
cholesterol (mg) 0	protein (g) 1	

Nonstick olive oil cooking spray

2 medium Roma tomatoes, halved from top to bottom

1 medium zucchini, trimmed, halved lengthwise

1 medium green or yellow pattypan squash, trimmed, quartered

1 medium yellow crookneck or straightneck squash, trimmed, halved lengthwise

1 medium sweet onion, such as Maui, quartered

1 medium carrot, unpeeled, cut crosswise into ¼-inch slices

8 medium green beans, trimmed, cut crosswise into ½-inch pieces

2 medium garlic cloves, peeled

1½ tablespoons balsamic vinegar

1 teaspoon fresh lemon juice

½ teaspoon dried ground fennel seed

½ teaspoon dried thyme

Coarse salt (kosher or sea)

Freshly ground black pepper

OPTIONAL ⅛ teaspoon dried red pepper flakes

1½ tablespoons freshly grated Parmesan cheese or crumbled feta cheese

FOR SERVING pita chips (*see Cook's Note*)

1. Arrange an oven rack in the middle position. Preheat the oven to 400 degrees F. Coat a rimmed baking sheet with cooking spray. Arrange the tomatoes, zucchini, squash, onion, and carrots cut-side up in a single layer. Add the beans and garlic. Spray everything generously with cooking spray.

2. Bake without stirring for 20 to 30 minutes, or until all the vegetables are fork tender. Put half the vegetables in a food processor. Pulse until they are coarsely chopped; some vegetables will be puréed, and others in tiny pieces. Use a rubber spatula to scrape the contents into a medium bowl. Repeat with the remaining vegetables. Add the vinegar, juice, fennel seed, and thyme; season with salt and pepper. Stir to combine. If desired, add the pepper flakes and stir to combine. Taste and adjust the seasoning as needed.

3. Transfer the dip to a serving bowl. Top with the cheese. Serve with pita chips.

COOK'S NOTE Pita chips are available at many supermarkets and natural food stores. Or, to make toasted pita bread triangles, preheat the oven to 350 degrees F. Cut several pita bread rounds into eighths and put them in a single layer on a rimmed baking sheet. Bake until lightly browned and crisp, about 6 minutes. Cool.

Pasta Salad with Crookneck Squash, Olives, and Basil

Marinating diced summer squash changes its character. The flesh absorbs the mustard vinaigrette, giving it enough aromatic succulence to make its mark in this pasta salad. Fine shreds of fresh basil add a final flourish. The easiest way to cut the tender leaves into chiffonade (skinny slices) is to stack several leaves, roll them into a cigar shape, then cut them crosswise into narrow slices using a sharp knife.

Yields 6 servings

NUTRITIONAL INFORMATION
(per serving without salami)

calories 320	sodium (mg) 360	vitamin A IUs 8%
fat calories 150	total carbohydrates (g) ... 33	vitamin C 25%
total fat (g) 17	fiber (g) 4	calcium 4%
sat fat (g) 3.5	sugars (g) 4	iron 10%
cholesterol (mg) 65	protein (g) 9	

2 eggs

2 tablespoons red wine vinegar

1 teaspoon Dijon mustard

½ teaspoon agave syrup

Coarse salt (kosher or sea)

Freshly ground black pepper

⅓ cup extra-virgin olive oil

2 medium, yellow crookneck (or straightneck) squash, trimmed, diced

8 ounces whole-grain small pasta shells

½ cup (packed) lengthwise-halved grape tomatoes

⅓ cup pitted kalamata olives, quartered lengthwise

¼ cup diced pepper Jack cheese

¼ cup diced hard salami (casing removed)

¼ cup (packed) shredded fresh basil

1. Put the eggs in a small saucepan with water to cover by 1 inch. Place them on high heat. When the water comes to a boil, cover and remove the pan from the heat. Allow the eggs to sit, covered, for 12 minutes. Drain and run cold water over the eggs. When they are cool enough to handle, crack and peel them in cold water, then place them in an airtight container, and refrigerate.

2. In a large bowl, whisk together the vinegar, mustard, and syrup; season with salt and pepper. Add the oil in a thin stream, whisking constantly. Add the squash and toss; set aside.

3. Bring a large pot of salted water to a boil on high heat. Add the pasta and cook until al dente (following the package directions). Drain well. Add the warm pasta to the dressing and toss. Let it cool to room temperature.

4. Add the tomatoes, olives, cheese, salami, and basil to the pasta. Toss. Taste and adjust the seasoning as needed. Cut the eggs into quarters and place them on top of the salad.

MEATLESS ALTERNATIVE Omit the salami.

TANGERINE

also Mandarin, Clementine, Fairchild, Murcott, Page, Pixie, Satsuma

Most often, a tangerine's bright orange skin is loose and well separated from the flesh, making it a cinch to peel. It only takes a gentle tug to pull the juice-packed fruit into petite crescent-shaped segments. Although the convenience is wonderful, it is outweighed by the irresistible taste—a profile that perfectly balances sweet and tart flavors. A citrusy floral fragrance also adds to the allure.

These citrus wonders offer a veritable pharmacy of nutritional benefits.

NUTRITIONAL INFORMATION
(per 1 cup raw sections)

Calories 103	sodium (mg) 4	vitamin A IUs 27%
fat calories 5	total carbohydrates (g)... 26	vitamin C 87%
total fat (g) 1	fiber (g) 4	calcium 7%
sat fat (g).........................0	sugars (g) 21	iron.............................. 2%
cholesterol (mg) 0	protein (g) 2	

ARTHRITIS HELP

The combination of antioxidant phytochemicals called flavonoids has proven so effective against inflammation and pain associated with osteoarthritis—especially that of the knee—that a drug was created from the same flavonoids. Tangerines have especially high concentrations of a form of carotenoid called beta-cryptroxanthin. A major study of thirty thousand women showed that high intakes of this vitamin A–type compound significantly lowered the risk of rheumatoid arthritis.

BIG C

As with oranges and other citrus, tangerines are big on vitamin C, which has proven effective at blocking the development of several types of cancer in research studies. Other compounds in tangerines, called polymethoxylated flavones and flavanone glycosides, have shown to be especially effective at protection from cancer of the cervix.

SNEEZE CONTROL

Tangerines often contain significant amounts of synephrine, a natural product that can help relieve the symptoms of colds and allergies.

AVAILABLE

Clementine: Almost year-round, peaks November to July

Fairchild: November to January

Murcott: January to February

Pixie: March to May

Satsuma: December to February

KEEP IT FRESH

Look for tangerines that feel heavy for their size, without soft spots or discoloration. Store them at cool room temperature for up to 1 week, or refrigerate loose up to 3 weeks. Both the zest and juice can be frozen.

LAST-MINUTE PREP

Rinse with cold water. Peel off the skin and separate the flesh into segments. If seeds are present, remove them with the tip of a paring knife.

QUICK COOK

Tangerines are most often eaten raw. The peel can be candied or dried. The juice can be used in sauces, vinaigrettes, and marinades.

try it!

IN COLESLAW

Add tangerine segments to your favorite coleslaw.

IN SALAD DRESSING

In a glass measuring cup with a handle or a small bowl, stir to combine ⅓ cup fresh tangerine juice, ½ teaspoon salt, 1 large garlic clove (minced), 2 teaspoons rice vinegar, 2 teaspoons finely minced tangerine zest, and 1 teaspoon minced fresh ginger. Whisk in 1 teaspoon Asian sesame oil and 1 teaspoon extra-virgin olive oil. Toss with mixed baby greens, tangerine segments, and coarsely chopped toasted almonds.

IN FRUIT SALAD WITH GINGERED YOGURT

Peel 3 tangerines and pull them into sections; cut the sections crosswise in half and put them in a medium bowl. Add 1 cup sliced hulled strawberries and 1 cup blueberries. Drizzle with 1½ teaspoons agave syrup and gently toss; spoon into four bowls. In the bowl used to toss the fruit, stir together 1 cup plain fat-free Greek-style yogurt and 3 tablespoons minced crystallized ginger to combine. Top each serving with a dollop of yogurt mixture. Dust the top of each serving with a small amount of ground cinnamon.

Couscous with Tangerines

Fresh tangerine segments make a luscious sweet-tart garnish on this cumin-spiked couscous concoction. It is delicious on its own or served as a side dish with curried fare.

Yields 8 servings

NUTRITIONAL INFORMATION
(per serving)

calories 310	sodium (mg) 300	vitamin A IUs 10%
fat calories 100	total carbohydrates (g) ... 49	vitamin C 35%
total fat (g) 12	fiber (g) 8	calcium 6%
sat fat (g) 1.5	sugars (g) 13	iron 10%
cholesterol (mg) 0	protein (g) 8	

COUSCOUS

- 1½ tablespoons extra-virgin olive oil
- ½ teaspoon ground cumin
- ½ teaspoon salt
- 1¾ cups dry whole-wheat couscous
- ¼ cup dried currants or golden raisins, coarsely chopped
- 2 tablespoons diced pitted dates

DRESSING

- ¼ cup unseasoned rice vinegar
- ¼ cup extra-virgin olive oil
- 3 tablespoons finely diced red onion
- 2 teaspoons dark honey
- 2 tablespoons chopped fresh mint

Garlic salt

- 6 green onions, trimmed and thinly sliced (including half of dark green stalks)

Fresh lemon juice

Coarse salt (kosher or sea)

Freshly ground black pepper

- 3 large or 4 small tangerines, peeled, segmented

GARNISH ¼ cup slivered almonds, toasted (*see Cook's Note*); chopped fresh mint

OPTIONAL GARNISH sprigs fresh mint

1. To make the couscous: In a large saucepan, combine 2¼ cups water with the oil, cumin, and salt; bring them to a boil on high heat. Remove from the heat and stir in the couscous. Cover and let stand 5 minutes. Add the raisins and dates. Fluff with a fork.

2. To make the dressing: In a small bowl or glass measuring cup with a handle, combine the vinegar, oil, red onion, and honey; stir vigorously to blend. Stir in the mint and season with garlic salt. Toss the dressing with the couscous.

3. Add the green onions and season the mixture with lemon juice; toss. Taste and adjust the seasoning, adding more lemon juice if needed, plus salt and pepper. The amount of lemon juice needed will vary depending on the tartness of the tangerines.

4. Add the tangerine sections. Toss. Garnish the couscous with the almonds and chopped fresh mint and, if desired, sprigs of fresh mint.

COOK'S NOTE To toast slivered almonds, place them in a single layer on a rimmed baking sheet. Bake in a 350-degree-F oven for 3 to 4 minutes, or until lightly browned. Watch carefully because nuts burn easily.

Asparagus with Tangerines and Tangerine Gastrique

Gastrique, a reduction sauce made primarily of vinegar and sugar, can be used to garnish either sweet or savory dishes. Spiked with tangerine juice, it is delicious judiciously drizzled over cooked fresh asparagus. The recipe makes about ⅓ cup of gastrique and uses only half that amount. Leftover gastrique is delicious stirred into hot tea or drizzled over grilled scallops or chicken breast.

Yields 8 servings

NUTRITIONAL INFORMATION
(per serving without cheese, using half of gastrique)

calories 90	sodium (mg) 0	vitamin A IUs 15%
fat calories 0	total carbohydrates (g) ... 22	vitamin C 30%
total fat (g) 0	fiber (g) 2	calcium 4%
sat fat (g) 0	sugars (g) 19	iron 10%
cholesterol (mg) 0	protein (g) 2	

Coarse salt (kosher or sea)

1½ pounds trimmed asparagus

½ cup sugar

¼ cup fresh tangerine juice

¼ cup unseasoned rice vinegar

1½ teaspoons minced tangerine zest

2 to 3 tangerines, peeled, halved top to bottom, and cut crosswise into ¼-inch slices

OPTIONAL GARNISH shaved Parmesan cheese

1. Bring a large, wide pot of salted water to a bowl on high heat. Add the asparagus and cook until it is just tender-crisp, about 3 to 4 minutes. Blanching times vary depending on the width of the stalks. Drain it in a colander and refresh with cold water. Drain again.

2. In a small, heavy-bottomed saucepan, combine the sugar, juice, and vinegar. Move the handle of the pan in a circular motion to redistribute the sugar and combine the ingredients. Bring them to a boil on high heat. Reduce the heat to medium-low and simmer. Rapid bubbles should dance around the edge of the pan. Simmer for about 15 minutes, or until syrupy. Bubbles will form at the center of the pan. To test doneness, drizzle a drop or two of gastrique on a plate. It should stay in small droplets. Remove it from the heat.

3. Arrange the asparagus on a platter. Drizzle half of the gastrique in a thin stream back and forth on top of the asparagus. Sprinkle the zest on top. Season with salt. Arrange the tangerine slices around the edge of the platter. Top with the cheese, if desired, and serve.

Tangerine Arabesque Salad

In this tasty salad, tangerine segments are accented by the briny saltiness of kalamata olives, as well as the up-front sweetness of dates. This quick dish also includes chopped fresh mint to give it a shot of herbal perfume.

Yields 6 servings

NUTRITIONAL INFORMATION
(per serving)

calories 180	sodium (mg) 80	vitamin A IUs 70%
fat calories 130	total carbohydrates (g) 15	vitamin C 40%
total fat (g) 14	fiber (g) 3	calcium 4%
sat fat (g) 1.5	sugars (g) 11	iron 4%
cholesterol (mg) 0	protein (g) 1	

5 small or 4 large tangerines, peeled, segmented

⅓ cup halved pitted kalamata or niçoise olives

2 tablespoons diced dates

⅓ cup extra-virgin olive oil

2 tablespoons white wine vinegar

¾ teaspoon ground cumin

½ teaspoon smoked paprika (*pimentón*)

⅛ teaspoon cayenne pepper

¼ small red onion, cut into narrow slivers

2 hearts romaine lettuce, torn into 1½-inch pieces

Coarse salt (kosher or sea)

Freshly ground black pepper

1 tablespoon minced fresh mint

1. In a large bowl, combine the tangerine segments, olives, and dates.

2. In a small bowl or glass measuring cup with a handle, stir the oil and vinegar together with a fork. Add the cumin, paprika, and cayenne; stir rigorously to combine. Stir in the onion and allow it to rest at room temperature for 10 minutes.

3. Add the dressing to the tangerine mixture and toss. Add the lettuce; toss. Taste and season with salt and pepper. Divide the salad between plates. Sprinkle it with the mint and serve.

WATERCRESS

The mellow peppery taste of crunchy green watercress leaves adds a tangy attitude to a wide variety of dishes. Sandwiches and salads or soups and appetizers all benefit from its bright green presence. The spiciness varies, but all watercress seems to complement something sweet, whether that is a little honey in vinaigrette, a handful of raisins, or the herbal charm of a vine-ripened tomato.

Watercress is a true "supergreen," with more calcium than milk, more vitamin C than oranges, and more absorbable iron than spinach.

NUTRITIONAL INFORMATION
(per 1 cup raw, chopped)

calories 4	sodium (mg) 14	vitamin A IUs 22%
fat calories 0	total carbohydrates (g).....0	vitamin C 24%
total fat (g) 0	fiber (g) 0	calcium 4%
sat fat (g)........................0	sugars (g) 0	iron...............................0%
cholesterol (mg) 0	protein (g) 1	

BLOOD CELL BOOSTER
With iron, folate, and pyridoxine (vitamin B_6) critical to the body's ability to manufacture healthy red blood cells, watercress is a star blood builder. And as a rich source of vitamin C, it also helps the body absorb more iron from vegetarian sources. Healthier blood cells are able to transport oxygen better, which translates to less fatigue, more durable energy, and overall better health.

DISEASE DETERRENT
Vitamin B_6 is also necessary to make the antibodies that form the core of our immune system. Vitamins C and E, also abundant in watercress, help protect the specialist cells of the immune system from free radical damage and their natural barriers from injury and contamination by foreign invaders and oxygen radicals. Meanwhile, glucoside compounds in watercress activate cell defense to protect against carcinogens, especially in the liver.

AVAILABLE
Year-round

KEEP IT FRESH
Look for bright green leaves that are crisp, without wilting, and stems without discoloration. Trim off and discard large lower stems and swirl the leaves attached to thin stems in a large tub of cold water to wash. Shake to remove excess water; wrap the leaves in a clean kitchen towel or paper towels and place them in a partially closed plastic bag. Refrigerate in the crisper drawer. Watercress is very perishable, so use it within 1 to 2 days.

LAST-MINUTE PREP

Use a paring knife to cut the thin stems into 2-inch portions to make bite-size pieces.

QUICK COOK

Although watercress is most often eaten raw, it is also delicious stir-fried or lightly steamed. To stir-fry it, wash and thoroughly dry the watercress. Heat some canola or vegetable oil in a wok or large, deep skillet on high heat; swirl the oil to cover the sides of the pan. Add some minced garlic or finely chopped shallots and cook just a few seconds. Add handfuls of watercress and stir-fry until they are wilted. Remove the stir-fry from the wok and, if desired, serve it drizzled with ginger dipping sauce (combine 1/3 cup sodium-reduced soy sauce, 3½ tablespoons unseasoned rice vinegar, 2 tablespoons water, 1 tablespoon sugar or dark honey or agave syrup, and 1½ tablespoons minced fresh ginger).

try it!

AS A BURGER PARTNER

Instead of lettuce, use a generous amount of watercress as a garnish on a hamburger or veggie burger.

AS A BED FOR GRILLED PROTEINS

Line a platter with watercress and top it with grilled fish, chicken, or tofu. The juices will flavor the cress, and the heat will wilt it just enough to make it irresistible.

ATOP PIZZA

Place a handful of watercress in the middle of a hot pizza.

ON FAST APPETIZERS

Mince a handful of watercress in a food processor; add either fat-reduced cream cheese or strained yogurt cheese (*lebni*), and pulse to continue. Stir in finely chopped dried apricots and chopped toasted walnuts. Place spoonfuls on Belgian endive leaves.

Watercress and Green Bean Salad

Watercress serves as a crunch-packed bed for this delicious vegetable salad. The combination of blanched green beans, ripe tomatoes, and red onions is classic. Throw in a garnish of roasted cauliflower florets, and this salad becomes over-the-moon delicious. For a main course, cook (and cool) 1 cup of farro; sprinkle it over the watercress before adding the green bean mixture. To make this quicker to assemble, you can prepare the green beans and watercress several hours or a day in advance.

Yields 10 servings

NUTRITIONAL INFORMATION
(per serving, without cauliflower)

calories 110	sodium (mg) 30	vitamin A IUs 35%
fat calories 70	total carbohydrates (g).....11	vitamin C 50%
total fat (g) 8	fiber (g) 4	calcium 8%
sat fat (g).........................1	sugars (g) 5	iron.............................. 8%
cholesterol (mg) 0	protein (g) 3	

2½ pounds fresh green beans, trimmed

OPTIONAL roasted cauliflower florets with garlic (*see Cook's Note*)

1 medium lemon, zested and halved

1 teaspoon Dijon-style mustard

Coarse salt (kosher or sea)

Freshly ground black pepper

⅓ cup extra-virgin olive oil

½ medium red onion, cut into thin wedges

2 bunches, about 14 ounces, watercress, trimmed and washed

3 cups baby heirloom tomatoes or cherry tomatoes, halved

1. Bring a large pot of water to a boil on high heat. Add the beans and boil them for 4 to 6 minutes, or until tender-crisp (cooking times vary depending on size of beans). Drain and refresh with cold water. Wrap them in a kitchen towel and place in a plastic bag. Refrigerate.

2. If adding the cauliflower, roast it as directed below, let it cool, and refrigerate it well sealed.

3. Add the juice of ½ lemon to a small bowl. Stir in the mustard and season with salt and pepper. Add the oil in thin steam, whisking constantly. Taste and adjust the seasoning with more lemon juice if needed. Add the onion and stir; set aside for at least 1 hour to marinate the onions, or cover and refrigerate up to 8 hours.

4. Just before serving, arrange the watercress on a platter. Toss the beans with the dressing and onion. Use tongs to lift the beans from the bowl and place them in the center of the watercress. Arrange the tomatoes around the beans and spoon any leftover vinaigrette over the tomatoes. If using, push the cauliflower florets in between the tomatoes. Season tomatoes with salt and pepper if needed. Serve.

COOK'S NOTE To roast cauliflower, preheat the oven to 450 degrees F and blanch the unpeeled cloves from 1 head garlic in boiling water for 25 seconds. Drain and peel the garlic. If the cloves are large, cut them in half lengthwise. Toss them with 1 large head cauliflower (cut into 1- to 2-inch florets) and 3½ tablespoons extra-virgin olive oil. Roast on a rimmed baking sheet for 20 to 25 minutes, tossing twice during roasting, until the cauliflower is tender-crisp and lightly caramelized. Season with salt and pepper.

Open-Faced Hummus, Tomato, and Watercress Sandwiches

Simple watercress sandwiches are de rigueur fare at proper English teas. These open-faced sandwiches are much more rustic. They showcase ripe tomatoes and a tasty hummus in addition to the peppery greens. If you like a spicier hummus, add a squeeze of Asian hot sauce to the mix, such as Sriracha.

Yields 4 servings

NUTRITIONAL INFORMATION
(per serving)

calories 240	sodium (mg) 450	vitamin A IUs 20%
fat calories 60	total carbohydrates (g)... 36	vitamin C 30%
total fat (g) 6	fiber (g) 9	calcium 10%
sat fat (g) 0.5	sugars (g) 7	iron 15%
cholesterol (mg) 0	protein (g) 11	

1 large garlic clove, peeled

One 15-ounce can garbanzo beans, drained, liquid reserved

1 tablespoon extra-virgin olive oil

1 teaspoon ground cumin

½ teaspoon coarse salt

4 slices rustic whole-grain bread, about ⅜ inch thick

½ cup watercress leaves, washed and patted dry

2 medium, ripe tomatoes, cut into slices

Coarse salt (kosher or sea) to taste

1. In a food processor with the motor running, add the garlic through the feed tube to mince it. Stop machine. Add the beans, oil, cumin, and salt. Process until they are puréed, adding enough of the reserved liquid from the beans to make a spreadable consistency.

2. Adjust an oven rack to 6 inches below the broiler element; preheat the broiler. Place the bread on a rimmed baking sheet in a single layer. Broil until it is toasted, about 1½ to 2 minutes; watch the progress because bread burns easily.

3. Spread a layer of hummus on top of each slice. Top with some watercress and the tomato slices. Season with a little coarse salt, if desired, and serve.

Warm Watercress Salad with Roasted Fingerling Potatoes

Honey-spiked warm vinaigrette and roasted fingerling potatoes tame the peppery edge of watercress in this scrumptious salad. For the most color and flavor, select a variety of fingerlings such as Purple Peruvian (bright purple interior and deep blue skin), Russian Banana (yellow flesh with tan skin), or Ruby Crescent (yellow flesh with a chestnut-like flavor and pink-tinged skin). If you like, sprinkle grated Parmesan cheese on top just before serving.

Yields 8 servings

NUTRITIONAL INFORMATION
(per serving)

calories 100	sodium (mg) 330	vitamin A IUs 25%
fat calories 60	total carbohydrates (g) 9	vitamin C 40%
total fat (g) 7	fiber (g) 3	calcium 6%
sat fat (g) 1	sugars (g) 2	iron 2%
cholesterol (mg) 0	protein (g) 2	

12 ounces assorted fingerling potatoes, washed, halved lengthwise

2 tablespoons dry white wine

5½ tablespoons extra-virgin olive oil

1 teaspoon coarse salt (kosher or sea)

Freshly ground black pepper

3 tablespoons finely diced red onion

1½ tablespoons red wine vinegar

2 teaspoons Dijon mustard

1½ teaspoons honey

9 (packed) cups watercress with large stems removed, torn into bite-size lengths, washed, patted dry

1. Preheat the oven to 375 degrees F. In a small roasting pan, combine the potatoes, wine, 1½ tablespoons of the oil, and the salt; toss to coat. The potatoes should be snug but still in a single layer. Cover them with aluminum foil and bake for 20 minutes. Uncover and roast them an additional 5 to 10 minutes, until the potatoes are lightly browned and fork tender. Season with pepper. Set aside.

2. In a small saucepan, stir together the onion, vinegar, mustard, and honey and season with pepper. Whisk in the remaining 4 tablespoons oil in a thin stream. Put the pan on low heat. Stirring occasionally, cook just until the mixture is hot. Remove from the heat.

3. Put the watercress in a large bowl. Pour the warm dressing on top and toss to coat the leaves. Place the salad on plates and garnish around the edges with the potatoes. Season potatoes with pepper.

WATERMELON

Over the past few years, seedless watermelon varieties have become commonplace. Whether they are red fleshed or yellow fleshed, their hard "spit-out" seeds have disappeared for the most part, replaced with seeds that aren't developed. They are small, soft, empty white "pips." A pip is the portion that surrounds the seeds in seeded varieties.

The lack of seeds in a watermelon makes the flesh firmer and helps it to stay fresh longer, whether left whole or cut and refrigerated. As for 30-pound humongous watermelons, mini-melons have taken a growing share of the market over the last several years.

Baby melons average about 5 pounds, and a hungry watermelon devotee might cut one in half and devour the entire half section. Whole, they are a lot easier to fit in the fridge.

Delectable in cold soups and salads, beverages and desserts, these tasty melons have several nutritional advantages.

NUTRITIONAL INFORMATION
(per 1 cup raw, cut into small balls)

calories 46	sodium (mg) 2	vitamin A IUs 18%
fat calories (g) 2	total carbohydrates (g)....12	vitamin C 21%
total fat (g) 0	fiber (g) 1	calcium.........................1%
sat fat (g).........................0	sugars (g) 10	iron...............................2%
cholesterol (mg) 0	protein (g) 1	

HIGH C
While other fruits such as guava and oranges provide abundant vitamin C for immunity and skin health, watermelon is a low-acid source of the vitamin. Just 1 cup has more than one-fifth of your daily C in fewer than 50 calories.

A PLUS
Watermelon scores well with vitamin A; it has almost one-fifth of your daily needs for that strong antioxidant vitamin. Watermelon has B vitamins and the minerals magnesium and potassium, too. All are needed for building and facilitating the actions of the enzymes that run the body's complicated machinery.

CODE RED
The red color in some varieties points to an abundance of the carotenoid lycopene. Although associated most often with its ability to help protect against prostate cancer, lycopene also benefits women, having demonstrated protective propensities against cancer of the breast and endometrium.

AVAILABLE
Year-round, but yellow flesh is difficult to find in late fall and winter.

KEEP IT FRESH

For cut watermelons, they should look moist and fragrant, without flesh that has pulled away from the seeds. For whole melons, they should feel heavy for their size. If it is large, look for an area on the melon that is creamy yellow—the spot where it rested on the ground as it matured; that can be a sign of ripeness. Avoid those with cracks or soft spots. Store melons at room temperature out of direct sunlight for up to 1 week or refrigerate them whole up to 2 weeks. Or cut and refrigerate in an airtight container, up to 3 days.

LAST-MINUTE PREP

Remove the rind and cut the melon into slices, wedges, or balls. The easiest way to remove the rind from a whole watermelon: Cut off a small slice at top and bottom (blossom and root ends), then cut the melon in half through the equator. Place the cut-side (equator) down on a cutting board and cut off the rind in strips from top to bottom, following the contours of the melon. If desired, cut-up and peeled watermelon can be frozen, airtight, up to 3 months.

try it!

WITH ALMOND CREAM

Toast ¼ cup slivered almonds until lightly browned; let them cool. Combine 8 ounces vanilla yogurt with ½ teaspoon vanilla extract and a pinch of ground nutmeg. Divide 2 cups seedless watermelon cubes between four small bowls. Top with the yogurt and almonds and serve.

IN A COOLER

In a blender, purée ¼ cup raspberries, ¼ cup seedless watermelon cubes, and enough chunks of peeled and pitted white peaches to make about ½ cup. Strain. Place a generous spoonful of strained fruit purée in champagne glasses and top with cold Chardonnay. Stir and serve.

IN MIXED GREEN SALAD

Toss bite-size chunks of watermelon with mixed baby greens. Top with a simple vinaigrette and toss.

Watermelon and Arugula Salad with Feta and Cucumber

Full of crunchy, clean flavors, this salad is a taste bud wakeup call, offering a lovely balance of sweet, tart, and bitter. To make it a main course, add a handful of baby spinach to the mix and top each serving with grilled shrimp or slivers of roast chicken. A small cluster of seedless grapes, placed on the plate next to the salad, makes a beautiful garnish.

Yields 6 servings

NUTRITIONAL INFORMATION
(per serving)

calories 120	sodium (mg) 410	vitamin A IUs 15%
fat calories 80	total carbohydrates (g) 9	vitamin C 10%
total fat (g) 9	fiber (g) 1	calcium 10%
sat fat (g) 3.5	sugars (g) 8	iron 4%
cholesterol (mg) 15	protein (g) 4	

2 tablespoons white wine vinegar

Coarse salt (kosher or sea)

Freshly ground black pepper

2 tablespoons extra-virgin olive oil

4 ounces crumbled feta cheese

½ small red onion, cut into thin slivers

1 Persian or Japanese cucumber, unpeeled, thinly sliced

4 cups baby arugula

3 cups chilled ¾-inch watermelon cubes, preferably seedless

1. In a small bowl or glass measuring cup with a handle combine vinegar, salt, and pepper. Whisk to dissolve salt. Whisk in oil in a thin stream. Add the feta and onion; toss and set aside.

2. In a large bowl, toss together the cucumber and arugula. Add the dressing and toss. Taste and adjust the seasoning as needed. Add the watermelon and gently toss. Divide among six plates and serve.

Watermelon Agua Fresca

Agua fresca, which translates from Spanish as "fresh water," is a refreshing beverage made most often from fresh fruit, water, and some kind of sweetener. Instead of fruit, some Mexican agua frescas showcase hibiscus or a combination of rice and cinnamon. Here the star is fresh watermelon, cut into chunks and puréed in a food processor with water. Agave syrup and fresh lemon juice add perfect balance to this refreshing drink.

Yields 5 servings

NUTRITIONAL INFORMATION
(per serving)

calories ... 45	sodium (mg) ... 5	vitamin A IUs ... 10%
fat calories ... 0	total carbohydrates (g) ... 15	vitamin C ... 20%
total fat (g) ... 0	fiber (g) ... 1	calcium ... 2%
sat fat (g) ... 0	sugars (g) ... 14	iron ... 2%
cholesterol (mg) ... 0	protein (g) ... 1	

5 cups 1-inch watermelon cubes

1 teaspoon agave syrup, or more as needed

3 tablespoons fresh lemon juice, or more as needed

Ice, preferably crushed

GARNISH 5 sprigs fresh mint; 5 thin lemon slices

1. Place a medium-mesh sieve over a medium bowl; if you have a batter bowl with a spout and handle, it is handy for this.

2. Put 1 cup of the watermelon and ⅓ cup water in a food processer or blender. Pulse until the melon is puréed. Strain it in the sieve. Repeat, using another 1 cup melon and ⅓ cup water, until all the melon is used and strained. Discard the solids from the sieve.

3. Add the syrup and lemon juice to the watermelon juice. Taste and adjust the seasoning, adding more syrup or lemon juice, or additional water.

4. Fill five glasses with ice. Stir the mixture and pour it into the glasses. Garnish each glass with a sprig of mint and a lemon slice.

Grilled Watermelon Slabs

Served while still warm, these thick slices of watermelon soak up a little white balsamic vinegar before they sizzle on the grill. Use them as a side dish for grilled meat or tofu, topping them with a little cheese and baby arugula to give them additional personality.

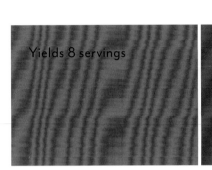

Yields 8 servings

NUTRITION INFORMATION
(per serving, without cheese and arugula)

calories 110	sodium (mg) 100	vitamin A IUs 35%
fat calories 15	total carbohydrates (g)... 25	vitamin C 40%
total fat (g) 1.5	fiber (g) 1	calcium 4%
sat fat (g) 0	sugars (g) 21	iron............................ 4%
cholesterol (mg) 0	protein (g) 2	

1 large, ripe seedless watermelon
½ cup white balsamic vinegar
2 teaspoons sugar
Vegetable oil or canola oil for brushing on grate
Coarse salt (kosher or sea)
Freshly ground black pepper

OPTIONAL ½ cup crumbled feta cheese or shaved ricotta salata; 1 cup baby arugula

1. Cut two 1½-inch-thick crosswise slices from the middle section of the watermelon. Cut each slice into quarters. Marinate the quarters in the vinegar in a nonreactive baking dish for 1 hour, turning them after 30 minutes.

2. Build a medium-hot fire in a charcoal grill, or preheat a gas grill to high. Sprinkle one side of the watermelon quarters with the sugar. Brush the heated grill grates with oil. Place the watermelon sugared-side down on the grill. Cook for about 3 minutes, until the melon has grill marks and becomes caramelized. Turn and grill the opposite sides for 30 seconds.

3. Place the watermelon on a large platter, turning so the sides with the grill marks are facing up. Season it with salt and pepper. If using, sprinkle the cheese and arugula on top.

Index